This Book Is for You, if You're Going to Move...

LEARN WHAT TO DO ABOUT—

- √ BUDGETING YOUR NEW LOCATION
- √ TODDLERS' FEARS AND TEENAGE REBELLIONS
- √ NEW JOBS
- √ "TRAILING SPOUSE" CONFLICTS
- √ THE DEPENDENT-PARENT SYNDROME
- √ GETTING A PIANO INTO A HIGH-RISE AND A POOL TABLE THROUGH THE REC ROOM DOOR
- √ DOUBTS ABOUT MOVING
- √ EVALUATING A DEAL TO BUY A TERRIFIC NEW HOUSE IN A NOT-SO-TERRIFIC NEIGHBORHOOD
- √ RADON, ASBESTOS, WATER CONTAMINATION, OR LEAD PAINT IN YOUR NEW LOCATION
- √ EVALUATING RETIREMENT CHOICES
- √ HIRING A PROFESSIONAL MOVER . . . OR DOING IT YOURSELF
- √ DAMAGE CLAIMS MOVING COMPANIES BALK AT PAYING
- √ THE EMOTIONAL LETDOWN YOU FACE AFTER YOU MAKE YOUR MOVE

YOU'LL GET THE SMART SOLUTIONS HERE
IN . . .
STEINERS COMPLETE
HOW-TO-MOVE HANDBOOK

Quantity Sales

This book, Steiners Complete How To Move Handbook, as well as Steiners Complete How to Talk Mortgage Talk are available for quantity purchase for use as premiums, in promotions, and as appreciation gifts to clients. The covers can be imprinted with your name and/or slogans in reasonable quantities at very attractive price points.

Please contact Linda Tan at IIP (415-643-8600)

STEINERS COMPLETE

HOW TO
MOVE
HANDBOOK

By Clyde and Shari Steiner

From the Authors of
Steiners Complete
How to Talk Mortgage Talk

Design by
Lionel Storch

Independent
Information
Publications
Consumers
Series
San Francisco, CA
94110

www.movedoc.com

Published by the IIP Consumer Series, an imprint of **Independent Information Publications**, San Francisco, CA 94110. For information on where to purchase this book, please call 1-800 444-2524 Extension 1. For information on bulk or premium sales, please call the Bulk Sales Desk at 415 643 8600.

First Printing May 1998
Second Printing September 1998
Revised Second Edition April 1999

Steiners Complete How To Talk Mortgage Talk, **by the same authors, covers all aspects of financing your home, and is also available at better bookstores or by direct order from 1-800 444-2524 ext 1.**

Library of Congress Cataloging in Publication Data
Library of Congress Catalog Card No: 99-62111
Steiner, Clyde L.
      Steiners complete how-to-move handbook/by Clyde and Shari Steiner
      Includes glossary.
      Includes appendix.
      p.   cm.   10 9 8 7 6 5 4 3 2
      ISBN 0-913733-14-8
      1. Moving Guide — United States.
      2. Real estate business — United States — finance.
      I. Steiner, Shari Y. II. Steiner, Clyde L. III. Title.

Printed in the United States of America
Published simultaneously in Canada

Acknowledgments

People on the move often find they belong to a passionate club. Upon discovering one another in the supermarket line or (more likely) at one Of the local shipping company offices, we start by swapping war stories and end up with friendships strung out around the country.

We want to acknowledge the insights we've received from all these wonderful people and give an even more heartfelt thanks to those who've taken the time and energy to respond to our annual moving surveys. We invite readers who have more to add to this compilation of information to contact us at our e-mail address, steiner@movedoc.corn, to keep the circle ever widening.

We'd like to thank the many who've commented on individual sections of this book, particularly tax expert Julian Block and ex-president of the National Association of Realtors Harley Rouda, for their insights from their specific fields.

We'd like to dedicate this book to our daughter, Vienna, who knows a thing or two about the necessity to keep in motion.

While we've been writing this book, the great stalwart has been fellow mover Goldy VanDeWater, who organized and conducted much of the research, reviewed everything, and helped rescue us from lost research material and other disasters. Abby Albrecht tracked down the Internet addresses for you.

—Clyde and Shari Steiner

Contents

Preface

We decided to write this book while speeding along an interstate highway. We were returning from apartment hunting in Sacramento, California, and debating the pros and cons of moving yet again. We have moved more than twenty times since marriage, and we thought it was time to organize our ad hoc expertise into some logical step-by-step plan that could help us and others.

The Census Bureau says one out of five American families moves each year. We surveyed frequent movers for the data service of Independent Information Publications. The respondents, like us, all exceeded the U.S. average in number of relocations. Predictably, these people like to move. Overwhelming they picked "Change of Lifestyle" as the biggest advantage of moving. Besides presenting their insights and practical tips, in this work we've tried to bring out a sense of their thrill at the challenge of a new beginning.

This book contains the collective wisdom and experience of thousands of moves. We've drawn not only on what we and others have done, but also on the insights of moving industry experts.

As a real estate broker and a property manager, we have helped, advised, and observed many clients on their moves. Recording all the input, sorting, and organizing took us months of effort. Now all that information is ready to help you, the reader, make the most of your move.

There are loads of tax saving ideas and cautions that affect the relocation process. We give you the ideas, but we are not accountants and you should check with your tax advisor before making any of these dollar decisions.

A word about pronouns. We've opted to use "she" as the universal pronoun. Grammarians will note that this doesn't jibe with generic proper nouns like "landlord." Since writers of the past chose to use "he" ubiquitously, we feel it's time for a change.

Introduction

Mental health specialists say moving is one of the major traumas of modern life. Do you have to be one of the victims? No!

This book will guide you through the decision making, planning, and implementation stages of moving. You'll take advantage of research by dozens of industry experts. You'll use insiders' tips to defeat problems and make moving a fulfilling experience.

The pointers in this book will give you the power to:

√ Make the IRS fork over for moving costs.
√ Whip the moving company at its own pricing game.
√ Beat the market in buying and selling your house,
√ Master the secrets of rental bargain hunting.
√ Win your perfect new home in a one-week blitz.
√ Extract the money you deserve from your employer and landlord,
√ And more.

Use this book as a guide whether you are just beginning to think about moving, relocating at the request of your employer, or dreaming of starting a new life in a brand-new location.

You'll find practical advice for college seniors, retirees, job seekers, transferees, divorcees, and newlyweds. The information is based on people's real-life experiences and a knowledge of industry practices and legal standards.

Some scenarios are the same for renters and homeowners. Others are tailored to your individual circumstances. You'll do best by looking over the table of contents to select those parts that apply to you and your family. Everyone will want to know about documenting your moving expenses—you can save the price of this book and more in taxes. Ask your tax advisor!

Don't neglect the Appendixes. They are filled with easy-to-use checklists and contact information to make organizing a relocation a snap.

Happy moving!

ONE

Taking Control from the Beginning

DEALING WITH THE DANGERS OF INDECISION

You've just won the job offer. After interminable weeks of looking, the new position offers a better salary, a better title . . . and relocation to a city you've never even visited, much less considered living in.

Faced with this proposition, most of us rally a rah-rah act for our psyche. We've won the job-hunt marathon, now think of the nice new home we'll have and the kind of lifestyle we'll be enjoying. There we are basking by that giant pool or bantering with new friends getting ready for a football game.

Maybe the decision to move comes for other reasons. We need a new home because there's a baby on the way or another major life event that makes the current home obsolete. Even if the new location is only a few blocks away, we spend time and energy imagining what life will be like after the change. This time, we resolve, we're going to have space for that traditional kitchen or that woodworking shop in the garage. Ah . . . the joys of change!

Then the doubts creep in—to move or not to move? Stress arrives and clouds the picture even more. Indecisiveness can lock us out of a genuine opportunity. Conversely, it can force us into a move we don't want but feel helpless to resist. Psychologists tell us that when we feel stressed about a decision, we make nearly twice as many bad choices as we do when we feel unthreatened and in control.

Don't let indecisiveness happen! Ambivalence attacks everybody, but you can keep it from grabbing the driver's seat. The way to break out of that whirlpool of indecision, stress, and more indecision is to take control of the process. This chapter will show you how to:

√ *Identify which fears are holding you back.*

√ *Overcome the most common fear, fear of the unknown, by setting specific goals for what you want to have in your destination and researching how specific locations measure up.*

√ *Use your own "City Evaluator" (see sample in this chapter and the blank in Appendix A) to organize and divide your needs, feelings, and hopes into manageable parts so you can evaluate the picture one piece at a time.*

√ *Tackle the fear of not being able to afford the change by working out a budget based on reality.*

√ *Go through the timetable exercise at the end of this chapter to give yourself more structure.*

AMBIVALENCE IS NOT A MYTHICAL BEAST

All of us have days when we're ambivalent about a change, but if you find yourself continually feeling out of control and unable to tackle the practicalities of moving, you need to identify the specifics that are holding you back. Is it leaving good friends? Leaving a comfortable job? Leaving a fabulous ski slope?

To find what you want out of the place where you'll be living, look for the things that make you feel at home now. Maybe it's the corner espresso bar where you can hang out and write, or the mountain to climb within a half hour's drive. Maybe a friendly neighborhood or a home with a gourmet kitchen or a school with a great sports program is what it will take to make the perfect home.

Isolate the things you've been building your life around, then see how other locations can meet the needs behind the things that are precious to you. As Barbara Sher says in her fabulously helpful book *Wishcraft, How to Get What You Really Want, a Unique, Step-by-Step Plan to Pinpoint Your Goals and Make Your Dreams Come True*, "There is nothing frivolous or superficial about what you want. It isn't a luxury that can wait until you've taken care of all the 'serious' business of life. It's a necessity."

Or perhaps the stumbling block is something you really dislike about the new place. Maybe it's a climate you can't stand or a steep cost of living. Once you've started to evaluate what's important to you, you can decide whether a problem is fixable or not.

Don't be surprised if your investigation alone "fixes" the ambivalence. Fear of the unknown is the biggest cause of indecisiveness.

THE SCIENCE OF SITE SELECTION

Corporate site selection experts, who are paid six-figure fees to help Fortune 500 companies make decisions on where to locate a new plant or office, have made this evaluation process into a science. Although many of their concerns are "bottom line" and numbers oriented, quality-of-life factors rank very high.

Dr. Tapan Munroe, chief economist for Pacific Gas and Electric, explains that site selection can include searching out communities with "a sense of place, stability, and participation." George Maegoto, principal architect for Takenaka International, finds his Japanese clients select locations where "... people are friendly, there are already a couple of good Japanese restaurants and perhaps even a Japanese school."

USING SITE SELECTION TECHNIQUES

The way to put site selection expertise to work for you as an individual or a family considering a possible move is to break it up into three parts:

√ *city or area selection*
√ *neighborhood selection*
√ *house selection*

In this chapter, we give you the information resources and evaluator you'll need to tackle the first cut—city selection—because having the city evaluation in hand is essential to overcoming fear of the unknown. Later chapters will give tips and insights on dealing with the neighborhood and home specifics, how to handle family issues and get the best tax benefits, and how to do a trial move, so you don't commit yourself until you've had a chance actually to experience life in a new community. From there, we cover how to implement the moving process itself.

THE SIX MOST IMPORTANT CITY SELECTION FACTORS

In preparation for doing this book, we conducted the Frequent Mover Survey for Independent Information Publications (IIP). In it we collected information from people all over the country who had moved recently. Collectively, they represented the wisdom garnered from nearly 500 moves, both inside and outside the United States. The majority of these people (66.67 percent) were frequent movers—they had moved ten or more times as adults. They were fairly consistent in the items they listed as important considerations for finding new locations that were both comfortable and practical.

The "City Evaluator" is derived from their responses. It includes six main personal priority categories—job availability, climate/environment, entertainment/leisure, cost of living, social life/personal safety, and children's world.

We combined these personal priority items with the principles of corporate site selection in order to tailor the professional system to your individual needs. We have given you a good range of priorities to get you started evaluating, but you should add your own priorities as you go along. Self-selected items will make it all the easier to start painting a picture of your new area.

Photocopy one blank "City Evaluator" from Appendix A for your existing city and one for each prospective location

SAMPLE CITY EVALUATOR

Mark only those items important to you. Use a scale of low=1 to high=5. Use separate charts for your current & each possible new location.

Location SAN DIEGO

Info Contact CHAMBER OF COMMERCE

Phone 619 - 232 - 0124

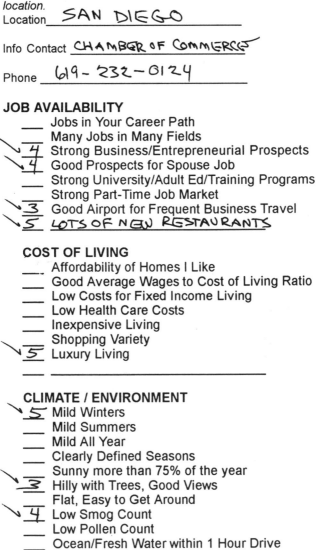

JOB AVAILABILITY
___ Jobs in Your Career Path
___ Many Jobs in Many Fields
_4_ Strong Business/Entrepreneurial Prospects
_4_ Good Prospects for Spouse Job
___ Strong University/Adult Ed/Training Programs
___ Strong Part-Time Job Market
_3_ Good Airport for Frequent Business Travel
_5_ LOTS OF NEW RESTAURANTS

COST OF LIVING
___ Affordability of Homes I Like
___ Good Average Wages to Cost of Living Ratio
___ Low Costs for Fixed Income Living
___ Low Health Care Costs
___ Inexpensive Living
___ Shopping Variety
_5_ Luxury Living
___ _____

CLIMATE / ENVIRONMENT
_5_ Mild Winters
___ Mild Summers
___ Mild All Year
___ Clearly Defined Seasons
___ Sunny more than 75% of the year
_3_ Hilly with Trees, Good Views
___ Flat, Easy to Get Around
_4_ Low Smog Count
___ Low Pollen Count
___ Ocean/Fresh Water within 1 Hour Drive
___ Mountains within 1 Hour Drive
___ _____

CHILDREN'S WORLD
___ Good Schools/Child Care
___ Friendly Neighborhoods
___ Many Supervised Activities
___ Much Open Space or Parks
___ Active Parent Groups
___ Strict Upbringing Prevalent
___ Liberal Upbringing Prevalent
___ Many Newcomer Children in Area
___ Good Colleges and Universities
✓ _?_ ICE HOCKEY _____

SOCIAL LIFE / PERSONAL SAFETY
✓ _0_ Relatives/Friends/Business Contacts in Place
✓ _4_ Openness to Newcomers
___ Active Singles Community
___ Active Family Community
___ Cultural/Ethnic Homogeneity
___ Cultural/Ethnic Variety
✓ _?_ Political Orientation
✓ _4_ Active Church
___ Active Club(s)
___ Many Health Club Options
___ Many Hospitals/Health Service Options
✓ _4_ Low Crime Rate
✓ _4_ Good Freeway System
___ Good Public Transport
___ Good Newspapers/Libraries
___ _____

ENTERTAINMENT / LEISURE
___ Variety of Cultural Activities
___ Special Cultural Activity (fill in interest):
___ _____
___ Variety of Sports Activities
✓ _5_ Special Sports (fill in interest):
___ GOLF _____
___ Good Restaurants
___ Elegant Clubs
___ Fun Clubs
___ Many Weekend Getaway Places
___ _____
___ _____

_59_ **TOTAL POINTS**   ©C&S Steiner 1999

you're evaluating, so that you can compare what you've got with what you'll get. Make a set for each family member to fill out on their own. If you're moving by yourself, it's fun to have a friend fill out a set and compare answers. You'll get more out of your own choices if you discuss and defend them.

SAMPLE CITY EVALUATOR NOTES

This sample has been filled in by Lois Franklin. At the time she was a Denver restaurant supply store owner/manager. Her husband, Don, a CPA, had a specialized clientele of midsize real estate developers.

During the previous two years, Lois had had three serious bouts with flu and pneumonia, her business had gone from fantastic to not very good, and Don's client base had been deeply eroded by Denver's real estate recession.

Their two boys were avid ice hockey players. The youngest was getting ready to graduate from high school, and they were both slated for an East Coast university in the fall. Lois and Don had decided it was time for a move.

The Franklins had two "absolutely necessary" criteria— getting away from winter and finding good business opportunities for both of their businesses. Lois's research showed that San Diego and Miami both "fit" those two requirements. The sample is her evaluation of San Diego.

After she photocopied her set of "City Evaluators," Lois thought through which items were most important to her and checked them off. She rated only these personal items using scores from 1 to 5. When she totaled the points, she found that San Diego rated higher than Miami.

Let's review the Franklins' personal priority categories from the "City Evaluator."

Job availability, strong business and entrepreneurial prospects were really the prime concern for both Lois and Don, and involved several subissues. She needed lots of restaurants and, even better, lots of *new* restaurants as a customer base. As many of her wares were imported, she wanted a good international airport.

Climate items all seemed important at first, but Lois wanted to isolate the most important considerations, so she limited her important items to mild winters, low smog, and hilly with views.

Thinking about their *entertainment/leisure* needs, she and Don discovered a surprising consensus. Neither had played golf since college, but they discovered that they both were enthused about taking it up again, now that they were going to be living in a location where they could play all year around. Golf became their only checked-off leisure item.

Under *cost of living,* Lois assumed they'd be able to afford a reasonable home in the beginning, and she wanted to have a selection of luxury housing to move up to if they were able to establish themselves as she hoped they would. Also, she was considering marketing her wares to amateur gourmet cooks as well as the restaurant trade, so again, she wanted a strong luxury market in the area.

For *social life/personal safety,* she felt community openness to newcomers and having an active church were most important. She would have preferred having friends or relatives already living there, but she didn't have advance contacts in either Miami or San Diego. Still, she felt confident the church she'd always attended would offer the best place to make new friends, so long as people were generally friendly.

A low crime rate and her business' need for a good freeway system were other social life/personal safety items that she checked, investigated and ranked for both locations.

With both sons already registered in a university, Lois didn't check any of the *children's world* items, although she made a note to herself to investigate the existence of indoor ice hockey facilities in whatever city they chose, as that might make vacations at home more fun for her kids.

Lois found it easy to research how her two locations stacked up against each other in terms of her priorities. Both cities' Chamber of Commerce were very helpful. She contacted the National Restaurant Association for more industry information on both locations. Her husband called commercial real estate brokers to sound out his prospective clientele. She checked with three major international freight service vendors and discovered that San Diego's airport was not nearly as good as Miami's, but would still be sufficient for her importing needs.

Don did the home affordability research and nearly vetoed San Diego because homes there were twice as expensive as in Miami. As they checked further, however, they found that San Diego property taxes were lower and so was the crime rate.

They decided to leave the final decision until after they'd been able to visit both places. On the San Diego trip, Don made two business connections that clinched their decision. They headed west.

"The whole experience has been great for us," says Lois. "We both know we got what we wanted, and both of our businesses have flourished because we were able to position ourselves before we arrived. Oh, and not only have we gotten to be great golfers, our sons have dropped ice hockey and are now into tennis!"

BUDGETING YOUR NEW LOCATION

Since costs vary enormously from location to location, it's important to do a draft budget for any new community you're seriously considering. In Appendix D, we give you a "Monthly Budget Estimator" to fill in as you do your research. If you research on the Internet, several sites have assembled many of these numbers for you. Try www.Realtor.com, www.HomeFair.com and www.MonsterDate.com.

Otherwise, most of these numbers can be dug up individually. In the "Contacts and Resources" directory (Appendix C), we've included lists of real estate/rental photo advertiser magazines that can help you get an idea of house prices and rents in various areas. Local newspaper classified ads can offer further information. Often real estate companies and Chambers of Commerce can help with local taxes and average living expense figures. Calculate your salary from what you've been offered, from area newspaper want ads, or from trade publications.

If you have a job in hand, you may already have been contacted by a very important information resource person—the company destination services counselor. This person can be a bonanza of budget numbers, local lore, and advice on everything from the neighborhoods where colleagues live to where you can get your lawnmower fixed.

 Tip: If your company doesn't offer this service, but you can afford a private consultation, and/or you're going to be buying an expensive home, try a large real estate firm or consult the latest Employee Relocation

Counsel's directory of real estate brokers and destination services.

The biggest relocation service, PHH Fantus, now part of Deloitte & Touche, (203) 834-8500, offers services worldwide. Another big location research company, Runzheimer International, (800) 558-1702, www.runzheimer.com, can send you customized comparative cost-of-living reports by mail. Independent networks, including Relocation Consultants, Inc., (800) 643-7222, Independent Relocation Consultants Association, (800) 432-1RCA, and BTA Economic Research Institute, (800) 627-3697, also issue compiled demographic and budget reports on various locations.

Finally, if you or a member of your family is or has been a member of the Armed Forces or National Guard, you can get a PHH Fantus affiliated relocation consultant and discount real estate agency services by joining USAA, (800) 582-8722, an affiliation group, which offers a wide variety of insurance and other services.

Fill out the "Monthly Budget Estimator" in Appendix D using the most accurate figures you can find. P 312

DRAFTING YOUR
DECISION / ACTION TIMETABLE

Nothing motivates like deadlines. If you're up for a job transfer, of course, you already know you have to decide by a specific time. If your impending move depends entirely on internal forces chattering away inside your head, however, you can keep putting the decision off to a point that you become immobilized. If this is happening to you, use this timetable to break out of the pattern.

Decision / Action Timetable

Pinpoint the best time for you to make a move. This may be before the next summer heat wave hits, after you've had six months' experience with a new job responsibility, or the day you reach a milestone birthday. You know what your inner clock is talking about. Write down your "Must Move" date. Then:

July, 2005

√ *Count backward four months from the "Must Move" date.*
Write down this "Decision Due" date: April 2005
√ *Commit to making a decision by this date. Tack your "Must Move" and/or your "Decision Due" dates up on your bulletin board or refrigerator to jog your memory. Review the rest of this book to keep the decision making process in gear.*

If you can't face setting a "Must Move" date, look over your "City Evaluator" for your current location. Reevaluate whether you really want to move. Is your current location scoring better than your other choices? Is there any new location that offers *at least most* of your important items?

Delve into other options in this book. Maybe what you need is a solution to a family issue from Chapter 2 or a trial move from Chapter 3. Read Chapter 4 so you can set up your move schedule to get the best from Mr. Taxman. Browse through all the possibilities—knowing the options can save much effort and hundreds, even thousands of dollars.

If you still can't set that "Must Move" deadline, put this book away and stop researching for three months. Keep it out of your conscious mind as much as possible. At the end of that time, do a new evaluation. Putting your subconscious to work for you may be all it takes to clarify your needs.

family Issues

PSYCHING UP THE WHOLE FAMILY FOR CHANGE .

When psychologists Holms and Rahe did their seminal study on how events trigger stress in our lives, moving scored right up there on their Social Readjustment scale as a major stress factor in our lives.

When we're about to move, we're often going through other major changes as well. Job wise we're finding our first job, retiring, evaluating a new career. Personally, we're leaving friends and family behind. We may even be going through a divorce or the death of a spouse. The cumulative effect can be overwhelming.

We're usually moving more than just ourselves. We have family. We have pets and belongings. We have responsibilities and routines. Sometimes there are wrenching decisions about family members who can't move for one reason or another. As soon as you begin contemplating any move farther away than the same school district, children's friends and school become a big part of the process.

Since we all do have to face moving, and since economists predict we'll be moving even more in the 2000s in order to meet the economic challenges of the job marketplace, how do we cope?

The first thing to acknowledge is that every member of the family is likely to have a different approach. The youngest child may be the type to jump into a project at the deep end; the mother may want weeks of researching and analyzing; the father may want to hash plans over with his buddies; the oldest child may want to jump in one day and spend the next three not thinking about the move at all.

Although approaches vary, gathering concrete information and developing a clear game plan works wonders for everyone. So does your attitude. Studies by psychologists M. Scheier, Wientraub, and C. Carver indicate that people who have general expectancies of good outcomes of a situation experience less physical illnesses during times of stress.

Those who cope best:

√ Look at problems as challenges.
√ Discuss a problem in terms of how it can be solved, not how terrible it is or how awful it makes them feel or what bad luck it is.
√ Get help from friends to deal with whatever has to be done.
√ Make specific plans.
√ Carry out the plans as quickly as possible.

TIME OUT FOR THE DAY SCHOOL DANCE

If one of your most important moving criteria is a good facility for a preschooler—particularly if you're a working parent—your advance research has to be thorough.

Dr. Stevanne Auerbach, director of the Institute for Childhood Resources in San Francisco and author of numerous books for parents, including *Keys to Choosing Child Care*, advises:

1. Contact the Child Care Information and Referral Agency in the new community for a list of child care alternatives. The national number is (800) 424-2246.
2. Look through the local parenting newspaper for additional resources. Contact Parenting Publications of America,

(210) 492-9057, for information on local parent-oriented newspapers.
3. Contact several other parents working in the new company for advice. Sometimes the company itself gives referrals.
4. Check the Government pages in the local telephone book for the licensing agency, and ask for a list of licensed centers and homes.
5. Check the yellow pages for nursery schools, child care facilities, and nanny agencies.
6. Ask for suggestions from any pediatrician and/or pediatrician's receptionist you contact.
7. Put an ad in the local paper under domestic/child care help wanted, or look for people offering their services. Follow up with telephone interviews and check referrals.
8. Make sure the arrangement you select has room for your child and that all enrollment requirements are met prior to your arrival.

ANTICIPATING CHILDREN'S CONCERNS

If both spouses like the idea of the move, and it's all systems go on the job front, tell your children about the move as soon as there are no more questions about the date. When making the announcement, describe something about the move that will be particularly advantageous to them—a chance to live in a bigger house or to go skiing, swimming, or mountain hiking, or perhaps it will be time to adopt a new pet.

Older children will accept the idea of moving "sometime in the spring," but patience is never a virtue of the preschooler. If anything, the constant questions, what ifs, and squirming uneasiness about the move will help you completely believe in the process. Another big help—the preschooler is far more reliable than any daily newspaper for getting the word out to your friends and neighbors.

When a Move Is Not Decided

If there are uncertainties about a move—either because a job offer may not come through, or because both parents aren't convinced they want to relocate—how to tell the children becomes a major issue. If they're likely to sense the uneasiness, explain the entire situation to them as clearly as possible, tell them some positive things about the move if it does happen, and give them the date when you think you'll know for certain what will happen.

As soon as the course is set, start helping them to adjust. No matter how young they are, they will be somewhat apprehensive. Even a three-month-old has already started making observations about the familiar vs. the unfamiliar, and is often frightened by anything out of a routine. Reactions can range from mild to nightmares and bedwetting to serious long-term problems due to loss of a trusted friend or inability to cope in the new locale.

Involve the children as much as possible. Just like adults, many of their fears will center on losing control of their lives. Get their help on research tasks. Tell their teachers, and ask if they can have assignments connected with their new location. See about finding pen pals with the children of friends and future coworkers.

Don't forget to spend time with each child alone to talk. Discuss good things about your adventure, but also share misgivings and sadness about leaving good friends and good times. Don't oversell the new location. Unrealistic expectations can lead to disappointment. Sometimes it's a good idea to leave some special goodies about the new location to be "discovered" after you move.

Separation Questions

Families that have gone through a divorce have especially complex problems to solve. Diedre Schwartz, a single mother I helped move to San Francisco from Philadelphia after her company offered her a promotion she couldn't refuse, brought her daughter with her, but left her son behind with her ex-husband.

"The choices were just zilch," she commented. "I didn't want to leave either child behind, my husband didn't want me to take either. Neither one of the kids wanted to move. I consider myself lucky that my ex and I have worked out an agreement, so we're not still pecking and clawing at each other. And the kids are happy with the arrangement, although neither one seems to look forward to the July-with-the-other-parent trip. Long term,

I just have to hope that my son will reach an age where he'll want to spend some time out here—maybe at college."

Tips and Traps for Parents

The following are some strategies to consider:

√ Don't make all the decisions without child input. *Children's resistance to moving is heightened when they feel forgotten and left out. One mother was horrified to overhear her son asking a friend, "My folks are giving our dog to the Entzes, but could you get your folks to take me? I don't like the Entzes."*

√ Don't take the children with you on a long-distance house- or job-hunting trip. *Air flights are no fun for most children under seven, and even older children are rarely helpful on house-hunting trips. Except for teenagers who are enthusiastic about the move, try to arrange for someone to look after them rather than taking them along during the reconnaissance stage. But don't forget to bring back pictures of the three most likely homes and research material for the projects they're interested in.*

√ Investigate all the consequences of school changes. *Children participating in special programs (sports, music, dance, art, language) may have trouble finding these classes in your new location. Teenagers nearing graduation and/or on special programs may have particular needs.* Be sure to notify your child's school and all extracurricular leaders as soon as you know about the move. *They can help you research what's available in your new location—and perhaps advise you on neighborhoods for house-hunting, as well.*

√ Consider a mid-schoolyear moving date. *The National Association of Realtors statistics show that year after year, house sales go up in the spring and peak in April and May. A large number of people "feel like moving" at that time of year, but even more say they've been motivated by trying to make their move so that the children have time to settle into a location before school starts. This is the way our parents did it, and we have carried on with the tradition. We were surprised to find that a significant number of parents we've worked with did it differently. They had their children arriving in the middle of the school year, and they swear by that program. Their children settled in faster than when they started school as new enrollees in the fall.*

These parents theorize that this schedule works because the teachers can focus on a newcomer more easily in the middle of the year, when there are fewer problems with all the other students finding new classrooms and wanting to switch teachers.

Children I've talked to who've moved several times say they were most miserable coming into a new community at the beginning of summer, when there was no school to provide an easy access to others in their age group.

√ If you do move during the school year, make certain the children are enrolled before you move. *Enrollment can be a lengthy process, and it's disastrous to have to go through the wait after you've arrived.*

√ Make it a family priority to find an extracurricular activity that each child wants. *Again, keep children informed and get their input before making a decision. Don't use a move as an opportunity to enroll a child in a sport Mom or Dad always wanted to play, but the child doesn't like.*

√ Plan so that your children's good friends can spend some time together next summer. *Either arrange for your child to go back or have the friend come stay with you.*

When It May Be Right to Leave an Older Child Behind

If your teenager, or a significant member of his or her school/extracurricular activity advisor team, has some serious reason for advising that the youngster stay behind, discuss the possibility seriously. Finishing a special course may be vital to future advancement. Your son's football coach may be the best one to get him into the college of his choice. If your research shows tile schools ill your new location don't have the same opportunities or may have a team where your child doesn't fit, other options need to be investigated.

These include:

√ Staying with friends or relatives both you and the teenager trust. *Make sure arrangements include a clear understanding of what duties the teenager has to fulfill (helping at a job, baby-sitting, etc.). Write up "house rules" with the host family regarding daily routines such as how much TV, how much homework, weekday and weekend curfew, off-limits language, music, dress, and the like. Have the teenager review and sign in blood (just kidding).*

Also, sign a written agreement with the host family as to whether you're paying for room and board. Without everybody thinking through the practical details, misunderstandings can deep-six the arrangement very quickly.

Finally, have a code phrase with your teenager that translates "Get me out of here immediately." Some problems, such as harassment from the host family or a serious run-in with someone at school, can't be explained over the phone, much less dealt with by a teenager. In that case, you need to be able to step in instantly.

√ Working as an au pair or other household help. *This takes a serious commitment and a responsible attitude. Some teenagers already have exhibited good social sense and the ability to keep working at a job, even when it's unpleasant and boring; others haven't.*

You can't expect an employer to shoulder parenting "Have you done your homework?" responsibilities, so you and your teenager should set up a weekly report schedule that both of you treat as a professional obligation. Practice this new relationship before the teenager gets the job and the rest of the family moves—one or both of you may hate it.

√ Renting a room at the YMCA or some other dorm facility. *We don't recommend this. Several families we've talked with tried it but have had problems with teenagers getting into trouble because living on their own attracted friends who, according to one father, "were just out to trash everything, themselves included."*

However, there are some possibilities. Sometimes you can find a boarding facility connected with your school or church. Obviously, some institutional places are better run than others. Investigate thoroughly.

THE "TRAILING SPOUSE" SYNDROME

Every time a family moves, no matter how democratic the decision process has been, one partner is being transferred or taking the lead on the decision to move and the other becomes the "trailing spouse." According to Glenn Williams, a career consultant with Hardy Freeman & Associates, the trailing spouse has several problems that make the move particularly difficult.

For example, he explains, prospective employers in the new location may be suspicious because the trailing spouse is going through a "voluntary" move. There are questions of how committed that spouse is to his or her career. It's difficult to talk to friends about fears and resentments, without their asking, "Then why did you agree to move?" Williams suggests that the "trailing spouse" vent feelings with a career counselor, then move forward to explore the positive opportunities for growth that will come out of the change.

It used to be assumed that the trailing spouse was always the wife, that she'd adhere to the biblical admonition to go "whither thou goest," and that was that. In the 1960s, when the widely read *Help Your Family Make a Better Move* was written, less than a third of married women worked outside the home. The book's authors (both women) described the trailing spouse's role this way: "As wife and mother, you arc the person in the family whose attitude toward moving can help every other member of the family. Your feelings are highly contagious. Your enthusiasm affects your husband's morale and determines your children's reaction toward the move. If you accept the move and decide to make the most of it, your family will follow your lead."

These admonitions still ring true, but they're no longer for women only, and "accepting the move" almost always also means "finding a new job" for the trailing spouse. The 1990 census showed 58.4 percent of married women work. When tile Employee Relocation Council later polled its members, it found that 78 percent were relocating female employees with working spouses.

Today's couple is almost as likely to find the wife being transferred and the husband needing to find a job as the other way around. It's not unheard of for both partners to be notified of a transfer—to different locations—the same week.

Large corporations, looking over the growing lists of employees refusing to transfer, have devised relocation incentive programs that include spousal employee assistance plans. If you need these services, ask what options are available during the initial "how would you like a change of scenery?" interview, whether you plan to accept the transfer or not. Then review the options we list in Chapter 5 in the section "Negotiating Your Best Deal with Your Employer" and keep your ear to the ground.

If you decide to move, you need to know what others have won for their relocation packages in order to know what concessions the company can and will make.

If your company doesn't offer official programs to help the relocating spouse, ask if you can have some ad hoc assistance. The company may say it will be glad to try to help and what do you have in mind? Even if you don't get help this time, voicing your desire for a program may mean it *will* be available the next time a transfer comes along.

And remember, even if the company already does have a spousal assistance program, finding a new job is rarely easy. Not only should you deploy whatever forces an employer offers, you should turn to the section entitled "Long-Distance Job-Hunt Strategies" in Chapter 5 for information that can be tailored specifically for your situation.

SOLVING THE DEPENDENT RELATIVE DILEMMA

"We solved the problem of how to care for my father-in-law by taking him with us when we moved," said one Bank of America employee who moved from California to Arizona when the company took over a large data entry center there. "We pooled the sale money on both homes and bought a duplex. He loves the weather, and there are all kinds of community center activities here to keep him busy. He has arthritis, so I have to keep his fridge stocked with pre-opened meals, and once in a while we have to go by and fix something, but mostly this new arrangement means we all have the freedom to lead our separate lives, yet still know we're right here if there's a problem."

The dilemma of what to do about semi-independent parents or other relatives or close friends was one of the biggest problems encountered by the people we surveyed. Not only did it put people in a quandary about moving away, respondents reported that moving into an area in order to help a parent was a prime motivator.

How to Help—Some Points to Consider

If your family is worried about an elderly or disabled person, keep the following in mind as you investigate what can be done:

√ What do your parents feel about the move? *Would they rather go with you or stay where they are? One school administrator explained, "My mom was really on my case about our moving, 'And stealing my grandchildren away.' as she put it. Then I said, 'Okay, let's evaluate this. How about your moving too?' We sat down and looked at the possibility, and she finally said, 'You know, I'm going to have to say no. But I'm not going to fight your decision anymore. Thanks for asking me to come.'"*

√ Who else offers support? *Are there several friends and other relatives in your current area who all take care of each other? Get in touch with these people, and see if everyone feels that the gap you'll leave can be filled. Don't forget that an important part of your parents' lives may very well be that they in turn are caring for someone in their current neighborhood.*

Be sure to keep everyone's telephone numbers, so that you can check in from time to time from your new home. Hearing how your parents are doing from a friend is often very reassuring, and keeping up to date with the whole community makes the distance between your lives seems smaller.

√ What kind of community centers and other services are available? *Do local chapters of clubs such as the American Association of Retired Persons (AARP) have networking services with the new location? Go over Appendix C for national and international services. Check the yellow pages under "Elder" and "Senior Citizen" headings for both your current and your new locations. Subscribe to senior newspapers in both areas. You may find your parents already live near a senior day care facility that offers just the daily meal program and exercise class that's needed.*

√ What kind of physical changes in the *home* will make a difference? *Check the Internet for sites like www.barrier-free.com, which has products for independent living. Look over your parents' home to see what can be done. Railings, easy jar opening devices and a voice-activated telephone may be just what's needed to make for independent living. You also may want to install a daily call service and emergency help such as Lifeline, (800) 635-5156.*

Financing Exotica to the Rescue

Often the biggest problem to face for our parents (or sometimes for ourselves, for that matter) is being "house rich and pocketbook poor." The way around this obstacle is to investigate several exotic refinancing techniques that have become popular since the mid-1980s as ways to help the person who wants to stay in a home but doesn't have enough income without tapping into the home's equity. Here are three of the possibilities.

Reverse Mortgages. These work exactly the opposite of a conventional mortgage, where a person borrows a lump sum to buy a house and then pays it back (with interest) in monthly increments over the course of thirty years. With a reverse mortgage, a lender pays the individual monthly amounts for a set number of months and is repaid a lump sum when the individual dies or sells the house. Some programs charge lower origination fees and interest in return for participating in the home's appreciation.

Sale Leaseback. The individual sells the home to a member of the family or an investor, then rents it back. This frees the equity in a lump sum, with the first $125,000 profit tax free for individuals over fifty-five. It works well for the investor if the rent can cover expenses and mortgage payments, and the appreciation gives a reasonable return.

Refinance. Lenders won't allow a conventional refinance unless a borrower has a regular income to cover payments, so planning to repay out of the equity freed doesn't work. However, sometimes a bank may allow a loan if a working family member cosigns. Otherwise, a retiree should refinance several years before retirement.

 Tip: For more information on financing possibilities, send a request with a large postage-paid envelope to the American Association of Retired Persons Home-Equity Information Center, P.O. Box 2400, Long Beach, CA 90901-2400. Ask for "Home-Made Money: A Consumer's Guide to Home Equity Conversion" and a list of reverse-mortgage lenders across the nation.

Another information source is the National Center for Home Equality Conversion, 348 W. Main Street, Marshal, MN 56358, which supplies a list of reverse mortgage lenders and information on sale leaseback.

HEALTH HURDLES

As you plan your move, take into consideration the health of all family members. No matter what, you'll need copies of your records to take with you. Call your health providers, tell them about your plans, and find out if you need to sign a particular form and/or pay a fee for copying your records. Get a typed list of medications and their generic names. Ask if they can refer you to colleagues in your destination city. If your child sees a pediatrician, ask if she can refer you to any day care facilities or authorities.

You may want to have a general physical before you move, as this may assist getting health insurance in your new location. If you're moving abroad, ask if your health provider gives out health reports on the destination area listing what to look out for and what inoculations you'll need. Also, get sufficient prescriptions (including glasses prescriptions) filled to last you at least six months.

 Tip: Diabetics and others needing special medications have several specific travel health needs. Contact The Diabetic Traveler (a quarterly newsletter), P.O. Box 8223, Stamford, CT 0690.5. Also, call Sugar Happy Diabetes Supplies at (800) 473-4636. Order their catalog of hard-to-find diabetic supplies, including the Diapack, a traveling case for insulin or other temperature-sensitive medicine, which will keep it cold for hours without refrigeration.

Have a doctor's letter to show immigration officials why syringes are necessary. Never pack any medications you need regularly in the moving van or even in luggage that you don't carry with you on your flight—if the flight gets delayed or the bag gets lost, you could have a serious problem.

Have your teeth checked and cleaned. We've never seen research to back this up, but it's our theory that the stress of moving often triggers dental or health problems.

OF PETS AND PITFALLS

Moving often involves so many lifestyle changes that what to do with a pet becomes a big issue, particularly if you're going from a rural situation to a city. Except for Manhattan high-rise managers, very few apartment people commonly allow dogs, and, nationwide, apartment associations report more than 50 percent refuse to accept any pets at all.

If you're going to be giving away your pet, the sooner you start asking friends and relatives to help find a new home and put an ad in the paper, the better. Other possibilities are to put notices up at the local Society for Prevention of Cruelty to Animals, veterinarian offices, pet stores, and the library.

Tip: Every year the SPCA finds thousands of pets that have either gotten lost or have purposely been left to fend for themselves by owners who have moved away. By the time they're found, these pets are often victims of accidents, have been attacked by wild animals, or are starving and diseased. If you can't find a home for your pet, don't think she can fend for herself, even if she's an independent cat. Take her to a shelter and enlist its help in giving her the best hope for finding a new home.

Paws on the Road

No moving company will transport a pet because the storage area is neither insulated nor air-conditioned, and a car trip of longer than a day, particularly during freezing weather or a hot summer, is not good for any animal.

Two months before you leave, take your pet to your veterinarian to have a physical, get an interstate health certificate including an up-to-date rabies inoculation verification, pick up all records, and discuss the moving trip. If you're likely to be in an area where mosquitoes carry heartworm, you'll need to start a preventive program.

Talk with your vet about any medicines, prevention precautions that need to be mounted ahead of time, or items that should be taken with you. Get input on the best ways for your animal to be transported. Megan Walker, one of our survey respondents, emphasizes that pets should be vaccinated against Lyme disease.

Tip: If you're moving to one of several states, your pet will have to be quarantined upon your arrival. Hawaii, for example, requires 120-day quarantine.

Overseas quarantine requirements can be even longer, and you may need different inoculations. Check with your state veterinarian, State Office of Animal Husbandry, or write the ASPCA, Education Department, 441 East 92nd Street, New York, NY 10128. Its $4 booklet, "Traveling with Your Pet," gives animal travel regulations on a state-by-state and a country-by-country basis.

Your veterinarian may recommend a light sedative, although pet's reactions are erratic. It's a good idea to have your pet tattooed or microchipped with an ID name and a contact telephone number. Use the number of a relative who doesn't move very often or a pet identification service your veterinarian recommends. Be sure the pet also has a collar with name and contact telephone number.

If you're taking a pet on an overnight trip, make sure to reserve ahead, particularly during vacation months. Besides the national ASPCA, you can ask the local SPCA branch or your veterinarian for a list of hotels/motels that will take animals.

If you're taking your pet in your car, have her accompany you on short trips in advance, so that her carrier and the vehicle become "home territory." Always keep her in a carrier in the car. If she hangs her head out the window, a flying stone can blind and a closely passing vehicle can do worse. Letting her loose inside the car can result in her tangling up the driver or being very badly hurt in an accident.

Tip: Never transport pets (even hibernating snakes in a vivarium) in the car trunk or with the furniture. Loads shift. Uninsulated compartments quickly become freezers or ovens. The potential for disaster is infinite. We've had a very sad ending to moving a hamster in our own car, because small animals are much more likely to collapse from heatstroke than humans. Our frequent-mover respondents report cats and dogs fare better.

If you're moving long distance, investigate shipping through your veterinarian or with a pet shipper. Air Animal, (800) 635-

3448, ships both nationally and internationally. Make sure your pet's plane comes in at least 24 hours after your arrival.

Often it's economical for a member of the family who is flying to take the pet along. Some airlines even will allow a pet in a carrying kennel under the seat, provided you have certification of her rabies or other shots—always ask what documentation you need. We have had good experiences with air trips for larger pets.

Air shipping costs for an unaccompanied pet will run approximately $80 for anything parakeet size up to 100 pounds. Large animals weighing more than that (kennel included) are $100 per 100 pounds. You need to buy a fiberglass or plastic carrier kennel separately. It must be air cargo recommended and large enough for the animal to move around in. It should have a built-in water dish. Check with your veterinarian or one of the discount pet supply stores such as Petco.

Charges for Air Animal and other such services, which take care of getting the best cargo service for your pet and can do everything—including pickup and delivery—start around $250 for small pets to $550 for larger ones.

If you're driving with your pet, remember that animals need as many (or more) rest stops as children. Schedule one for every two to three hours. If there's an accident, just clean it up without comment. The animal is too distracted during this time to learn from any discipline measures.

Even if your pet is accustomed to traveling with you, it's not a good idea to let her off the leash. In strange surroundings she might bolt into traffic, or the sudden appearance of a rabbit or a squirrel could lead to a disoriented, lost pet.

A friend of ours lost her cat temporarily because he was able to wriggle out of his leash. Not too scary, except that it was at the Grand Canyon! Don't put yourself through that extra worry. It's better to leave smaller pets in their carrier cages and in a secure, protected spot by the car, if you're going to make a side trip. Make sure she's in deep shade that won't disappear half an hour after you leave and be sure there's a big bowl of water.

Tip: If your pet does get lost, contact the local SPCA immediately. Provide complete data on your pet, including name, identifying markers, a photograph, and where you can be reached at your new location.

You also should run an ad in the local paper describing your pet, offering a reward, and giving your telephone number. Ads produce amazing results. An SPCA office recalls getting a call from Tokyo, where a vacationing local reading the paper en route had noticed an ad about a pet she'd taken to the shelter. The SPCA was able to reunite the pet with her owner.

THREE

Alternatives

RELOCATION STRATEGIES FOR GETTING YOUR FEET WET WITHOUT GETTING IN OVER YOUR HEAD

You're moving. That is, so fate, your boss, your significant other, or your inner itch has decreed. But there's a war going on inside your head with another voice that doesn't like the decision. Some part of you doesn't want to go.

Does this mean your only option is crawling into a hole and pulling the hole down after you? Of course not. A number of alternatives to outright relocation can make the process significantly less risky.

What about the "commute move," where you spend only part of your time in the new location at the new job? What about a "homeshare" arrangement to split housing costs and make easing into a new lifestyle that much easier? What about the "trial move;" where you don't have to make the commitment involved with a full-scale relocation? These alternatives can be achieved with a surprisingly small amount of effort. And they offer the big advantage of not having to burn your bridges or publicly recant if you go back to your current location/lifestyle.

The drawback? Somewhere down the line you may be facing two move—the "alternative" arrangement and the "real move" later. While this may be daunting, nevertheless it is preferable to two full-scale relocations—one there and another one back.

 Tip: *Alternative moves present some complications when writing off relocation expenses on your tax return. Chapter 4 examines the pitfalls and lists possible alternative moves that might be better for you, tax-wise.*

You'll want to explore the possibilities of an alternative move if:

√ *You don't feel comfortable with your new location for any reason.*

√ *A partner moving with you doesn't feel comfortable with your new location for any reason.*

√ *You don't feel comfortable with your new job or you don't have one yet.*

√ *Ditto your partner.*

√ *A better job offer may come up in some other location down the road.*

√ *You can't (or don't want to) sell your existing home, or you don't want to give up a lease on a great apartment you've loved living in.*

If any one of the above (or a combination) applies to you, read on! We've talked with dozens of people who've had direct experience with the following possibilities. We've tried a number of alternative moves ourselves, and highly recommend them.

ALTERNATIVE POSSIBILITIES

The Commute Move

The commute move is probably the most customary solution for couples with that increasingly common problem—one spouse has a enticing job offer in the new locale, the other one has a great existing job right where you are, thank you very much. The arrangement works best for locations not more than three hours' drive away, where weekend and holiday commutes are relatively easy. We have a relative, however, who has commuted between New Jersey and Orlando over two years, and one of the couples we've interviewed commuted between South Carolina and California for more than nine months.

Note: Commute moves rarely qualify for any tax deductions on traveling between the two locales. (See Chapter 4.) If you're going into a situation like this, discuss it with your tax advisor to see what you might be able to do.

This alternative works particularly well if you have:

√ *An "assignment" job that makes it possible to take on one project in the new location without giving up work in your current area.*
√ *A possibly more enticing job opening up back in your current hometown.*
√ *Not sold your existing home, and someone has to remain behind and finish this task.*
√ *Children finishing a particularly important class in school that can't be duplicated in the new location.*

Tips to Remember:

√ *Make it a priority in the new location to find yourself a comfortable place in a neighborhood that feels friendly. You won't get any insights into how well you like living there if you plonk yourself into a sleazy furnished room that gives you the creeps. Also, you'll have no success convincing a reluctant partner to change his or her mind about the move.*
√ *Sublets are good. Also try furnished apartments, short-term rentals, vacation rentals, corporate interim housing (which is available for individuals—see "Finding Accommodations" at the end of this chapter). Sometimes you can find a room rental in a home that turns into the perfect space for your stay. Remember, you're trying to evaluate what your new life will be in a new location, so make your temporary home as much "you" as you can.*
√ *Furnishing a small apartment with secondhand things or with*
√ *Rental furniture is viable if the arrangement is likely to last more than three months.*
√ *Both spouses should commute back and forth between the old and the possible location if you're serious about*

making a change. Otherwise, it's all too easy for one or the other never to feel ready to make a decision.

√ *Don't forget, children enjoy "trying out" a new hometown too. They'll have much more appreciation of the pros and cons of the new location if they have a chance to see it for themselves on weekends and vacations.*

Relocation-Research Vacation

A relocation-research vacation is by far the most popular approach, and it's fun and easy. Anyone armed with this book can do a month's advance research, spend two weeks on a research vacation, and come away with a very good idea of how well a prospective location "fits" their needs.

This works particularly well if you have:

√ *Moved several times before and have a solid idea of what things are really important to you.*
√ *The time and the budget to prepare for the vacation, an evaluation period afterward, and launching a new search if the first location doesn't turn out to be to your liking.*
√ *People who recommend this method:*
√ *Businesspeople who do research business trips, and add the important ingredient of sounding out possible new employers to their list of things to investigate.*
√ *Parents who want to incorporate school vacations and children's reactions in their relocation planning.*
√ *Prospective retirees who can spend several years' worth of vacations "location shopping" for just the right place to return to later.*
√ *College students who can spend their summer vacations working in different locations to test viability.*

Tips to remember:

√ *Rent a room in a home or stay with friends rather than in a hotel. Staying with a native offers the great advantage of having someone to show you around. Be sure to select someone with a similar lifestyle to yours—a city type won't get many insights out of staying in a suburban home.*
√ *Check college bulletin boards for short-term sublets located in residential areas you want to explore.*
√ *Other very doable options can be found in the local newspaper under "Furnished Apartments," "Short-term Rent-*

als," "Vacation Rentals," and similar headings. Even if you have to take a place for longer than you want to stay the total cost often is less than you'd spend for a shorter stay at a hotel.

√ Rooms in several national hotel chains, such as Embassy Suites, have individual kitchens, which give you the opportunity to "live like a native," and the concierge usually can give you local insights.

√ Look under "Mobile Home Parks" in the yellow pages; sometimes you can find short-term furnished rentals that way.

√ To investigate several communities during one trip, or to explore living in a wilderness area, you might rent an RV. Like mobile home parks, RV parks usually are full of friendly people sharing information about a location. Both mobile homes and RVs come complete with kitchen and can accommodate up to six people. Look under "Recreational Vehicle Rentals" in your destination yellow pages or call a national agency such as El Monte RV Center at (800) 367-3687

√ Check bed and breakfast travel books for intimate places. In the off season, hosts might give you the run of the kitchen, and generally they'll treat you like a visiting cousin.

Homesharing

It used to be that getting a roommate was a mark of the young and underfinanced. In today's financially subdued climate populated by smaller families that often are fragmented into several different geographical locations, getting a roommate has proven very versatile. The change in attitude, of course, is marked by a new term, "homesharing."

Whether you want to share your current home with someone, or you're looking to move and find a homeshare in your new location, there are numerous possibilities to explore. An important decision to make at the outset is what you want from the arrangement. Are your needs monetary, practical task sharing, emotional, or a combination of all three? Accommodations range from the "pay the rent and stay out of my part of the house" situations, to carefully orchestrated peer programs for people matched with common interests, needs, and preferences, to informal ads that turn into deep friendships. Don't forget, the traditional turn-of-the-century boardinghouse hostess/host always ended up marrying one of the guests.

You'll want to investigate homesharing if you:

√ Want to slice your current housing costs without "moving down" to a smaller place or a less desirable neighborhood.

√ Want the freedom to leave your home for extended periods and have someone there who gets along with your pet and knows how much water to give the plants.

√ Want to have someone around to share an occasional evening at home watching TV or doing a crossword puzzle.

√ Have a physical situation that makes you vulnerable to falls or other accidents.

√ Have at-home duties of caring for children or others that conflict with work.

√ Have a part-time job that makes it easy for you to supplement your income by helping with someone else's home responsibilities.

√ Want to get to know foreigners, academics, entrepreneurs—the list is endless—staying for a short time in your area, perhaps with a view toward staying with your guests at their place later.

People who recommend this method:

√ Singles of all ages, including single parents.

√ People who enjoy having other people around and are curious about newcomers to their region.

√ People wanting to cut housing costs.

√ People who work at home or have a part-time job and enjoy shouldering domestic chores for others.

Tips to remember:

√ In Appendix C, we give you "Contacts and Resources" for setting up all kinds of alternative moves. Appendixes B and E contain forms to use when setting up the actual arrangement.

√ Don't limit yourself just to the national sources of homeshares. Local bulletin boards, newspapers, and clubs are usually the best sources.

√ *Homeshares can be either short or long term. We've only done short term, but several of our interviewees highly recommend long-term stays after a three-month trial period.*

The Trial Move: The In's and Out's of Home Trades and Term Rentals

We love home trades. Our family has enjoyed home trades several times, and once ended up living in the charming home of a future Nobel Prize winner. We've also been happy subletting someone else's fully furnished home.

The advantages of these types of trial moves are numerous. You can "try on" a whole way of living without any of the hassles of sorting and shipping furniture, of selling and buying a house, of figuring out what to do with your car and your plants. If you're job hunting, you can start organizing in advance with stationery listing your new telephone number and address.

Your new home often comes with everything ready to go, including a car with a list of local filling stations and a wonderful note describing "the best supermarket, dry cleaners and bookstores are . . ." (See Appendix B for checklists.)

But trial moves do have drawbacks. Sometimes it's impossible to set up one of these arrangements in your chosen location on the dates you need. The trade/furnished rental can also suffer from a housekeeping problem. Nobody ever takes care of the home you leave behind like you do. Either they're too neat or you are. Valuables in both homes may get broken (particularly it' both of you have children). Gardens will be changed. We once returned to our original home to find a terrible mess because our trading partners had invited four extra people to stay.

You can rent your home and find another furnished place in the new location more easily than doing a swap, but you often don't get the same stimulation of "trying on" someone else's lifestyle. Also, this type of renting can be costly, as furnished places invariably seem to be difficult to rent in your existing location and expensive to rent where you're going. (See the next option of renting unfurnished places.)

Home trades/furnished rentals work particularly well if you already:

√ Have a job but aren't sure you want to keep it.
√ Love the area but aren't sure you can get a job there.

People who recommend this technique include:

√ Career changers who yearn for big transformations in lifestyle as well as work but aren't sure this yearning is going to stay with them.
√ People returning to a location with mixed emotions.
√ People who can't sell their home in a down market.
√ People who want to save on rent during a job search in the new location.
√ Anyone with a "portable" job who has several location options.

Tips to remember:

√ These arrangements work best for situations where your trial move is scheduled for two weeks to six months. Shorter periods aren't worth the trouble. For longer stays, unfurnished rentals usually work better.
√ If some of your belongings are fragile, lock them away. If most of your belongings are fragile, consider trading your home unfurnished.

Renting Your Home Unfurnished

When some good friends won a two-year scholarship to an advanced studies program at MIT, they chose to rent their home unfurnished. The reasons?

√ It was easier and faster to arrange than a trade.
√ The rent received covered the rent they paid in Boston.
√ They could sell or give away some of their furniture, store the things they loved, and not worry about damage. In Boston they picked up the necessities secondhand.
√ Pets could go along—a difficult requirement if they'd been looking for a furnished rental at their destination. (This also could be a consideration if children are involved.)

This option works particularly well if you:

√ *Know that your trial move definitely has a cutoff date, and all signs are that you'll be moving back to your original home.*
√ *Don't have time to set up a home trade.*
√ *Don't want to have strangers living with your possessions.*

Tips to remember:

√ *You'll almost certainly have to leave large appliances behind—few renters can cart these things around, particularly if they're only staying in a place a few months.*
√ *Expect to be gone at least six months. Anything shorter than that makes the whole rigmarole of storing furniture too time consuming.*
√ *Leaving your home vacant for over two weeks is inviting break-ins, roof leaks, and burst pipes. If you can't bear to have someone renting your place furnished for a month or two, make arrangements for a friend or a professional housesitter to come in and check things.*

THE NUTS AND BOLTS

Now that we've talked about the major moving alternatives, their advantages and best uses, here are some guidelines for making them work.

Getting Your Home Ready

Obviously an advantage of either the commute move or the research vacation is that you don't have to do anything at all to get your existing home ready. Outside of making special arrangements for care of pets and plants while you're gone, you can focus most of your energy on investigating the new location.

Preparing your home for a homeshare, a trade, or a furnished rental and "checking out" from your partners' home when your visit is over isn't difficult either. Many people don't do anything more than figure out how to lock up areas where there are fragile items. You'll also want to check Appendix B, the "Home Trade Move-in/Move-out Checklist." This is based on the list used by one of the largest home exchange clubs in the world, Intervac, (415) 435-3497, which was founded by European teachers in 1953.

The option of putting your furniture in storage and renting your place vacant entails the most up-front work—we recommend this method only if you're going to be gone for six months or longer.

Tip: Even if you're not clearing out your furniture, start garage sale planning now. When you're freeing up closets for other people to stay, harden your heart against those unfinished projects and un-reparable gizmos. Get rid of them. Today. If you decide not to transfer after your trial move, you'll find the lack of clutter in your home inspiring. If you go for a full-fledged move, getting the most questionable stuff out of the way now will make the next steps easier.

Marketing Your Term Rental or Trade

Although you save time and energy on preparing a home with a trial move, you'll need to focus on marketing as much as if you were making a full-fledged move—maybe more so.

To do a good job, take the time to think through why your home is fun and desirable, and "sell the dream." People who do trial moves are individualists who enjoy the personal aspects of their adventure. Keep these people in mind as you put the word out.

For marketing strategy, don't just run an ad one Sunday and forget the project if nothing happens. Go over the list in the next section on where to look for trades and term rentals in your destination. Launch a similar bulletin/notice attack in your current hometown. Review the "Potential Occupancy Agreement Letter" in Appendix E and add your home's selling points. If you're describing a home in Albuquerque, New Mexico, for example, you might include information about skiing at Taos, exploring ghost towns in the mountains, and enjoying campfire food in the desert.

Tip: Don't forget to make it very easy to contact you. Seasoned trial move people state that first contacts are invariably by telephone.

Finding Accommodations

Finding accommodations at your destination often takes the most work of all, particularly if you're doing a trade. Trades, the cheapest and most enriching way to do a trial move, take the most time. Teachers, performers, and professionals who do home trades usually start a year ahead of their swap date, but give it a try even if you've only got three or four months. Here's how to approach finding a temporary home:

√ *Be as flexible as you can about your move date and location. Flexibility increases the number of opportunities offered.*

√ *Use a shotgun approach. Go over the contacts in Appendix C. Call friends, family, business colleagues, and fellow church and club members in every potential location. Ask if they or anyone they know might be interested in a term rental or a trade. Call people you know who used to live there.*

√ *Besides asking everybody you contact about accommodations, ask which local publications would be best to advertise in, and what ad categories are available for vacation home and home trade want ads.*

√ *Seek out publications in your destination area that cater to college staff, school teachers, musicians, artists, or retirees. If friends and family don't have suggestions, telephone the local librarian for publications that have the highest percentage of readers interested in doing a trade or term rental of their furnished home while away on sabbatical or a year abroad.*

√ *Think about reaching special interest people who might want to come to your area. For example, if you're in New Orleans, advertise offering a trade or a term rental in the* International Musician *magazine; if you're in Denver, you might find someone through* American Hunter *magazine.*

√ *Place "apartment wanted" ads in the daily newspapers. If your swap is for four months or less, put it into a vacation rental or short-term rental category. If you want to stay longer, you might try the regular rental apartments/houses or the personals. Before you place the ad, be sure to ask the publication's advice as to what would be the best category to list it under.*

√ *Send bulletin board notices to be posted in college and universities for both students and teachers in your new area. Graduate schools are particularly good. State that you are interested in doing a home trade or finding a term rental or a rented room homeshare, so you can generate as many responses as possible. If your alternative move is over a summer, be sure to send notices to be posted in the teachers' lounge for local schools.*

√ *Send the same notice to colleges and schools or other possible groups in your origination area—people there may know of someone arriving who can do just the trade you want.*

√ *Join the trading clubs listed under "Alternative Move Lead Sources" in Appendix C. You can write trade seekers in their catalogs even if you're too late to place your own ad.*

√ *If you haven't found accommodations by two months before you must start your move, shift gears and mount a blitz for renting your home either furnished or unfurnished. Run ads. Post bulletins. Put a "For Rent" sign in your window. Start looking for a furnished or unfurnished rental in your destination location.*

Follow-up

When you've found some alternative move prospects that interest you, use the correspondence samples in Appendix E as a guide for how to respond.

√ *For people interested in staying in your place:*

√ *Describe what's good about your home and cover all the practical details. Include pictures of the home, some local scenic spots, and yourself. You'll want to trade with people whom you might choose as friends, and your prospective partners will feel the same way. It's also good to include a map, showing where your home is in relation to local highlights.*

√ *For people looking for a trade:*

√ *Write a number of possible trading partners, James Dearing, author of* Home Exchanging, *a book that covers all the ins and outs of the process, advises writing not five or ten people, but to fifty! The more people you query, the better chance you'll get just the location and dates you prefer. He also suggests that trades, which don't work out the first time around, may be perfect if you decide to continue your search next year. As you get closer to completing the arrangement:*

√ *Whether you're doing a trade or a term rental, if you're working with people arriving from out of town, you'll want to give them as much info as possible. Send them your personalized version of Appendix E's "Home Trade Query*

Letter" and two copies of the "Potential Occupancy Agreement Letter"—one you've filled in about your place and a blank one for your potential trading partners to fill in. Everybody should review and sign both checklists, to keep misunderstandings at a minimum.

Offshoot Possibilities: As responses start coming, you'll find some can't offer you the arrangement you want. The people arc interested in the location but something else won't work for them. Ideally, you'll find a person or family to fit at least three parameters:

1. They're reliable.
2. They're in a location you've targeted or they're coming to your location.
3. They are willing to do a term rental so you can at least rent your place and find a sublet at your destination.

Some people add a fourth criteria—the size of the destination house. We've successfully stuffed our family of four into a one-bedroom for a three-month trade and still loved it, so I don't think that exact size is an important criterion, but everyone wants different things, so be sure to add this or any other criteria that's important to your list.

Don't discourage prospects who fit only some of your criteria! Another date, another location, another trade/term rental arrangement than what you originally envisioned may turn into a fabulous opportunity.

Send everyone the same "Potential Occupancy Agreement Letter" (Appendix E) as you send your most likely prospects. Do a different cover letter, explaining your preferred plan of action, and add you're intrigued by their response and may go forward with their proposal. Be sure to detail how you see working out their plan—for example, if they want to rent, specify how much rent and security deposit you want. Then ask them to let you know if they're interested and give them a date when you'll decide what you want to do.

Tip: Be absolutely sure to follow through with information on your decision! Don't ever say "yes" to more than one party or forget to let people on your "maybe" list know that you've made other plans.

Credit Checks and Referrals

It's easiest to check out whether a prospective tenant or trading partner is reliable if someone in your town can vouch for the person. When you're considering your own accommodations, this kind of reference is also important for you to supply. If you're not employed in your prospective location and you don't know anyone there, what do you do? Supply letters of recommendation, such as the "Personal/Business Referral Letter" in Appendix E, from people in your existing location. The letters should be written by your current landlord, your banker, your business partner, and/or friends who can vouch for your reliability and can describe how you care for your home. They should give name and telephone number so your potential trading partner or term rental landlord can follow up questions.

Property managers who sort through tenant applications every day always insist on referrals *and* a credit check, and this is a good policy for informal trades and term rentals as well. You can check with a local credit agency to get your own or a prospective tenant's credit record. You will need written authorization from the other party. Have their birth date, their Social Security number, and their current address ready.

Written Agreements

For anything but a trade, you'll want everyone to sign a legal rental agreement as well as the informal checklist "Potential Occupancy Agreement Letter" in Appendix E, but you don't have to send the rental agreement until everyone's agreed on the rental, and you need their good-faith deposit.

Getting a rental agreement from a local property management company is preferable to buying one from a stationery store, as the management company form should address local legal restrictions such as rent control. Read it over to familiarize yourself with how to fill it out.

Be especially careful about subletting your rented place for long periods, as your landlord may get uneasy. It's best to tell your landlord and give her a copy of your sublet or trade agreement, so that she knows it's temporary.

Get your landlord's acknowledgment in writing, and be sure that she knows where to contact you if there's a problem. If it's not possible to get an acknowledgment from your landlord, be sure you let your sublessee or trade partner know, and explain why.

In many states, agreements pertaining to real estate *must be in writing* in order to be valid. Whether it's the law or not, don't settle for a verbal agreement. Misunderstandings can arise when there is nothing in writing.

The major concern in all agreements is to be as complete and as concise about your specific situation as possible. The more everyone understands each others' expectations, the easier the trial move will be.

Leave-Behind Checklists

Appendix B has other lists to help your exchange partners get oriented quickly: the "Info/Emergency/People/Phone List," the "Fun Things to Do List," and the "Bill Tracking List." You might want to send your exchange partners a blank copy of these lists to fill in so you'll have them waiting for you at the other end.

fending Off Mr. Taxman

THE GOOD NEWS AND THE BAD NEWS

Moving is a big investment of money, time and energy. Hiring a moving company is always a hefty chore. Even those traveling with few possessions have to budget for loss of wages. Costs are particularly high if you're a homeowner. Big ticket items include loan origination fees for the new house, closing costs on both old and new properties, the daunting possibility of having to carry the mortgage on both the old and the new home after you've already moved.

The Employee Relocation Council, a nationwide professional group of human resource relocation specialists, estimates that companies currently reimburse an average of more than $45,000 to move a homeowning family of four. Company costs are usually higher than individual costs, because they include moving bonuses and extra insurance. Still, anyone moving on their own needs to plan for a substantial outlay.

Fortunately, particularly if you're a homeowner, the IRS turns up on your side with a number of significant deductions. These benefits can amount to thousands of dollars, so be sure to consider IRS rules and deadlines as you put together your moving plan.

As with practically everything governmental, to save IRS dollars, you have to know and follow the rules precisely. You don't want to be like a couple we know who closed their house sale four years after they'd moved out, thinking they'd qualified for the $500,000 tax exclusion, because they'd owned it the past five years. They were wrong. They didn't meet the use test (see later in this Chapter).

Be Aware: We are not accountants, and tax laws and regulations change constantly. If you're moving abroad or are employed by the military, time deadlines can be longer and ceilings on deductible amounts can be higher than the ones detailed here. If you are married and filing separately, your deductions can be lower. Check with your tax advisor on the specifics of any program that may apply to your situation.

DEDUCTIONS, DEDUCTIONS, DEDUCTIONS

The first deductions described in this section are for people changing jobs at the same time as moving. They apply to a person being transferred within the same company, as well as someone looking for a job and/or moving to a new company.

Later we'll talk about other tax breaks. Each deduction has different "tests" for qualifying, and there are several different forms involved. In addition to the information below, in Appendix D we've given you a list of the related IRS Forms and information booklets.

JOB SEARCH DEDUCTIONS

As long as you're looking for another job *in the same line of work*, job search expenses can be deducted. Pass this test, and it doesn't matter how far away your job is, whether or not you find a job on your job search, or even if you decide to keep your current position. The IRS considers *the same line of work* to be the whatever you are doing (or did) for your existing (or last) employer.

Job search writeoffs must be tracked on Form 2106, then transferred to Schedule A under miscellaneous job expenses. Details of exactly who can take the deductions and what deductions are allowable are explained in IRS Publication 529. They are subject to minimum amounts and they phase out if your Adjusted Gross Income is above a specified amount.

*Tip: If you're already tracking all your expenses and doing your taxes on your computer, your tax program will automatically calculate these qualifications, once you get them assigned to the proper tax form. Otherwise, do a rough calculation on your Adjusted Gross Income and on all your other Schedule A items **before** you carefully detail the entire list.*

*Unless your itemized deductions are **more** than your Standard Deduction, or you're better off simply taking the Standard Deduction. Also, your allowable job hunting expenses must total more than two percent of your Adjusted Gross Income, as only the excess above the two percent "floor" is tax deductible. Be sure to check with your tax advisor on all these deductions, as Congress constantly changes the rules.*

Three Disqualifiers

There are three biggies that will disqualify you from taking Job Search Deductions, but won't disqualify you from taking Moving Expenses (see next section). If you're looking for your first job, changing from being an employee to being self-employed or looking for a job in a new line of work, your Job Search expenses are not deductible, even if your job hunt is successful.

Tip: If you're self-employed and moving your existing business, you'll usually be better off deducting these exploratory trip expenses as expansion research against your Schedule C business income rather than as a Schedule A job search expense, because business deductions don't have the Schedule A limits and they also cut your self employment taxes. Check with your tax advisor.

HEALTH-RELATED DEDUCTIONS

The deduction for expenses incurred due to a move for serious medical reasons are depressingly small and complex. Occasionally the IRS has allowed deductions for traveling expenses, but not for the much larger costs of moving furniture and the family, even for those suffering incapacitating allergies.

The only major break is for homeowners who suffer debilitating illness soon after moving into a new home. They can sometimes qualify for the full exclusion (up to $500,000 for a married couple) on any capital gain, after only one year of living in their home.

MOVING EXPENSE DEDUCTIONS

You're eligible to deduct the most significant items on your moving expense list if your move is due to a job change or transfer. These expenses are deductible whether you're a renter or a homeowner, whether you get transferred by your company, stay in the same line of work or move into a totally new career.

You can write off these expenses if you are starting your first job or you have been out of the job market for a "substantial" period of time. The IRS generally defines substantial as more than a year, but check with your tax advisor about your specific situation.

Deduction Qualification Tests

Here are the three tests the IRS requires you to meet in order to qualify for Moving Expense deductions:

1)   The Move Must Be Closely Related in Time to Starting Your New Job. In general, the IRS considers "Closely Related" to mean within one year of starting work. This requirement makes it possible to move to a new location before you look for a new job. If you can't find one within the "Work Time Test" deadline, however, you won't be able to take the deduction (see later in this Chapter).

Strategy: Review the concept of a "Trial Move," as described earlier in Chapter 3 "Alternatives." If you leave the furniture behind until your job hunting is successful, then you can be sure the moving expense deductions will qualify.

Be aware, however, that if you rent your old home furnished and can't move the furniture until longer than one year after you start work, the IRS may not allow the deduction (see "Trial Move Pitfalls," below).

2)   Distance Test. This test says the new job must be *located at least 50 miles farther from your old residence than your old job was from your old residence.* If you are starting your first job, or have been out of the market for a "substantial amount of time," the IRS allows you to count your miles starting at your old residence.

Here's an example of how the distance test works. Say you're a Boston software engineer living in the suburb of Brookline. You drive 10 miles to your current office. You get transferred to an office just over the New Hampshire border in Nashua. You drive up there, and find you've clocked 58 miles. Do you qualify? Fill in this chart to calculate:

Distance Calculations

Distance of the "shortest, most direct route available by conventional transportation" from your old home to your new workplace:

<u>58</u> *Miles*

Subtract the distance from your old home to your old work place

- <u>10</u> *Miles*

Total Qualifying Miles   = <u>48</u> *Miles*

In the case of the Boston software engineer, the Total Qualifying Miles are less than 50. Even though the new job is in another state, Uncle Sam usually won't help out on these moving expenses.

Tip: *There are several reasons you may be able to get the IRS to bend the 50 mile rule. If your employer requires you to move as a condition of employment—as a property manager, for example—you don't have to meet the distance test. If your move is costly and job related in any way, even if you're simply shortening your commute, you may be able to qualify for various deductions. See your tax advisor.*

3) Work Time Test. The third requirement you must meet is that you must work at your new job *at least 39 weeks out of the 12 months following your move.* According to *The Arthur Anderson Tax Guide and Planner,* this requirement is even more stringent for the self-employed, who must provide proof of working full time *both* for 39 weeks during the first 12 months, *and* for a total of at least 78 weeks of the 24 months following your move.

These time requirements become particularly important if you move a second time. If your second move is required by your employer (not a transfer requested by you), or is due to death, disability or getting laid off (for anything but willful misconduct), you *can* claim deductions for both moves. Otherwise, you must keep working in the same location through your time limit in order to qualify for any deductions.

Tip: You don't have to stay at the same job or even in the same line of work in your new location, so long as you do work for the number of weeks required within your new area. You can even change from being salaried to being self-employed, although you then have to satisfy the full 78 week time test for the self-employed. Consultants on intermittent projects, seasonal workers and the military have special rules. See your tax advisor.

Tip: A married couple can qualify if either one of them meets the time test. Note, however, that they can't combine weeks to qualify.

Warning: You must claim your moving expense deductions the year you incur them, unless you are subsequently reimbursed by your employer. If you claim, then subsequently don't make your "Work Time" deadlines, you have to either amend your return for the year you claimed the deduction or claim the deduction as income the year you fail the test.

Remember, for any job-related moving expense to qualify as tax deductible, it needs to be "closely related in time." This is usually considered to be within one year of your finding a new job or position.

If you have to postpone moving your household goods past that deadline, this is one of the few cases where the IRS might be willing to listen to proof that meeting the deadline was "prevented by circumstances." They have, for example, allowed moving expense deductions incurred more than a year later, when family members had to stay behind with a teenager graduating from high school.

On the other hand, they've denied deductions for people who weren't able to get their new home built within the one-year deadline.

"Trial Move" Pitfalls

Problems with meeting the time test often occur with trial moves. For example, you might transport some of your furniture to a small rental but put the rest of it in storage, while you're deciding about the new job and new location.

Once you're ready to commit and find the right home, you can run into problems ducting the costs of the second transportation (which can easily be the more expensive) because it isn't "closely related" to getting your new job.

This is another one of the many cases where you need to keep tax deadlines in mind as you plan. The trick is to be sure you don't deduct the first household goods transportation. The IRS has allowed these expenses to be deducted after a year as elapsed, but they never allow two transportation expenses. Check with your tax advisor.

The "Commute Move" Quandary

People doing a "Commute Move" run into a Catch 22 from Uncle Sam. If you are working in your new location, it becomes your "tax address" even if your family isn't there. Trips to that location from your family home are therefore not considered business tax deductions. Return trips to your family's location are for personal reasons, and therefore not tax deductible.

Tip: If both you and your spouse work, your spouse's trips to visit your location and look for a new job may be deductible as a job search expenses. Document all telephone calls to prospective employers, interviews, etc. to prove how your time was spent.

What You Can Deduct

You can deduct the costs of one actual moving trip for each member of the family. Deductions can include the cost of staying in a hotel close to your old home the first night after the furniture is moved, accommodations along the way, and another night close to your new home the first night you arrive. There is no longer any other temporary housing deduction, unless you're moving abroad.

Meal expenses are *not* deductible at all on the moving trip, but you can include the expenses of moving your pets, connecting and disconnecting utilities, shipping your car, and briefly (currently defined as up to 30 days) storing your things while you househunt and/or close the deal on your new home.

If you drive your car to your new location, itemize gas and oil car expenses, otherwise you can only presently write off ten cents a mile. This ten cents is adjusted from time to time, but the IRS has consistently kept moving expense mileage much below the amount allowed for business expense mileage.

Moving trip expenses can't be lavish, and a good way to get yourself audited is to include a hotel receipt for Orlando on your move from Dallas to Savannah.

Reimbursement Income

Employers offering relocation incentives to employees are required to report reimbursements for non-deductible moving expenses on your W-2. These reimbursements are reported as ordinary income, and are subject to withholding. When they're for IRS authorized deductible expenses, like moving your furniture, they're *not* subject to withholding, so long as your employer pays them via an "accountable plan." Under an "accountable plan," both you and your employer are required to keep track of all moving expenses and reimbursements.

If your reimbursements and moving expense deductions don't match up, you'll need to file Form 3903 showing the reimbursements as income and offsetting it against your deductible expenses. If your employer reimbursed you more than your deductible expenses, you must add it to your taxable income. If less, you can take an extra deduction.

Strategy: Meet with your employer's relocation expert and work with her to set up an accountable plan. You should also ask if your employer will "gross up" the taxes you'll owe on reimbursements, i.e., the company will pay your taxes on non-deductible items, so that your relocation benefits come to you tax free.

CHANGE OF ADDRESS, PAYMENT COUPONS AND REFUNDS

To let the IRS know about your new abode, send Form 8822 "Change of Address" to the Internal Revenue Service where you filed your last return. Be sure to include Social Security numbers for all the family members who are moving.

Form 8822 is particularly important if you'll be receiving a refund after you move, or you are currently paying your own withholding with payment coupons. Continue to use your old payment coupons, *with no changes on coupon address*, until the IRS sends you new ones.

If you receive your old mailing label on your tax return package, however, you *should* make corrections on that label when you send in your return. Your federal return should go to the IRS office that serves your *new* address, even if you spent the entire tax year at the old address.

If your refund takes longer than eight weeks (less, if you filed electronically), check your telephone book for your local Tele-Tax IRS number or call 1800 829 1040, or go online to www.irs.gov for information. The wait to get through the 800 number voice mail can be aggravating, but their email communications aren't always speedy, either.

STATE DEDUCTIONS

Most states allow the same moving deductions as the IRS. To find out, check with your local state income tax office. Be aware that you'll probably have to pay taxes to both your old and your new state in proportion to the amount of time you live in each.

Tip: Many states have extra benefits and deductions. California, for example, from time to time has allowed renters a tax credit similar to the homeowner mortgage interest deduction.

It's in your best interest to either interview a tax preparer in your new location soon after arrival or go directly to a local state tax office, get the literature and talk with a representative there.

THE HOMEOWNER'S HIP HOP TAX DANCE

We've been exploring deductions geared to help those moving more than 50 miles because of a job change, but if you're a homeowner, you have some major deductions even if you're only moving across the street.

All of us are familiar with the home mortgage interest deduction, which is almost always the biggest writeoff on your Schedule A. And when we're going through a sale or purchase, we have even more significant items to help our tax bills.

The largest savings are for homeowners with big profits from the sale of their home, but Uncle Sam gives a helping hand to medium priced homeowners and first-time buyers, too.

Predictably, the route to the biggest deductions is careful record keeping. The good news is that not only are there bigger tax savings on a sale, tracking information has become easier. Once you've sold a home where you'd "rolled over" pre 1997 capital gains, you can just keep that one box of all your purchases and sales and in-between capital expenditures, and start a clean slate from there on.

IRS reporting for others involved in the sale transaction, however, has gotten worse. Your home sale closing agent is required to file verifying statements on how much sales price you received, and, if you're a seller taking back a loan, buyers and sellers have to give the IRS each other's Social Security numbers, along with IRS forms to record the payments.

THE HOME PURCHASE—MR. TAXMAN APPLAUDS THE KICKOFF

Low Income / First Time Homebuyer Goodies

The government has been concerned about first time homebuyers being priced out of the market, of late. The solution? Increased government tax incentives and mortgage subsidy programs.

Numerous individual communities have buyer assistance programs, but the biggest works through the IRS. As a low income and/or first time homebuyer, you can qualify for a Mortgage Credit Certificate (MCC) tax credit in many locations.

Credits are better than income deductions, because you subtract them, dollar for dollar, from the actual tax amount you
have due on the back page of your 1040.

MCC Rules
To be eligible for these credits, you must:

√ *Buy in an area where MCCs are available. Some states
offer MCCs in many, but not all, counties. Other states
don't offer the program at all.*
√ *Obtain your new mortgage from a lender participating in
the local MCC program.*
√ *Have an income below the median income for the area
where you buy.*
√ *Be a first-time and/or a low income buyer. Participating
communities may have areas where both first time homebuyers and low income buyers can obtain the credit, and
other areas where only first time homebuyers are eligible.*

*Tip: The definition of "first time" varies. In Califor-
nia it currently includes anyone who has not owned in
the last three years. And in some communities there's
no stipulation about being a first-time buyer at all.*

To find out about obtaining a Mortgage Credit Certificate
and other community subsidies, check with your Realtor and
lender, then call your city or county housing authority or your
local IRS information line.

If no one seems to know whether or not MCC credits are
offered in your new area, check with the office of a prominent
city or county politician, or get on the Internet and check in
www.irs.gov for buyer assistance office locations. MCC Credits are somewhat complicated. They are often not well publi-
cized. But they offer exceptional tax benefits:

√ *You're typically able to deduct twenty to twenty-five percent of your interest payment directly from your income
tax bill.*
√ *Once you have the certificate, you don't have to do anything to requalify year after year. All you have to do is stay
in the same house with the same mortgage. As long as
the IRS doesn't cancel the program, you can continue your
deductions for 30 years till your mortgage is paid off.*

Lender's Origination Fees

All home purchasers can deduct one of their biggest items on their escrow closing statement—the "points." These are also called loan origination fees, maximum loan charges or premium charges. This deduction can be prorated over the life of your loan (IRS preference), or all at once in the year incurred (many taxpayers' preference). Here's how.

Loan Origination Fee Deduction Tests

"Points" may be deducted in the year incurred so long as they are:

√ *For a loan used to buy or improve your main home, i.e., where you live most of the time, not a vacation or second home.*

√ *The loan must be secured by your main home.*

√ *In keeping with the established business practice and established rates of the area where the loan is made.*

√ *For the use of the money, not for other services. It's important to provide documentation on this. Keep your settlement statement, your loan disclosure statement and/or the HUD-1 from your lender.*

√ *Incurred by a person using the cash method of accounting, which almost all individuals do.*

√ *Paid for by funds you did not borrow from your lender or mortgage broker.*

You'll need to have proof of how the points were paid. Although you're no longer required to do so, the best way to clarify this issue is to write a separate check from your own account and deposit it to the escrow holder for the specific amount of the points.

Under recently revised provisions, you can now also write off points in the year incurred, *even if the Seller pays the points for you*, so long as you pay an amount equal to or greater than the points into escrow.

In this latter situation, besides meeting the above tests, you also have to have the points specifically calculated as a percentage of your loan amount and detailed as such on your settlement statement. The emphasis is on documenting that the points are specifically a charge for the use of money, and can therefore be categorized as an interest deduction.

You can also deduct any points for a Second or Refinance during the year incurred, *so long as you took the loan in order to improve your main home.*

Finally, if you were spreading the points you paid on any loan on the old home through the life of that loan, you can finish writing them off at the sale.

Caution: Be sure to check with your tax advisor as far in advance of any sale as possible. These deductions have been heavily tweaked recently, are likely to be changed again, and you may need to meet new deadlines and/or tests at the time your property transfer goes on the county record.

THE OLD HOME SALE—THE IRS GIVES A FLOURISH OF TRUMPETS

All Around Preferential Treatment

Uncle Sam loves the homeseller. Homesale profit protection includes:

√ *Treating all profits on selling your home as capital gain, which is subject to a lower tax rate than ordinary income.*
√ *Use of an installment sale to cut windfall profit brackets.*
√ *The tax free exclusion of up to $500,000 of profit for a couple selling their home.*

Treating the Profits as Capital Gain

As long as you've owned your home longer than a year, if you do *not* qualify (or *completely* qualify) for other exclusions or deductions (see below), you still qualify for the lower capital gains tax rate on your profits. Currently this qualification can save you nearly $2,000 in tax dollars for every $10,000 of profit.

Installment Sale

If you don't meet exclusion test qualifications, or your profits exceed the IRS maximums (a very possible scenario, if you've lived for years in an area with exploding property values), you'll want to explore other tax saving techniques.

We've already discussed the fact that your profits will be taxed on capital gains rates (unless you owned for less than a year), not as ordinary income. You should also explore an installment sale to keep the sales windfall from being taxed in the highest brackets.

When you're considering carrying back a note on the sale of your home, your primary evaluation should be whether or not the buyer is creditworthy and whether or not you'll be getting enough cash out of the sale to go on to your next residence.

It the concept meets those two criteria, the installment sale offers a bonus, tax-wise. It allows you to "spread the taxable gain" over the course of the years that the note is paid back.

Besides giving you a tax benefit by breaking up the large taxable gain into more than one year, the installment sale can often win you a higher price from the buyer if you carry back your note at a lower interest rate than what the bank is charging.

Warning: If you set your rate ridiculously low, the IRS will impute the current Applicable Federal Rate. This rate can be obtained by calling the IRS at (800) 829-1040, and asking for information on installment sales. Remember the interest you receive is taxable in the year you receive it. Only repayment of the profit on the homesale can be spread out to lower your tax bracket.

If you own a home, and you want to move to a rental or a less expensive home, consider taking an installment note amortized over 15 or 20 years, to minimize taxes and provide a regular income.

Discuss this option with your tax advisor before putting the house up for sale. See the section on selling your home for insider tips on how to use this sales tool.

AND NOW... A $500,000 SALUTE!

By far the most important tax benefit for homeowners is the exclusion of up to $500,000 of your sale profits from any taxes whatsoever. This legislation can currently save you up to $140,000 in federal tax dollars *plus* state tax breaks, if you're a couple and meet the qualifying tests described below.

Tip: If tax benefits are a big part of your home sale decision making, you'll want to do more research. Talk with your tax advisor and carefully read a number of IRS info books including publications 523 "Selling Your Home," 544 "Sales and Other Dispositions of Assets," and 551 "Basis of Assets," for current deductions and exceptions. See Appendix D for a complete list of the relevant tax publications.

Some Home Sale Tax Exclusion Terms You Need to Know

Basis—What you paid for your very first home, plus or minus "adjustments."

Adjusted Basis—Your basis may have been adjusted "up" by subsequently buying a more expensive home or making allowable capital improvements, such as a room addition or a pool. Ordinary maintenance, including repainting, reroofing and other similar costs, are *not* included.

Your basis may also have been adjusted "down" by some insurance reimbursements or being paid for items like "rights of way or easements" or other items.

Costs of Sale—The IRS allows you to deduct sales commissions, advertising fees, legal fees and any loan charges you've paid for, before you calculate the profit.

Recognized Gain—The part of your sale profit that is taxable.

Caution: If you've "taken cash out" with a refinance, that early profit wasn't taxable at the time, but will be upon a sale if you've built up more gain than your exclusion. If you've done a number of refinances, you may find your recognized gain is higher than the cash you receive out of escrow after you pay off your current mortgage.

Calculating basis and recognized gain for a couple who've bought and sold numerous times since their original basis home is also complex. Get the help of an experienced tax preparer.

Qualifying Tests

To elect to exclude large taxable gains on the sale of your old home, here are the major qualifying tests:

1) The sale must have taken place after May 7, 1997, when the current exclusions took effect.

2) It must be the sale of your "main home." This may be a house, a co-op or condo, a mobile home or even a houseboat, but it can't be a vacation home or any other home you own but do not occupy most of the time.

3) You must have owned and used the your main home for two out of the five years prior to the date of the sale. The two years of ownership and use can be before the May 7, 1997, date, do not have to be continuous, and do not even have to coincide.

4) You must not have used the exclusion on the sale of any other residence during the past two years.

5) If you are an individual who meets the above tests, you can exclude up to $250,000 in gain. If you are a couple, either married or unmarried, you can each exclude up to $250,000 in gain calculated on your percentage of interest.

Reduced Exclusion Tip. If you have to move due to a serious illness or change of employment before one or more of the two year time tests are up, you may still qualify for a pro rata reduced exclusion. Congress continues to fine tune this tax benefit, so check with your tax advisor any time you're contemplating a sale to be sure you qualify for as much exclusion as possible.

THE DOWNSIDE

We've been discussing the friendly IRS rules for folks who make a profit on their homesale, but what happens if you're selling and you *lose* money? Any help for the taxpayer in that situation?

The quick answer is no. The IRS allows no writeoff for a loss on the sale of a personal home, any more than they allow a writeoff for selling your family car for less than your purchase price.

Conversion of Home to Rental Property

In the past, tax advisors did offer one alternative to simply taking the loss without any tax writeoff—convert the home to a rental property.

This option rarely saves big tax dollars, but can be considered if there's a slow sales market that you believe will improve or you're planning to return to live in the house later.

During the interim, you get income from the rental and the expense/depreciation tax benefits of income property writeoffs against the rental income you make.

If you're able to sell the home during the three years after you move, you should still qualify for the $250,000 per person tax exclusion, so long as you meet the other tests.

If you can't (or don't want to) sell within the exclusion time limit, you can still continue to receive rental income. When you finally do sell, any loss of value in the property *subsequent* to your turning the home into a rental can be written off as an investment loss.

The theory behind this strategy is that by converting your home into rental property, you pull out of the falling market, and sit on the sidelines with rental income and tax deductions... and the possibility that the market will get better.

Make sure to file the conversion and use of the home as a rental properly with your tax advisor.

Caution: The traditional real estate rule of thumb was that market cycles last five years. In the roller coaster 90s, however, places like Houston, Boston and Los Angeles saw deeper, longer swings than five years.

*Do **not** try turning your home into a rental unless you've worked out how to manage the property, you've researched what renters are paying in the low to medium range for other homes like yours and that the rent covers your maintenance and mortgage costs. You'll be better off taking a one time loss than an ongoing beating.*

STRATEGIES FOR HOMEOWNERS—SOME CAUTIONARY TALES

Below are situations you, as a homeowner, may face in your move. It's important to be familiar with the concepts in order to save tax dollars, but if you're confronted with similar problems, don't assume that you qualify exactly. Review your situation with your own tax advisor. Many tax dollars can be saved!

Problem: You've bought your new home but your previous home has been sitting on the market four months with no takers.

Strategy #1: The house can be rented and treated as a rental income property, while gain from the subsequent sale (within the three-year deadline) can still qualify for the $250,000 per person exclusion.

Strategy #2: Try offering the house on a one- to two-year lease option to buy. You'll greatly increase the number of people who will be interested in buying and you'll get rental income to help pay for the insurance, taxes and other upkeep. You should be able to qualify for rental property tax deductions on the old home as well as the $250,000 exclusion.

If the optionee doesn't buy, you still have time to find another buyer before your deadline is up.

Problem: You've just met a wonderful person you want to marry. Both of you have expensive homes, you've owned and lived in yours for more than two years, but he's only been in his place a year and a half. You want to sell both homes and take off on a two year round-the-world extravaganza.

Strategy #1: Since you already qualify for the $250,000 exclusion on your home, you can complete that sale first, and move into the other home. Wait six months, and then sell the second home when the second person qualifies for his $250,000 exclusion. Finally, head off to Tahiti celebrating saving taxes on $500,000 worth of profit.

Strategy #2: Same situation as above, but you don't want to wait the extra six months for your trip. Again, sell your residence, and elect to exclude your gain. Convert the other home to a rental with a two year lease, and take off on your trip. Your new spouse can still qualify for the exclusion after returning and living in the home again for six months.

STATE DEDUCTIONS

As with moving expenses, most of the big IRS homeowner deduction guidelines are followed by the states, but it's important to check for variations. Homesellers older than 55 in California, for example, can often transfer their previous (usually much lower) real estate tax to their next residence.

FURTHER INFORMATION

Any time you're filing unusual deductions, it's important to check with your personal tax advisor to get the most advantageous writeoffs for your particular situation.

In Appendix D, we've included a list of the free IRS booklets and forms covering special relocation circumstances for general moving, the military, students, emergency moves, retirees, etc.; where to get the publications for free, and an explanation of IRS Form 3903, where job-related moving expenses are calculated.

FIVE

Employment Considerations

LONG-DISTANCE JOB-HUNT STRATEGIES

Budgeting

If you don't already have a job in your new location, your number one priority probably will be to find one. Looking for a job long distance can be more fun than looking in your existing location. A job in another city or state offers the adventure of taking off for a new life. Jobs in a foreign country are so attractive, people sometimes end up paying employers for the opportunity, instead of the other way around. No matter how thrilling the prospects, however, you have to be certain you can afford a long-distance search.

Three Scenarios

Long-distance job hunting involves three possible scenarios—hunting on the sly while you continue to hold down your current job; moving in tandem with someone else who already has a job in the new location; or being out of work and moving with no safety net.

Hunting on the Sly. If you're currently employed and figure you'll be able to remain in your job at least six months, count this as a budgeting blessing. It may be difficult to wrangle a vacation long enough to investigate possibilities in your targeted locale, but it's easier than maintaining yourself on a shrinking bank account.

Moving in Tandem. Here again, your budgeting basics are covered or, at least, partially covered. Often the transferee's company will offer both consulting and monetary support for a spouse. With the basics in hand for several months, you'll have time to analyze your situation and mount a search for more than just a living wage. Use the change as a catalyst to break out of old work patterns if you find them stifling.

Moving with No Safety Net. If you find yourself without a job, and you know you want to change locations, should you move first and then find a job? Our advice is no. A rule of thumb in today's economy is that a job search can take three months to a year. Budget accordingly against your savings.

If you relocate, you'll have to figure a "newcomer allowance" of at least 30 percent, because you won't know how to find bargains and cut corners in the new location. Do you have enough capital to cover this expense? Spend it on exploratory interview trips, not on carting your furniture long distance.

More and more resumes now make the rounds with "Willing to Relocate" in big letters on the top. Others state "Renter, Willing to Relocate" or "Willing to Relocate at Own Expense." Comments like these let prospective employers know that not only will people trek across country to follow the job, they'll do so for little to no relocation assistance dollars.

Since employers are looking at prospective employees long distance, since you might not like your targeted location once you get there, and since your next job might be somewhere you haven't even thought of yet, save your shipping money and cast your job search net in all directions. Get your job in hand before moving, particularly before moving a large household. If job opportunities in your current location are slim to nil, try an alternative move strategy from Chapter 3. The only time moving your household without a safety net makes sense is when you've just left school and/or your household is limited, and you can schlepp everything with you in your car.

Job Search Tactics

Whenever you set out job hunting, you know you need to hone your research skills seriously. Accomplishing your goal long distance is the same process, magnified. There are three major items to keep in mind:

Mine Your Current Location. This comes highly recommended by job-change guru Richard Bowles in *What Color Is Your Parachute?* He points out that your existing local library, plus online computer search facilities, plus other local sources will go a long way in helping you find which communities have a good supply of jobs in your field. Ask even casual acquaintances in your existing location for source lists of names and addresses to contact.

Tip: Call the libraries in your area to find The Directory of Executive Recruiters *or order one directly from Kennedy Publications, (603) 585-6544. Not only does this excellent reference categorize headhunter firms by specialty and location, it also has a complete listing of trade and professional organizations nationwide.*

The library also may have the Surrey How to Get a Job *or the Adams JobBank career directory series for the specific city you're interested in or guides such as Casewit's* How to Get a Job Overseas. *Look them up in* Books in Print, *under the subject heading "Jobs." See also the "Contacts and Resources" directory (Appendix C).*

Network. Rack your Rolodex for names in your targeted location. Ask your college/high school alumni organizations for names of graduates who have moved there. Contact members of any trade organizations in your field, explain your search, and ask for specific information about the job market, salaries, and the location in general. If you have time, attend conferences and trade shows in the new location. If no conferences are coming up there, attend conferences in any location, and seek out attendees from your target locale.

Evaluate. As you start finding out about the job market in various locations, review the "City Evaluator" you filled out from Appendix A. (Also see the "Sample City Evaluator" in Chapter 1.) You may find new elements and/or different cities are more important to you than the ones you originally ranked. You may even find, as did a music composer in our IIP Frequent Mover Survey, who did a trial move from Los Angeles to New York, that the original location was the best one for her career progress.

NEGOTIATING YOUR BEST DEAL WITH YOUR EMPLOYER

Relocation assistance dollars played a big part in the executive perks in go-go times. Figures in excess of $100,000 extended to university and corporation top guns were splashed across the news, and corporations reported an *average* expenditure of over $45,000 to move their employee homeowners.

Getting Yours and "Reasonable" Requests

With across-the-board belt tightening on relocation assistance, what kind of a deal can you negotiate if you're looking at a transfer or you're being hired by a firm six states away?

When you've been working for a company and are asked to transfer—even if you've already been moved several times as you progressed up the company's rotation ladder—you need to research the assistance that may be available to you currently. Don't just glance over the company relocation policy statement and say yes. The more you review your situation and point out places where you need help, the more they'll try to oblige... As long as they really want you in the new position.

 Tip: This is a negotiating game. Your best ploy is: 'I'll be happy to move... So long as you make me whole." If they want you in the new position, this simple phrase says you're an experienced relocation negotiator, and

you deserve the full smorgasbord of relocation services that they're prepared to offer.

The concept behind an employee's need to be "made whole" is that, although you like the position and the opportunity, you don't suffer from insatiable wanderlust. You're telling them that moving is not a perk. If you have to suffer financial loss as well as significant emotional hassle... Well, who needs it?

Besides knowing that being "made whole" is a reasonable request, you need to know what possible services to ask for. The best-known perk—the moving bonus, for example—may be a policy no-no with the government or other employers. Try for other options. They may be perfectly willing to pay for an extra month's work that you accomplish while still at your old location. You never know until you ask.

Transferee and New-Hire Bargaining Points

Most companies have different policies for people in different categories—existing employees or new hires; exempt (salaried) or nonexempt (wage earning); domestic, foreign, or group moves. According to a poll taken of Employee Relocation Council (ERC) members, the following are the most common big-ticket items and the probability of a company's offering the programs.

Household Goods Shipping. The most commonly offered assistance. Universal to existing, exempt employees; 86 percent of companies offer this to new hires and/or nonexempt employees.

Low Interest Loan on New Home. Also very common. Universal to existing, exempt employees; 70 percent of surveyed companies offer this to new hires and/or nonexempt employees.

House Purchase and Closing Costs. Again, universal to existing, exempt employees, but only 53 percent offer this assistance to new hires and/or nonexempt employees.

Temporary Living Expenses, House-hunting Trips, Lease-breaking Penalties, Home-sale Assistance. Most companies have a cap on the maximum amount of reimbursement available for expenses of these types. Don't expect to spend more than sixty to ninety days in company-subsidized interim housing, for example. A significant majority offer these reimbursements to existing, exempt employees. About 80 percent of those companies offer them to new hires and/or nonexempt employees.

Loss-on-Sale Assistance. This is the biggie that currently separates the best relocation assistance programs from everybody else. Say you're now in a down market, selling a home you bought in 1989. Say your home is now worth $25,000 less than when you bought it. Companies offering a loss-on-sale program can end up having to hire a third party to sell it for you *and* reimbursing you the $25,000.

Given the ongoing problems of some real estate markets, a number of alternative programs are being offered; the most common is to cap the reimbursement at somewhere around $15,000. Result: A poor real estate market is a common reason employees give for refusing a transfer.

Although more than 70 percent of the companies polled said they offer some kind of loss-on-sale assistance for existing, exempt employees, less than a third offered it for new hires and/or nonexempt employees.

Duplicate Housing Costs. Another big item—particularly for homeowners transferring from an inexpensive part of the country to an expensive one. The employee moving into a more expensive area is reimbursed the difference between the old mortgage or rent payments and the new for a period of time ranging from one to five years. Your chance of winning this perk is not as good as of participating in the other listed programs. Only 60 percent of the companies offer this for existing exempt employees, and less than 30 percent offer it for new hires and/or nonexempt employees.

Other programs that are less likely to turn up on your company's relocation assistance menu include apartment search fees and equity/bridge loans for homeowners buying a new house before the old one's sale closes. Home marketing counseling has not been a favorite in the past but is now being encouraged in many companies, as it has been shown to cut loss-on-sale problems.

Destination Services. For help in your new location, these services include a wide range of programs including some of those already mentioned and some specific area counseling and homefinding help. These services help employees and their families rapidly narrow their search to desirable communities, taking into account factors such as cost, commuting times, and schools.

Spousal Assistance. Currently offered only to 54 percent of the existing, exempt employees and 28 percent of the new hires and/or nonexempt employees, these programs are surging in popularity, because a growing number of potential transferees have been citing spousal job loss as the reason for refusing to move. You can ask for a wide variety of services. The possibilities include:

- √ *Postponing the move for several months to accommodate spousal job hunting. Often it's impossible to arrange a delay of more than three months on the transfer, but you won't know till you ask.*
- √ *Your spouse's being hired by your company in a job suitable for his or her career path. Corporations used to have policies forbidding hiring a spouse, but those have largely disappeared.*
- √ *Free transportation to and from the new location for up to three spousal job search trips. Usually, it's expected that these trips will coincide with your "get-acquainted" and house-hunting trips.*
- √ *A bonus to cover up to six months' differential on the spouse's new job salary.*
- √ *Reimbursement for childcare costs while you conducts a job search/house-hunting trip.*
- √ *Reimbursement for spousal job training in the new location.*
- √ *Career change planning and counseling.*
- √ *Free research assistance on defining job markets for particular skills and/or facilitating simultaneous transfer by your spouse's company to a branch at the new location.*

√ *Free use of telephone and fax or reimbursement of these costs in contacting prospective employers and setting up interviews.*

√ *Career counseling, job aptitude tests, resume writing, and presentation assistance.*

√ *Telephone effectiveness training and seminars on how to evaluate an employment offer.*

√ *Videotaping and/or expert critiquing of job interviewing skills.*

√ *Financial counseling and help in negotiating better job offers.*

√ *Two or three coworker "contact" families you can call (or meet on orientation trips) who'll help your spouse with finding a job and settling in.*

√ *Networking programs with other employers in the new area. These programs include job fairs, exchanging resumes with other companies, introductions to other personnel officers, a resource library of employer contacts, and a subscription to the daily newspaper for the target community.*

Tip: Accompanying spouses should be able to qualify for unemployment insurance, so long as they have tried to continue working for their existing company in the new location. This coverage also may extend to those moving to care for ailing relatives. Contact your current state employment office for information.

Note to Retirees, "Rightsizing" Victims, and Resignation Candidates

If your move will be due to retirement, your company's work reduction, or resignation, you also should look to the Human Resources department for help with relocation. To begin with, you'll want to extend your current health program. Under the COBRA federal law, employers of twenty or more are required to extend health insurance for up to thirty-six months.

The company is allowed to charge you the full cost of what it actually pays for the coverage, plus an extra 2 percent for administrative expenses. Since most firms heavily subsidize employee health coverage, the premiums are likely to be much higher than you had to pay previously. But coverage under the group plan still is likely to be less expensive—or at least more comprehensive—than any individual policy. Check with your company about the COBRA program.

 Tip: This program is also good for recent graduates who were previously covered under a parent's employer-sponsored insurance plan. With COBRA, a graduate may be able to extend coverage, with the same stipulations just listed.

You also can profit from enrolling in many of the *destination services* programs that your soon-to-be-erstwhile company might offer. Ask particularly for help in researching other locations for cost-of-living information and neighborhood profiles.

If you've been hit by job layoffs, probably you are already working with job counseling, but expand on that. Today's job searches extend much farther than one city or even one state. You might come across a vital lead through a *spousal assistance* program your company offers in new locations you've targeted—so ask.

Pension Plan Distributions—New Requirements

Finally, be careful about any lump-sum pension plan payouts that may be due from your 401(k) or other company retirement program. You no longer have *any* time after job termination to decide what to do with the money. Arrangements have to be made to transfer into a new fund prior to payout in order to avoid paying taxes and penalties.

If you already have another job, you can transfer your funds into your new company's plan. Also, many accountants recommend the flexibility of having a bank, a stockbroker, or another investment administrator, roll the money into a new IRA, Keogh, or other retirement account. Consult with your tax advisor.

SIX

Giving Up the Old Homestead

DEALING WITH THE LEVIATHAN LANDLORD

Moving Out Before Your Lease Is Up

At no time in your relationship with your landlord will she seem more old-fashioned and calculating than when you announce you want to leave before your lease rolls over. From the landlord's point of view, you're unilaterally breaking a contract. You should be required to pay your monthly rent, whether you choose to live in her building or not.

So what can you do to get your deposit back? If you're able to provide a new, creditworthy tenant to take your place, most state laws consider that you've done your job and will not allow any other fines to be levied.

Taking on advertising and showing the apartment may be *less* work than you think. The landlord will hit you for the amount spent on advertising, anyway, and if you run the ad, you'll be able to arrange times to show your apartment when it's convenient for you, rather than the landlord, if you're the one answering calls. Also, you may know better than she does what's nice about your place, who works in the neighborhood, or a friend who'd like to move in.

If you can't find anyone, most state laws require landlords to accept the responsibility of rerenting, so long as you pay for advertising and the rent while the unit is vacant. Not paying your rent the last month you're there and walking away from the rest of your security deposit is rarely a good idea in today's electronically credit connected world. Review your rental agreement.

Some landlords will be more sympathetic to your financial situation than others. If you want to use your security deposit to cover your last month's rent, *be sure to check with your landlord first and get the agreement in writing.* You can use this agreement as an amendment to your lease and as documented proof of honest intent in case there is any problem with your landlord in the future.

Make sure both you and your landlord sign the agreement. Otherwise, the landlord may go after a judgment against you. She'll win if you're not in court to defend yourself, and even if bill collectors don't find you, today's credit companies will track the judgment. That means you won't be offered a lease at your next place or you'll be denied the next time you're looking to take out a credit card or car loan.

Move-out Notice

If your lease is up or you're on a month-to-month lease, be sure you notify your landlord that you're leaving within your deadline. Check your lease. If it says you're to give a thirty-day notice, *don't* try for twenty-nine, or the landlord may deduct one day's rent. Also, be sure to give *written* notice, stating the day you are leaving and when you'd like to schedule the move-out inspection.

Subleasing

If you're doing a trial move and/or want to return to your existing apartment, review Chapter 3 carefully. You'll need to have a subleasing or trade agreement with the people who'll be in your place while you're gone. It's important that you inform your landlord and get her to give you a letter verifying acceptance of the arrangement.

Warning: If you're in a rent-controlled area and you have a very favorable lease, your landlord is likely to forbid subleasing or even an apartment trade. *Check with a tenant lawyer or tenants' union to find out your rights.* If you decide to go ahead secretly, let your sublessee or your trading partner know what the situation is, and agree in writing that there is a risk of eviction for both of you.

"Key" Money

Although it's legally a gray area, renters in rent-controlled areas sometimes "sell" their leases to subsequent tenants. If you're considering doing this, investigate what other people are doing, particularly how much they charge and how they phrase their agreement or receipt with their subsequent renters. Usually, they "sell" some remaining furniture rather than the right to assume the lease. All of you should be aware that you might get sued for this procedure, and the subsequent renters might get evicted.

Cleanup Tips

Your lease almost certainly states something to the effect that you should leave your apartment in the same condition as you found it, "less normal wear and tear." Everybody agrees "normal" does not include indelible stains in the carpet, gouges in the wall where the rocker scraped, holes in doors and walls from hanging pictures, broken doors from frustration attacks, or torn drapes.

How clean the place needs to be is more debatable. Many landlords are sticklers for pristine cleanups. To figure out what you'll need to do in order to keep from having to pay a cleaning fee, go back over your move-in checklist, photos, and notes when you moved in. The landlord may give you a list of cleanup guidelines. If your apartment looked like someone had gone over every inch twice before you moved in, figure you need to make the same grade when you move out.

 Tip: If the apartment was a disaster when you moved in, you should have taken pictures and sent the information to the landlord at the time. It's still a good idea to leave it in good condition, however. You may want to use

*your landlord as a reference in the future, so depart on
good terms.*

Move-out Inspection

If at all possible, do the inspection *after* you've got all your
furniture out. Take current snaps or Polaroids to match your
move-in photos, and have your landlord sign off on the new
ones and your "Renter's Move-in/Move-out Property Condition Checklist." (See Appendix B.) This should cover you in
case there's any disagreement after you leave about what repairs need to be made.

If the inspection occurs before your furniture is out, don't
expect the landlord to return your deposit on the spot. Your
movers may leave an incredible mess, and, besides, problems
often turn up once large pieces of furniture are out and the
hidden floor or wall is revealed.

If all of your things are out, you've given proper notice, and
told your landlord you want your deposit back on that day, you
should be able to get it. This item is often forgotten, however,
so it's a good idea to double-check with your landlord the day
before, and remind her to please bring a checkbook. If the landlord refuses to make the refund at that time, the law usually
doesn't require a refund until some time after you move out—
the time span varies from community to community.

If you need to know the length of these time spans or to find
out about tenant rights in your community, look up the Rent
Board (government) or Tenants' Union (private) in your phone
book. Not every community has these. If yours doesn't, check
the Housing Authority, listed in the government pages. It may
not be able to help you directly, but it should be able to tell you
where to turn.

Delayed Deposit Refund Strategies

If you don't get your deposit refunded as you move out,
make certain the landlord has at least given you a signed, dated
verification of your move-out and the date the refund will be
mailed to you. It's not a bad idea to prepare this notice for the
landlord to sign. Be sure to include your new address and a
telephone number where you can be reached if any question
arises. We've provided samples of a "Home Trade Move-in/

Move-out Checklist" in Appendix B and a "Landlord/Tenant Move-out/Deposit Refund Agreement" in Appendix E.

PUTTING YOUR HOUSE ON THE MARKET

Doing the Hot-Market/Soft-Market Shuffle

When more than 30 percent of the shops in your hometown go out of business and/or sprout "Sale, Sale, Sale" signs, you can bet that your real estate agent's listing presentations will be filled with bad news. "Now is not the time to indulge in price fantasies," admonished Fred Sands, owner/manager of one of the biggest real estate agencies in Southern California, as he viewed the soft market of the early 90s, where prices had dropped by 25 percent from just two years before.

As you decide to move, the most crucial financial factor to take into consideration is the temperature of the current real estate market. Unfortunately, we sellers often feel the market is a lose-lose situation. If the market is hot, we're always afraid we're not getting a good enough price. If the market is soft . . . well, who wants to admit such a situation could ever happen to us?

How do you find out if your neighborhood is in a hot or a soft market, and what do you do about it?

Your local newspaper's Business News section will give you much insight and specific important information on whether companies will be hiring or firing during the next twelve months. The visual symptoms of large numbers of "For Sale" signs— or, even worse, "Foreclosure" notices and boarded windows— in a neighborhood, all point toward a very soft market. Conversely, during a hot market, you hear of homes being sold with no "For Sale" signs at all. Those that do appear usually admonish "Do *Not* Disturb Occupants" and are whisked away within weeks.

If you find yourself in a very soft market, reexamine your decision to move carefully. A bad real estate market has been the leading cause of corporate job transferees refusing relocations for the past several years, and this may be your conclusion as well. If you still opt for moving, consider the alternative move options in Chapter 3 until the market picks up. If none of them works for you, mount the loudest, hard-sell, price-bashing campaign you can.

If your market turns out to be very hot, give thanks, take the best offer you receive in the first month, and put a stake through the heart of that little devil who keeps whispering in your ear, "Maybe you could have gotten more…. "Sellers who change price and terms in the middle of a deal quickly get a sleazy reputation. Agents and their buyers desert you, and indecisiveness is commonly rewarded with months of waiting and a worse deal than the offers you got during the first thirty days.

Seller's Remorse

Prepare for seller's remorse at the outset. It's said that the horse traders of the Old West believed the best deals ended with both parties stomping out gnashing their teeth and rattling their pistols. Today, dealmakers believe in the "Everybody Wins" scenario. A good concept, but beware of that postpartum hangover even so. Real estate agents are all familiar with exhilarated people leaving a negotiating table in the evening, then all coming down with a serious bout of seller's (and buyer's) remorse the next morning.

The only way to deal with this flood of self-doubt is to review your priorities. Did you get the things that were most important? Then stop beating yourself up over might-have-been scenarios. A home sale weighs on us because so much money is involved, but actually, it's the same as selling a car—you never get the perfect deal. It's time to move on.

Timing Your Sale

Most of the time, the market is neither stone cold nor blazing hot. Its condition still is crucial to your sales and timing strategy, however. To begin with, you need to know what seasonal trends are predominant in your area.

Tip: Most locations see a rise in sales between March 1 and October 1. The exceptions to this rule are usually in retirement, Sunbelt locations. Not only do more homes sell during seasonal selling peaks, they typically sell for a better price. Try to time your sale for these peaks.

A number of other statistics are meaningful to you. Before you commit to selling, call one or two of the agents you may be interviewing to award the listing. Say you're thinking about selling and that you want to find out what kind of market you're in. Ask for the local quarterly or monthly averages for the last three to five years on three things:

√ 1. *Sales prices.*
√ 2. *Number of homes sold.*
√ 3. *Number of days on the market (DOM).*

Note that these numbers are averages and/or medians. They won't be much help in setting an asking price for your specific home. In order to do that, you'll need actual sales prices of specific comparable homes. Instead, the clues you'll be searching for in these numbers are "trend indicators." These are:

√ Seasonal trends. *Check whether your local market conforms to the national spring and summer seasonal selling pattern.*
√ Year-on-year trends. *This tracks long-term hot and soft markets by comparing prices, number of homes sold, and number of days on the market over several years. Check whether they're going up or down for the same period in previous years to find out if you're in a hot or soft market.*
√ Regional trends. *The home-selling market is subject to economic winds that blow much more fiercely in some places than others. The oil crisis, for example, drove the Texas market into disaster but had little effect on the two coasts. California was one of the hardest hit states with base closings.*
√ *For individual home sellers caught in a regional hurricane, understanding these forces is crucial. If you're thinking about moving "sometime soon," read your newspaper's Business and Real Estate pages, looking for the storm warnings of a soft market or comments on a heating-up market. Ideally, you'll want a hot market in your present area and a soft market where you buy your new home.*
√ Neighborhood trends, *if homes in your neighborhood sold for approximately the same price as homes in two or three other neighborhoods a few years ago but now sell for much less—or much more—your neighborhood is being influenced by something outside the regional trend. Neighborhood trends are particularly important if the difference is more than 1 0 percent per year, and they're crucial if the trend has continued over more than three years.*

√ *If prices in your neighborhood are going up faster than others, figure you can keep to the high end on your asking price, but you will take a little longer than average DOM.*

√ *If your neighborhood is going down, the wait-it-out possibility open to someone in a downward regional trend is more risky. Economists constantly are trying to get a better crystal ball to predict the permanence of neighborhood trends. One question that continues to befuddle—conflicting trends in moving out of, or back to, city centers.*

√ *An even more perplexing question is whether these trends have any discernible length or can be managed in any way. Many neighborhoods have turned their downward trend around, but the predictability of whether that will happen is weak. If you've got to move, leaving the unsold house with renters is unlikely to bring you back to an acceptable price level. Accept the worst and cut your price now.*

SAMPLE TREND INDICATOR

Take a look at the following California Association of Realtors statistics for 1987 through 1997. Note the late 80s inflation that peaked in 1991, and was followed by soft market of the recession. Over the period, home prices first inflated 49%, then fell 18% during the early 90's recession, then started back up again in 1998.

Annual Trends of Median Home Prices in Los Angeles

YEAR	MEDIAN PRICE
1987	$146,630
1988	$178,889
1989	$214,831
1990	$212,130
1991	$218,580
1992	$210,790
1993	$195,430
1994	$189,170
1995	$179,900
1996	$172,886
1997	$176,517

The average number of Days on the Market (DOM) will give you even more critical and specific information. Not only will it add insights to the market picture, it will give you as realistic a moving timetable as you can find.

The meaning of days on the market varies from location to location. In some places, it represents the period from the time you sign the listing until the day the sale closes. In others, it measures the shorter time from the date of the listing until the seller and buyer sign a purchase agreement. Ask which is true in your area.

Then start setting your strategy. If you need to move in 30 days, and your local average DOM is 90 to 120 (typical of a medium to slow market in San Francisco, where DOM is counted from listing to close), you need either to start off with a super bargain asking price, or to schedule yourself into interim housing or some other alternative move. (See Chapter 3.)

Tip: Nationwide, appraisers commonly use 120 DOM (from listing to contract dates) as the maximum a home should be available. If your market is showing a higher number, not only will you have trouble selling, your buyers will have problems with slow appraisers who may very well come up with an appraised value lower than your hard-won contract price. Often this leads to buyer demands for you to lower your price. Be prepared to counter with a larger seller- financed second mortgage instead.

A word of warning. Sometimes timing your sale is predicated on your finding a suitable house to buy first. Other times, you've had to transfer to a new job before your old house sold. By all means start your new home search while you've got your current home on the market, but try everything you can— including drastic price cuts—to avoid *buying* a new house before the old one is sold.

Your best bet is to obtain a sixty-day escrow period, after the buyer obtains her lender financing commitment, in order to negotiate your own purchase. If the buyer, or the lender, won't wait that long, go ahead and close, but ask to stay in your home and rent for a couple of months from the buyer, while you finish up your purchase. If neither of these proposals work, you're better off closing the first sale and living in a rental for several months rather than carrying two mortgages.

Selling It Yourself vs. Using an Agent

Shari is a real estate broker. She has sold our own property and we've used other agents, and we have to say we'd rather use another agent for selling our home. There are lots of reasons for this:

√ *A good agent is up to the minute on your neighborhood sales information and real estate legislation. Tracking these things is the job of a specialist, and the knowledge can keep you from making some expensive mistakes.*

√ *Buyers don't react to a home when an owner is there, they react to the owner. Often they feel the owner is "hovering," and they don't feel relaxed about exploring the kitchen or sitting down on the back deck to survey the terrain. The result is an uncomfortable impression of the house and no sale.*

√ *It's hard to be objective talking to buyers. You become so attached to your home, you never see its faults—much less how it stacks up in the general marketplace.*

Commissions

Everyone feels cost is the big disadvantage of using an agent. Agents' commissions typically run from 4 to 7 percent of the purchase price. With homes nationwide averaging a little more than $100,000, you're looking at between $4,000 and $7,000 in real estate commissions. Whoa! We're willing to hold a huge number of open house Sundays for that kind of money, we say to ourselves.

But wait. You rarely, if ever, save yourself the total amount of the commission when you don't list with an agent. It's a bad business decision—no, it's a *disastrous* business decision—to refuse to work with agents who want to show your house to their buyers. More than eight out of ten homes are sold through agents, and the price of your home will be seriously affected if you cut yourself off from 80 percent of your potential buyers. If a buyer is represented by an agent, that agent will need to be paid.

There's a small but growing trend for buyers to pay their agents directly, but such buyers often will expect you to give them a "wholesale" price that knocks off at least half your commission savings. Ditto with buyers confidant enough to represent themselves. Translation: Your savings are down to $2,000 to $3,500.

Then, without an agent to aid you legally, even if you've done a thorough job of researching current real estate law and you have a very simple purchase offer, you *must* have a lawyer review a contract before signing. Cost: $500 to $1,000. Other money you'll have to lay out will go for advertising and a good sign. Your savings on the real estate commission are now down to somewhere between $500 to $3,000.

Still worth a lot of work and hassle? It depends on how detail oriented and hands-on you are . . . also how much energy you have to devote and how much you value your time.

Listing with an agent doesn't mean accepting whatever fees an agent quotes. When you call agents tell them you're looking for someone to represent your home, let them know immediately that you're going to be talking to several agents and their commission will be negotiated.

Negotiating commission is your legal right, but don't expect the agent to bring up the subject. Broach the idea by asking what's their "commission schedule," then later ask what's the "best deal" they can give. After talking with several agents, you'll find that commissions can vary by as much as 30 percent. Count this into your decision on which agency to go with—it's one of the items on our "Seller's Real Estate Agent Evaluator" in Appendix A—but don't make commission cutting your only criteria.

Selecting an Agent

The first step in finding an agent is to ask for referrals from neighbors. It's an old real estate adage that there are three keys to a good real estate buy—location, location, location. Although we'd have to add timing, timing, timing to that list, location specialization is the key to a good agent for selling your home. If your aunt across town has a fabulous agent, talk to that person, but only to find out who's recommended in your neighborhood. If your uncle sells real estate in your area, consider a policy of not using friends or family—it may keep you from some nasty internecine strife.

Other good methods for developing your agent short list are to take down names and telephone numbers from area signs or area newspaper ads. If you know an agency name, but not which agent is right for your neighborhood, ask the agency office manager whom she would recommend.

Choosing agencies through the yellow pages is difficult, because you usually can't tell which agency specializes in your area. Don't call your local Board of Realtors. While it may confirm whether someone is licensed or not, it does not recommend.

Bonus Programs and Services

Large national chains and local agents often offer a number of bonuses and incentives. Always ask any agent you call if the agency offers a program, or if it has bonus coupons or other incentives from outside services. Here are the biggest opportunities currently available.

USAA, in conjunction with PHH Fantus (now with Deloitte, Touche) , one of the nation's largest relocation consultant companies, has a Movers Advantage program providing a list of local real estate agents who will award you a cash bonus for listing and/or buying a house through them. Bonuses usually run between $200 and $800, depending on the value of the homes involved and the formula used by the agent. In order to qualify for any of these programs, you must not already have listed your home, or seen the home you want to buy, with another agent.

You're eligible if you, or a member of your family (including either parent), have been a regular commissioned or warrant officer of the Armed Forces or National Guard, and you join USAA. The program provides you with a relocation consultant for free, plus the agent bonus. Telephone USAA at (800) 582-8722 (in San Antonio, 498-5522).

Century-21 has a national referral arrangement with Atlas Van Lines that includes discount coupons you can use on moving your household goods.

HomePool Cooperative Resource Services, (800) 321-8000, offers counseling on both selling and buying your home, gives references on real estate agents nationwide, and works with a mortgage company that can do a "home prequalification." They'll appraise your home and send you a letter stating that it qualifies for an 80 percent loan of a certain amount.

Discount Agencies

The yellow pages *are* a good place to check to find discount agencies—one way to go if you're willing to shoulder open houses and/or other traditional agent responsibilities for a lower fee. Help-U-Sell, a large, national franchiser, offers a menu of choices that range from set fees starting at $500 and paid whether your sale closes or not, to a reduced commission rate. Other agencies have other plans. Discounters should be interviewed like any other agent as you are making your listing decision.

POINTS TO COVER WHEN INTERVIEWING PROSPECTIVE AGENTS

Talk to five or six agents on the telephone to get a feel for people who seem easy to work with and knowledgeable. Take control of the conversation early by asking questions rather than answering their questions. Phrase your queries so their answers won't reflect what they think you want to hear.

Don't start scheduling presentations with them immediately. Instead, take notes on their responses on the "Seller's Real Estate Agent Evaluator" provided in Appendix A. You'll be able to see who the top candidates are by totaling their scores.

LISTING PRESENTATIONS—YOUR INSIDE TRACK TO MARKETING KNOWHOW

Evaluate all of your contacts, then call back the three you felt best about and set up listing presentation appointments. Try to schedule them for different days, so that it will be easier to assimilate their information. While these presentations can give you vital insights into your local real estate market, rarely are all the facts coherent without your stopping to think them through.

Ask all three to include in their presentations:

√ *A Comparative Market Analysis (CMA) of your property, listing:*
1. *All the homes that have sold in your neighborhood in the past year, their prices and attributes. Some people like the agent to weed out the complete sales list and present just three or four homes the agent feels are "most comparable" the homes appraisers are likely to use as comparisons when they set the lender's appraised value. We prefer to do our own weeding out.*
2. *All the homes that currently are listed in your neighborhood, their prices and attributes. Again, your preference may be to have the agent give you only a short list of "most comparables."*
3. *A three- to five-year quarterly tracking of median or average sales prices, number of homes sold, and number of days on the market for your neighborhood and several others in your city. As outlined earlier in this chapter, these numbers will help you analyze the market to determine whether you should try a high asking price and how long before you may have to consider reducing your price. If you get your price right at the outset, you can figure you'll close the sale in the average amount of time.*

√ *A marketing plan outlining any changes they think you should make—paint the exterior, clean out the garage, and the like; who she feels best fits your buyer profile; how to analyze when a price reduction is in order, and so on.*

√ *Background information on the agency and the agent with references. Look for at least two years in operation for the agent, five for the company. Although every year of experience can mean better skills at selling and solving problems, many times newer but established agents and companies try harder. Some agents can be very good after only six months of experience.*

√ *A marketing agreement nailing down in writing the minimum amount of advertising, promotions, and open house showings the agency will do.*

√ *The "Seller's Property Disclosure Form,"* which you'll *need to fill out, describing the condition of your home. (See Appendix E for a sample.) It will help develop a price and marketing strategy that won't fall apart when the buyer does inspections.* Note: *This form goes by different names, depending on which state you're in. In California, for example, it's called a Transfer Disclosure Statement (or TDS).*

√ The listing agreement *setting the commission and limiting the length of time the agency has an exclusive listing.*

 Tip: Before signing the listing agreement, check the number of complaints against your prospective agency with the state Real Estate Board and the Better Business Bureau. Even the largest firms may not treat clients ethically.

Setting Listing Price and Terms

Resist any urging to sign a listing agreement during a presentation. Wait till you've heard what all three agents have said and have had some time to think it over. Often my husband and I split appointments, then report to each other. Having to explain options to somebody else makes you organize and clarify the issues.

Before you sign a listing agreement, you'll be making some crucial decisions. You need to evaluate what the three experts have told you about price and the current market climate, what kind of financing you should be willing to provide a buyer, how much fix-up to do, how long you might have to wait for a sale if you start with a high offering price.

Try to be realistic in setting price and terms, but give yourself some "wiggle room" to negotiate. Weed out agent suggestions that seem out of line. If one agent suggests a price that's 20 or 30 percent higher than the other two, that agent may be trying to "buy" your listing or just may not be knowledgeable. Contrary to myth, more agents err by overpricing homes than by underpricing them. A higher price often gets the listing and, of course, presages a higher commission.

Go with the average-to-high end on price and terms if it's a hot market and/or if you can spend time waiting for a buyer and offer some seller financing. Be aware that Employee Relocation Council surveys show that overpricing not only leads to a longer time on the market, it also can result in a lower achieved price. If you're in a hurry for any reason, go with an average-to-low asking price.

Price and terms issues will come to a head when you've got a buyer on hand, who can tell you what her most important negotiating points are. Review all of the terms now, however, so that you'll already have mapped out your set of nonnegotiables.

The Seller's Property Disclosure Form—Friend or Foe?

As you're setting your asking price, review your "Seller's Property Disclosure Form" dispassionately. It's not some devious tool designed to create price reductions. More than half the states now legally require sellers to give buyers these forms, and real estate agents across the country advocate using them.

For good reason. Going over this list will keep you from forgetting some unrepaired flaw that could seriously impact your sales price and/or cause a future law suit. Property condition is an essential component of property pricing.

The ever-growing, post sale litigation problem is also serious. As Harley Rouda, past president of the National Association of Realtors, told us, "When sellers fill out a disclosure form, they not only give the buyer peace of mind, they do the same thing for themselves. Litigation resulting from problems that arise after the purchase of a home can be drastically reduced if the sellers disclose all they know about the property. It will make the home more salable, it will give the buyer more reason to buy, and, in the final analysis, it will eliminate the time, expense and uncertainty of litigation."

Rouda's not only been pushing for nationwide laws to protect buyers and sellers by disclosure, he's head of a major real estate agency in Columbus, Ohio, where he introduced the concept in the early 90's. He implemented it in his company before the state made disclosures mandatory. Since then, his company has sold more than 15,000 homes, and he's not heard from a single seller plagued with property condition litigation.

If your agent doesn't provide a "Seller's Property Disclosure Form," consider using the sample in Appendix E both for thinking through your asking price and for giving to prospective buyers. You'll certainly want one (or one like it) filled out by the seller when you go to buy your next home.

Along with the disclosure, be prepared to give buyers copies of your warranties for the roof, systems, and appliances, plus a list of any things that are *not* included in the sale, such as your favorite drapes or your new washer/dryer.

Length of Time for a Listing

The last item to be decided about the listing is its time duration. Agents usually want a three- to six-month exclusive listing. We always give three. It's difficult to mount an effective marketing campaign in less than a month, and you really need two additional months to test how the marketing effort is working. If things are working well at the end of three months, you can extend. If not, you'll want to change agents.

TRAPS TO WATCH FOR WHEN PREVIEWING THE CONTRACT

At your first meeting with your agent after you've signed the listing, ask to review a sample contract and open house and showing routines. You'll need her to explain any obscure phrases and go over how items typically are negotiated in your market.

If you don't have an agent, hire a lawyer or consulting broker to provide a sample contract and spend three hours going over it with you. You need to be familiar with the real estate laws of your state, because mistakes can be costly.

Obtain a complete purchase contract from your local real estate board. This form outlines the way most offers will come in to you. Being familiar with it before the tension of negotiating an offer means you're much less likely to overlook something vital.

THE OTHER EXPERTS ON YOUR SALES TEAM

Ray Brown, a well-known real estate broker and columnist, admits that 'selling and buying a home can be difficult. "A dentist I know once compared the home-sale process to having root canal work done without Novocain, but he was a master of the understatement," Brown comments.

The way to keep out of trouble? Set up a sales team of experts to help you sail through the experience. Besides the listing agent and her managing broker, the seller's team includes:

Company Home Sales Advisor. Large companies often have someone sit down with you and help you map out your home sale. These people explain corporate policies, including whether a home buyout will be offered at a reduced price if you can't sell after a set amount of time.

They also are trained to help you select a good sales team in your area. They usually give you a number of advisors, including several real estate agents to select from, and check in with you from time to time to troubleshoot if there's a problem. They can save you enormous amounts of time and hassle in the sales process.

Tax Advisor. In Chapter 4, we reviewed the importance of coordinating your sales game plan with your overall tax strategy. Always check in with your tax advisor as you map out selling your major asset, so you can be advised as to whether you should wait for an Over 55 Exclusion, how an installment sale might benefit you, and the like.

Attorney. Any time you have an unusual situation, such as a buyer requesting a lease option or a contractor's bill that's been recorded against your title, you'll want to check with your attorney. For states that do title and escrow work through bonded specialist title and escrow insurance companies, you may not always need a lawyer. In other states, attorneys always represent both buyers and sellers in every sale. To find out if this is true for your location, check with your real estate agent or call a local savings and loan, and ask a mortgage loan officer.

Lender. While you're talking to a loan officer, ask if you can have your home "prequalified"—receive a written appraisal on how much they'll lend against it. This service is not widely available. Lenders usually only prequalify buyers, as buyers are the ones who will be taking out the loan. Some lenders, however, will prequalify the home in the hopes of having buyers turn to them after an offer has been accepted. The house prequalification service is invaluable to you, the seller, because it gives you a very solid idea of how to price your home.

Appraiser. If you're selling your home without an agent, you may want to get a written appraisal to determine how much you should ask. Again, sometimes your local loan officer can give you a list of the local appraisers the bank works with. Otherwise, look in the yellow pages under "Appraisers" or "Real Estate Appraisers." Ads stating that a company specializes in local residential appraisal may be good leads.

Another source would be the National Association of Realtors at (312) 329-8200. Call and ask for a list of local members qualified for the residential accredited appraiser designation (RAA). You also may be able to check with your state board of real estate appraisers for a licensee list.

Escrow/Title Agency. The people at the escrow/title agency are not on "your side" per se. They're more like referees between the seller and buyer. They act as a neutral party, holding the buyer's good-faith deposit in escrow, verifying the title and issuing insurance on it, making certain that both parties actually are who they say they are, and—perhaps most important— prorating to the day of closing who owes what percentage of things such as taxes and insurance before calculating your proceeds from the sale.

Ask friends and relatives what escrow/title company they've used, and call to find out if they're typically paid by the buyer or the seller or both. They are paid differently in different locations. The responsibility can vary even within the same state. Also, check different companies' fees, as these too will vary.

If you're paying, select one, open an escrow account, and have them do a preliminary title search. The earlier you take a look at the title, the earlier you can resolve any problems. Look for remaining "clouds"—records of things such as the money Aunt Sally loaned you for the down payment (which you repaid five years ago, but forgot to update on the record), or the roofer's bill (which you contested and never paid). These "clouds" may keep you from being able to sell the property.

Tip: If "clouds" turn up, you'll need time to: Convince claimants to sign off on a quit claim deed to release the obligations. Take the issue to court. Post a bond to be held by a third party until the matter is settled.

Do not wait until two weeks before you're supposed to close to deal with these problems.

Tip: If you bought or refinanced your home within the past couple of years, check to see if you bought a "binder" for policy, this usually means that you paid extra on the last escrow in order to receive a cut rate when buying a new title insurance policy within a specified amount of

time. If you do have a binder, you can save yourself a significant amount of money by specifying in the agreement you eventually sign with a buyer that your binder title company be used.

SELLER'S INSPECTIONS—ARE THEY WORTH THE MONEY?

Historically, property inspectors were hired by the buyer, if they were used at all. Ten years ago, people often skipped contractor and pest reports, and nobody had even heard of radon, asbestos, lead paint, or submerged fuel tank inspections. Today a gaggle of reports are common to every deal, and many are paid by the seller and completed in advance of advertising the property for sale.

In many states, sellers are required to review the possibility of environmental hazards and make disclosures on specific forms, and/or include a licensed expert's report.

Tip: The California Department of Real Estate has had an independent research company, M. B. Gilbert Associates, develop a booklet describing environmental hazards. They describe asbestos, formaldehyde, lead, radon, and household waste; the hazards created; where they usually are in the home; and some methods of dealing with them. For a copy of "Environmental Hazards: a Guide for Homeowners and Buyers," send a self-addressed stamped number 10 envelope and $1.50 to Preferred Publications, 1300 E. Main Street, Suite 310, Grass Valley, CA 95945, (916) 273-6457.

The new popularity of owner inspections has come primarily because the legal responsibility for a home's defects has shifted from "buyer beware" to "seller disclose." Buyers have been winning big lawsuits against sellers (and their agents) who didn't disclose a roof problem, a cracked beam behind the washing machine, or all kinds of other problems. Result: Seller ignorance has been discouraged, and seller deviousness has been seriously punished.

So what do inspectors do for sellers? As a real estate broker I *always* advise sellers to consider inspections when:

√ *A home is in pristine condition.*
√ *It's a terrible wreck, commonly billed as "a delightful fixer-upper."*

If a home is in very good condition and should command a premium price, we want to be sure something doesn't turn up during a buyer's inspection that we didn't expect. Surprises like that not only ruin your day, they kill the deal.

If a home is in bad condition, having reports to spell out just how bad the problems are helps nail down the price ahead of time, so that negotiations with a buyer don't get strung out during the contingency stage and die the death of the thousand price reductions.

If a home is in standard condition, find out what other neighborhood homeowners are doing about inspections, and follow suit. If most owners are doing inspections, you should as well, or people will think you're hiding something.

Even if you do pay for inspections, many buyers will want to have their own. Don't be insulted. Think like a buyer. Given the expense of fixing some problems, a buyer feels more secure with input from different contractors. While this may result in further price reductions, future buyers are likely to make the same demands. The sooner you've diagnosed a problem's cost, the sooner you get the sale.

To Fix or Not to Fix

If an inspection turns up a problem or your agent says the outside really needs a paint job, what should you do? No one rule always works. Here again, your best guide is to do what other sellers in your market area are doing.

Prettifying items such as fresh paint or a weeded yard with a few flowers are usually a good idea. Even seasoned buyers attracted by "Your Creative Touch Needed" ads often turn away from a home with peeling paint and a ragged yard and purchase a place that looks nice and bright instead.

√ **Warning:** *Keep "fluffing up" renovations to the basic visuals. Decorate with light, neutral colors. This is not a time for hot pink. At this stage, big additions (even kitchen or bath renovations) rarely bring a price increase equal to cost, and the worst thing that can happen to a property is to be "the most overimproved house on the block." Buy-*

ers—those contrary souls—seem to resist stubbornly giving you the $20,000 back that you invested in the solar-heated indoor swimming pool.

If serious problems turn up during inspections, a "deferred maintenance holdback" may be the best way to go. A deferred maintenance holdback is essentially a price reduction. You leave the price in the purchase contract intact, but the buyer is credited back the amount needed to do the work in escrow. This gives the buyer the cash to do the project. This holdback is preferable to the delay of having the work done before you close. Buyers often seem more satisfied with a $5,000 deferred maintenance holdback for a new roof than with your having to replace the roof during escrow. Also, if you have the work done, you essentially have to worry whether the buyer is going to be happy with that roof for the next ten years.

Tax-wise, a deferred maintenance holdback should qualify as a directly deductible expense of sale, so it won't matter to the IRS. Be aware, however, that it will result in your paying higher real estate transfer taxes.

The lender may require that certain problems *must* be taken care of before the close of escrow. It may have a policy of not extending new loans against properties with certain deficiencies, particularly serious environmental or structural problems.

Tip: *If a lender balks at funding a purchase with a deferred maintenance   holdback, here are two strategies:*

√ *Try negotiating with the lender to oversee the deferred maintenance holdback and review the work before releasing the money to the contractor directly. To do this, the lender will need to have a licensed, bonded contractor give an all-inclusive bid and a guarantee to complete the work within a specified period.*

√ *Shop for another lender that specializes in this kind of loan. Do this as soon as you know about the repair problem. If you think inspections may turn up a serious problem, either fix the problem first, or do the inspections before you decide on an asking price, then find a lender that will lend with a deferred maintenance holdback. If you and your agent can't find this kind of lender, you must get the work done before putting the house on the market.*

One last strategy for the homeowner wanting to offer security to buyers about appliances and/or heating and air-conditioning equipment—see about buying a home warranty. These work like a service warranty and can mean peace of mind to all concerned. Ask your real estate agent for a recommended warranty program, or try American Home Shield at (800) 827-4663 or Buyers Home Warranty at (818) 841-2320.

Review several plans on coverage vs. cost vs. service reputation. If you and/or your buyer obtain(s) coverage before the close of escrow, usually you do not have to have any inspections other than those the buyer requests. Cost usually runs around $300 for a basic policy, with pool maintenance and other special add-ons costing more.

OPEN HOUSE TIPS

If you keep house like we keep house, the idea of having people through who have a throttlehold on your financial future is somewhat daunting. Somewhat daunting? Who are we kidding? Horribly daunting!

Don't let this natural aversion stop you. Open house weekends and appointment showings are the only way to get your house sold. There is absolutely no reason to wait until after you've moved your furniture out. Existing homes always sell better with furniture in place, because wall scrapes and discoloration doesn't show as much, and people have a clearer idea of how rooms might be arranged.

So, as Pippi Longstocking says, "Give yourself a good talking to, and if you don't listen, send yourself off to bed with no supper." Remember—clean everything and get rid of the clutter. You've set up a home business and have computer stuff strewn from one end of the house to the other? Rent a local garage or small office, and work there, while your home remains serenely spick-and-span. You only do dishes once a week? Have a box handy to put greasy dishes in and cart everything down to the car and stash it in the trunk (also good for dirty diapers).

Light sells. Light makes everything look bigger, happier, more inviting. Shine everything. *Wash all windows.* Make sure all lights have 100-watt bulbs, because a savvy real estate agent will turn them all on, even during daytime showings.

Clean all surfaces. Dirt turns everybody off. Take adhesive yukko stuff off with Goof Off or other products containing Xylene *(Caution:* dangerous flammable, poisonous vapors). Use cat litter or dry Portland cement to sop up the oil in the driveway. Steam clean the wall-to-wall carpets and drapes in bad shape. Fix dripping faucets and sagging doors. *Never* leave a half-re-paired vehicle on the front lawn. These efforts will more than pay for themselves at price time. Trust us.

Tip: You must prepare for weekend open houses, but during the week, try to keep special showing appointments to two specific periods. Buyers who come on appointment viewings are seriously interested in your house, and usually they can accommodate your schedule. If an out-of-town buyer turns up, however, you should try hard to accommodate their request.

OFFER, OFFER, WHO'S GOT AN OFFER?

Usually prospective buyers and/or agents will call ahead to let either you or your agent know that they are "going to be writing up an offer." If several agents say this, they all need to know that multiple offers may be coming in and the dates when you're going to review and respond.

Having multiple offers arrive in a flurry the first week a property is offered is a mixed blessing. The situation can mean that the home will sell quickly, but, just as often, it means that we sellers will sit back and dither . . . even sit back and state, "I'm upping my price." Sometimes buyers take this news gracefully. More often they go off to find themselves another deal.

If you're the seller in this situation, find out from your agent and everybody else you've talked with (friends, relatives, accountant, lawyer, lender and escrow/title person) whether multiple offers are common in your current market. If they are *not* common, you and your agent underpriced your home, and asking for more probably won't hurt. If they *are* common, you're in a hot market, buyers probably are making offers on more than one home, and indulging in too much negotiating can leave you with all your buyers going to other homes.

Huddle with your agent. If you're selling on your own, now you *must* have a lawyer on hand for immediate conference. Two buyers might accept your counteroffer at the same time, and you could get accused of selling the house twice—a sure route to spending your next year (at least) in the company of *lots* of lawyers.

A well-orchestrated multiple offer scenario goes like this. You and your agent give the buyers and their agents three or four days (often through the coming weekend) to prepare their offers. It's a good idea to contact any other buyers or agents that have expressed interest, and let them know a deadline is coming. The auction atmosphere encourages buyers to come up with the best offer they can.

On the day of the multiple presentation, all the buyers' agents are scheduled to present their offers in the order they called to say they are "writing up an offer." They either come by appointment or assemble in one room, then each presents an offer to the seller and the seller's agent in another room.

Sometimes your agent will listen to all the presentations separately, then relay them to you. This saves you time and shields you from agent pressure, but we dislike it. We love negotiating, and sometimes an important comment pops into the conversation that we never would have thought of, if we hadn't been talking to the agents and buyers directly.

Always tell everyone bringing an offer that you are going to review all of them before responding. Some people are able to make a decision the same day. We like a twenty-four-hour decision-making cycle. Longer than that will discourage serious buyers who need to know whether they must keep looking for another house.

 Tip: Unless you decide one offer is clearly what you want, here are two good strategies for handling competing bids fairly:

1. Rank the offers. (See the next section for guidelines.) Give your counteroffer to the strongest bidder, with the stipulation that if it is not accepted in writing and received in person, by you, the seller, at an exact time and place, your counteroffer is invalid. These deadlines are typically for twenty-four hours.

If the first bidder drops out, another counteroffer goes to the next offeree, and so on. Working with one buyer at a time keeps other buyers from presenting duplicate counteroffers, then claiming unfairness and suing, but it also means you might have had an even better revised

*offer waiting somewhere down the line that you never
find out about.*

*2. Have your agent prepare written counteroffers for
all the prospective buyers, but do not sign them. These
counteroffers may vary—you may offer to help with financing for one buyer who will give you a higher price,
but not for another buyer who is offering a quick close
with a lower price. Stipulate that only counteroffers signed
by buyers and back to you by a certain deadline (usually
within twenty-four or forty-eight hours) will be considered,
that you may select a buyer to work with for any reason,
and that your decision will* nullify all other offers.

Evaluating Competing Offers

How do you evaluate offers? Whether you're in a multiple
offer situation or not, if an offer comes in with full asking price,
should you be ready to agree to say yes immediately? *No! Never*
sign an offer without reviewing and understanding the *entire*
contract.

Be particularly careful about:

√ *A stipulation that buyers must sell their own home before
they can buy yours.*

√ *A requirement that you offer financing for more than you
want to offer.*

√ *A requirement that you offer to "wrap" existing financing—
that is, you continue to be responsible for the loan and the
buyer might not pass a lender's credit requirements.*

√ *A contingency period longer than two weeks for physical
inspections and/or four weeks for finding a loan.*

√ *Any contingency you don't understand. If you get an
explanation from your agent or the buyer that still seems
obtuse,* get the explanation in writing and check with a
lawyer.

Backup Offers

Seller's agents usually encourage buyers to come in with
backup offers, particularly when the offer in contract is with
someone the agent suspects may not qualify for the loan or is
not fully committed to the purchase. Backup offers are great

for sellers, because they help keep the existing buyer from making outrageous repair demands and will ensure that the sale process moves along, even if the first buyer stumbles.

Buyers often resist making backup offers because they understand this strengthens the seller's hand with the existing deal. Buyers also are concerned that having a backup offer in place will mean they can't buy another house. To help motivate backup offers, go ahead and sign acceptable ones that are revocable at the backup offeree's discretion. Stipulate what circumstances must occur for the backup to move into "first position" and become the accepted, contract offer. Make certain that once the backup has become the contract offer, neither you nor the buyer can revoke, except upon the conditions detailed.

THE ESCROW TIMETABLE— AVOIDING LAST-MINUTE SURPRISES

More often than not, moving dates become a point of contention in negotiations. Your buyers need to move in by a certain date in order to accommodate *their* buyers moving in by a certain date in order to... I've worked with closings that needed to orchestrate nine different moves.

Try not to do that.

But... given that this problem arises often, in Appendix B we give you a blank "Escrow Timetable and Checklist," which will help you maneuver this domino challenge. Fill it in with the deadlines detailed in your sales agreement. If you are under contract to buy another home with the money from this sale, *fill it in completely and check daily.* If you're not under a tight deadline, look over it, keep it tacked up beside your calendar, and make sure to mark the due dates that are most crucial to your situation:

WHAT TO DO IF YOU HAVE TO MOVE IN TWO WEEKS AND YOUR HOME HASN'T SOLD YET

If your agent hasn't sold your home within three months, particularly if you haven't had any offers, you'll want to re-evaluate. Even in a soft market, no offers means one or a combination of three things—your price is too high, your property is unusual, or your agent isn't doing her job.

Finding Out Why—a Diagnostic Tool

To isolate why a home hasn't sold, isolate the cause.

Asking Price Too High. Real estate agents always point to this as the key reason your home hasn't received an acceptable offer within the average amount of time for your existing market. Although we've seen home after home sell with a price reduction, typically we always resist this suggestion from an agent when it's *our* home. We've therefore developed the following list of "High Price Symptoms" to watch out for:

√ *Number of agents coming to look at the house drops off radically after the first two or three weeks. Agents know the market. If they think your place is fairly priced, they'll put it on their list to show to all their buyers looking in your neighborhood. Otherwise they'll stop coming, and the only people looking at your home will be novice buyers who aren't well versed with the market—and may not be very motivated to buy.*

√ *Buyers walking through during open house or special showings stay only three or four minutes.*

√ *Other homes on your comparable listings sheet sell at lower prices.*

√ *If offers do come in, the buyers ask for a deeply discounted price or extraordinary financing.*

 Tip: Many real estate agents set up a "price deadline regime" with their clients right from the start. In their marketing plan, they set a deadline—usually after two to four weeks of intensive marketing. If there is no offer within the deadline, they expect you to reduce your asking price by 5 to 10 percent.

This technique allows you to test the market with a high initial asking price. Beware, however. Without a fairly hot market and skilled advertising, it can get your home "shopped" to the point that only an agonizingly deep price reduction will create renewed agent/buyer interest. The best strategy if you find yourself looking at an "inventory sale" price reduction may be to arrange an alternative move and take your home off the market for six months to a year to reach the next season of buyers.

Unusual Property. This is a property that doesn't appeal to the regular buyer for your neighborhood. A Tudor mansion with extensive grounds nestled in the heart of a development of two-bedroom ranches would have this problem. So did a country cottage with a charming view but a sloping floor and a low ceiling that took us and several agents nearly a year to sell in the heart of one of San Francisco's most conservative neighborhoods.

The symptom of this problem is lots of people looking at the house, then making cruel comments but no offer. Be aware, however, that buyers who make cruel comments and then produce an offer many times secretly love the place but want the lowest possible price.

Price reduction is the fast fix for the unusual property problem. If you're in a hurry, push a big price reduction. If you have time, try something in a 5 percent range every two to four weeks. Otherwise, keep your price at the low end of what the market says is your range, and be prepared to wait a long time till the oddball buyer arrives. Of course, you'll love having your individualistic home go to that very special connoisseur buyer.

Agent Ineffectiveness. Keep track. Does she keep to the marketing plan? Do buyers come to the open house? Do other agents come often with buyers? The most common causes of agent ineffectiveness are disorganization and an attitude that puts people (particularly other agents) off. Another problem may be lack of enthusiasm for your kind of home.

 Tip: If you're thinking about changing agents, expect the new candidates to recommend a price reduction to add buyer interest. We had a very practical, organized

agent for a little Victorian home once. No offers. We thought the problem was that she didn't like Victorians.

We reduced the price 5 percent, switched to someone else who loved Victorians, and she sold it in two weeks. A price reduction does not have to go with an agent switch, but don't forget to consider it.

If you feel that it's the agent's fault your property hasn't sold, interview and evaluate several new agents, review their evaluations (from Appendix A) against the originals, and notify the current agent that you are changing when the listing expires. She will want to reserve the right to deal with prospective buyers already introduced to the property. Otherwise you should be able to make a change with no problem.

Fast Move/Soft-Market Options

What do you do if you have to move in a month and/or you find yourself in a Very Soft market? There are a number of options:

Company Buyout. If your transfer is being managed by your company, find out about its buyout policy *immediately.* Even if it doesn't have a buyout plan, it may be able to help by providing someone to oversee the sale process, staying on top of the showings and keeping the home looking nice after you've moved away.

Leave It on the Market. This is the most common option, but we recommend trying every other means to sell it or leasing it so it will be off the market for a while instead. Unless the market is fairly hot, an empty house that most agents in your city already have crossed off their list will only attract lowball offers.

If you have to continue to try to sell, however, make arrangements to get back to your place at least once a month to meet with your listing agent and be sure no problems, such as frozen pipes or roof leaks, have developed. If you have relatives or good friends nearby, you might pay them to do some of the physical checks. You *must personally call* your agent regularly, and put yourself on a price reduction deadline schedule.

Limited-Term Rental. We discussed this option at length in Chapter 3. This works particularly well if you think the soft market will end within the next year and/or there's a chance you might be moving back to your current location later. Your best bet is to rent to a friend at below market rates with a full understanding that within six months or so, you may be putting the house back on the market, and you'll need the person's help in showing it. Otherwise, particularly if you're moving more than two hours away, consider renting through an agency that comes highly recommended by your listing agent. Your listing agent should be aware that your granting a renewal of the listing is based on her maintaining a happy, rent-paying tenant relationship.

√ *Warning:* Always *have your full rental agreement in writing. Also, in order to avoid paying taxes on any profits you make later on the sale of your home, you need to be aware of the IRS 1034 two-year deadline. Check Chapter 4.*

Offer Seller Financing—of Installment Sales and Carrybacks. One of the selling points for your home can be seller financing. No matter how soft the market, the smaller the down payment required on a property, the larger the number of buyers who are interested. If you don't need all your equity dollars out of a sale in order to buy your next house, consider having the buyer give you a second mortgage on the property for part of the down payment.

This procedure is so common, it has several names. The IRS calls it an installment sale and treats sale profits specially, so that you aren't hit with one huge income tax bill. Publication #537, "Installment Sales," explains how to qualify. Your agent and prospective buyers may call it a "carryback," "taking back paper," or "a seller second loan."

A typical seller "carryback loan" would be for 10 percent of the price, interest only, for three to five years. The interest rate would run from one to three percent more than what lenders are charging for a thirty-year fixed loan. If you can carry a larger loan and/or offer a better rate, advertise this heavily to create buyer interest. Also, check Chapter 4 and with your accountant on the tax benefits of taking your profits through an installment sale.

Warning: Seller carrybacks can be tricky. Be sure to check out:

√ 1. *What financing other sellers in your market are offering. Seller second mortgage structure varies enormously from market to market.*
√ 2. *The creditworthiness of the buyer. Use the "Verification of Credit and Income Form" in Appendix E. Be sure to re-verify information by telephone.*
√ 3. *What a lawyer has to say about the contract before you sign off.*

Offer a Lease Option. Robert Bruss, the well-known syndicated real estate advice columnist, always recommends selling your home via a lease option during a soft market. Not only that, he usually sells his own investment property that way, no matter what market he's in. He reasons that he gets the best price from those who are eager to buy, but either haven't saved enough yet for a down payment or haven't established enough of a credit history to qualify for a bank loan. Banks and S&Ls typically require a person to have two years' of credit card history and a regular job as the minimum needed to establish a "ratable" payment record.

The lease option technique calls for careful implementation and in-depth analysis of your buyer, but, besides a better price, it offers a good way to maneuver the rough seas of a very soft market. See Chapter 9 for some suggestions, buy Robert Bruss's minibook, *How Home Sellers, Buyers and Realty Agents Can Profit from Lease Options* ($6, Tribune Publishing Company, 75 East Amelia Street, Orlando, FL 32801), and check with your lawyer before proceeding.

Auction Your Home. As more and more lenders have used auctions to sell off homes across the country, other owners, particularly developers, have become more interested in the process. Now many communities have home auction specialists who will sell your home this way. So long as you can fit into their regular auction dates, their advantage is speed.

Any seller currently not in a listing contract with an agent can contact auctioneers directly. If your home is listed with an agent, she also may be able to arrange the deal, with a price that includes some kind of commission for her. Be aware that many auction houses require owners to pay an up-front fee to cover their advertising/marketing costs.

However you come to investigate an auctioneer, there are several things to watch out for, according to Donald C. Hannah, president and CEO of USAuction, Inc., of Stamford, Connecticut. Here are his six points to cover:

√ 1. *What percentage of the homes offered by an auction house actually sell?*

√ 2. *Are you obligated to accept any price, or can you refuse to sell below your "reserve" price minimum?*

√ 3. *How does the auction house agree on a reserve priice with you?*

√ 4. *How much time passes between auction and closing?*

√ 5. *What does the auction company do to make sure the sale closes after the gavel goes down?*

√ 6. *And—most important—does the auction house have good credit and a sterling reputation for paying off home sellers?*

Offer a Deep Discount, Lender Workout, or Deed in Lieu of Foreclosure. These are everybody's least favorite options. Always review all the options just presented and Chapter 3 *carefully* if it appears the market has totally collapsed on you, and your financial situation makes it impossible to keep up the mortgage. If none of those alternatives is possible, try the following:

Figure out how much you need to receive to pay off your mortgage and closing costs. If you've probably got some margin above that, blast out a heavy ad campaign on "DESPERATE Price Reduction." Remember, you need to maintain a sales price with some margin to pay an agent commission, because you'll need her help too.

If the market is too soft, and/or the heavy discount doesn't work, and/or your situation is so critical you have no energy left over to fight the real estate fight, contact the Consumer Credit Counseling Service. It may recommend that you get in touch with your lender's loan customer service representative. Tell her you're going to have to do something as a workout.

These people see problems all the time. They won't be gentle, but they should appreciate your being up front about the situation, and they may be able to offer some "workout plan" that will solve your problem. If you're going through a difficult

period such as a job loss or an illness, there are several possibilities, so long as both you and your lender feel you'll be able to
return to a regular payment schedule within six months to a
year. These include a "loan modification" involving a partial
payment schedule (often interest only) and/or a "forbearance
agreement," where you defer several payments and add them to
following payments or extend the term of the mortgage.

If you aren't going to be able to resume a regular schedule
within the foreseeable future, try to work out a deed in lieu of
foreclosure rather than going through a formal foreclosure. This
process will mean your assigning the property to the bank vol-
untarily. Its advantage to you is that it usually is accomplished
without going on your credit record and costing legal fees.

Some lenders may refuse to accept a deed in lieu. Robert
Bruss recommends that as long as you don't have any other
loans against the property, your attorney may be able to record
the deed back to the lender, then send the lender a copy of the
recording, the house keys, and a certified letter explaining your
situation. He says this should stop the lender's proceeding with
other legal action.

> √ **Caution:** If you must go through any of these procedures,
> get help from a local consumer legal representative. Con-
> tact the nonprofit Consumer Credit Counseling Service at
> (800) 388-CCCS, for legal advocates near you. These
> counselors usually have very low fees and will review the
> documents with you. You need to be sure that you don't
> make any promises you find impossible to keep.

SEVEN

Your Plan-Ahead Strategy

ESTABLISHING A PRELIMINARY FORWARDING ADDRESS

An important step in the Steiner Smooth Move System is establishing a forwarding address as soon as possible. If you're doing a trial move of less than six months, you'll probably opt to have the Post Office simply forward it to you, so long as your length of stay qualifies for a temporary "vacation forward." But if your move is for a longer period—or a sure thing—get started changing addresses now.

If you're moving to a place where housing or your schedule is tight, you may want to invest in a cell phone service, so you can set home viewing appointments all day. If you've already found a place to move into, get the exact address, call up the local telephone company, and see if it will assign you a number. Some services will give you a number even though you're not going to turn it on for a while, others won't. Check to find out if you can establish a voicemail number that can receive calls, even though you won't be hooked up to your new address. Otherwise the telephone company may require that you use a friend's address or a mail forwarding service to receive your bills.

Change-of-Address Do-It-Yourself Kit

Assemble the following:

- √ The "Change-of-Address Checklist" in Appendix B.
- √ An accordion folder or box for important documents and research materials, this "traveling filing cabinet" will need to travel with you when you move, as undoubtedly you'll need to check several items the first week you arrive.
- √ Always request two copies of your records. That way, you can give one copy to your new school, accountant, doctor, or whomever, and keep one yourself.
- √ Finally, get a new telephone book where you can start jotting down new friends and practical information, such as the new school principal's name and telephone number.

Fill in the "Change-of-Address Checklist" and set up your forwarding address and telephone number about one month ahead of time. Check with your existing phone company to see how long they will provide number change service. Send all your notices out over the next thirty days, so that the forwarding assignment will be finished before that ultra busy last month before you move.

Checking in regularly with family and friends in your old hometown is important. Whatever support system you set up, be sure to touch base at least once a week. Anything is preferable to being unreachable. The greatest disasters always seem to have happened when we've been "between phone numbers."

Mail Forwarding Alternatives

- √ Have your mail delivered to a reliable friend in the new location. Be sure to check that your friend doesn't mind forwarding future stuff after you've found a permanent place.
- √ Consultants and other businesses often find it convenient to set up an account with a storefront mail company, such as Mail Boxes Etc. or the Postal Annex, and use this as their forwarding address. Such services runs between $12 and $25 a month—about twice as much as a P.O. box. The street address of such a company may have more prestige, however, and it offers other goodies, such as phone-in mail check, copiers and fax machines, and sometimes a voice mail or a telephone answering service. The firms are set up as a convenient way to operate your business out of a suitcase.

√ *The very cheapest solution is to have mail delivered to you "Care of General Delivery" in your destination city. This system harks back to the good old days, when you walked into your local post office, gave your name, and asked a real, live person for your mail. Each city has only one general delivery post office, so you don't need to know the zip or to set it up ahead of time. Your mail will be held only ten days before it is returned to the sender, though, so check in often. Also, be sure to give the post office a change of address card as soon as you have a permanent address.*

√ *If you're moving overseas, the clever people at American Express offer a mail desk at each office in major cities worldwide where you can pick up your mail. To use the service, you must buy their travel services or traveler's checks or have their credit card. Consulate offices also accept mail for Americans, but their office hours are much more limited, and they seem to have a much higher rate of lost mail than American Express.*

Once you've got a forwarding address, order sticky labels or an address stamp with the new address, so marking your notices and return envelopes is quick and easy. You also may want to use these to label your furniture, appliances, and so on, prior to shipping.

> *Warning: Be sure you don't put labels on polished surfaces that can be marred.*

People sending out resumes, consultants, and others needing to correspond with businesses should order stationery now. Your address in print creates an aura of stability and permanence, even if you're using a P.O. box.

> *Tip: We've found a reliable source of these items is Walter Drake. Return address labels are currently priced from $1.99, starter stationery sets of fifty printed letterheads and envelopes (small size) from $7.99, and 250 business cards from $4.99. Call (800) 525-9291 for the catalog or to order. Allow three to four weeks for shipping.*

Email Forwarding

Be sure to check whether your email provider has a local telephone number in your new location. If it doesn't, you may want to find another provider, to avoid big log distance calls. Try www.snap.com or www.askjeeves.com for a global search engine find of email providers, many of which also provide email forwarding services. You my also be able to find shareware software that will automatically forward for you at www.zdnet.com. Be aware that you'll have to keep paying for your old service in order to have the forwarding. Notify everyone in your address book as soon as possible. Then renotify the people who still send you stuff for two months, and that should catch everyone important.

LETTING PEOPLE KNOW

Once you've established a forwarding address, you need to let a whole passel of people know what's happening. Friends and family are on everybody's list, of course, but there are a number of other people whom it's crucial to notify as well. If you don't let these people know about your new abode—preferably including a telephone number as well as an address—all kinds of bad things can happen. You can lose the refund on your apartment deposit, the IRS rebate can get lost in the mail, your credit cards can get overdrawn without your ever having received the bill, ad infinitum.

We like to move, and we consider spreading the word about our change as a happy trumpet of exhilaration. As we've repeated the process, however, we've found that loudness is not as effective as organization in being sure the word gets to the right people. The "Change-of-Address Checklist" in Appendix B lists everyone we try to contact with our "We're Moving!" notices.

Start by dropping by any post office and picking up a Change-of-Address Kit, which contains an official Change-of-Address Card plus nine postcards you can send to others. You'll need a Change-of-Address Card for everyone moving with you who has a different last name. Ditto any business names.

If one person with the family last name is staying behind, you'll need to prepare individual cards for each family member who is moving. Be sure to include zip codes and apartment numbers for both your old and your new addresses.

www.usps.com/moversguide
to change address - even for magazines

Tip: The post office can furnish you with your "zip +4" code in both old and new locations. Adding these numbers will help speed rerouting your mail. The post office forwards 2.2 billion pieces of mail a year, and anything you do to help is useful.

Mail the Change-of-Address Card(s) to your *old* local post office. The post office automatically stops forwarding letters eighteen months after receiving the card. Cutoff for second-class mail (magazines and newspapers) is sixty days. Third-class advertising material is never forwarded unless you notify the post office that you'll pay for it. Cutoff for fourth-class parcel post is one year locally, but forwarding to addresses outside your area will also involve extra charges and a special notice to your post office.

For three months after the forwarding cutoffs, the post office will send all mail back to the sender with your new address attached. After that, everything addressed to you gets returned to the sender without any information on your forwarding address.

You can try the post office's "hold" form for mail if you don't have a forwarding address set up. While holds are supposed to work for up to thirty days (the system was designed for people on vacations), we've never known anyone to have good luck with this system.

ORGANIZATION BASICS—THREE STEPS

Whether you're arranging a move to different quarters within your own city or setting off across continents, your route through a Steiner Smooth Move involves three steps:

1. Evaluate your needs.
2. Research the possibilities.
3. Distill all you've collected into two or three "best choices," so that your hunting won't disintegrate into a desperate game of bobbing for apples blindfolded.

You've already started the process by researching and evaluating your destination city in Chapter 1. Now you need to review the "Neighborhood" and "Home" evaluators in Appendix

A to focus on more specifics, and the following resources zero in on exactly what you want.

INTERNET SIFTING

There's no denying the Internet has vastly increased our research capabilities. But what the Internet empowered term as glorious "surfing" is pretty much tedious "sifting" to the rest of us. Speaking as reluctant admirerers, we have to point out there are a number of sites that mix only a little chaf with tons and tons of great relocation information (including, of course, our own, www.movedoc.com, where you can see current moving surveys and others' experiences with the process). We've listed many speciality sites like the numerous mortgage and real estate malls, etc., etc., in the Contact Directory in Appendix C. Here's our shortlist of favorite relocation web information sources that will cut your sifting time and frustration level:

www.snap.com and www.askjeeves.com, two search engines that go through the other major information directories like Lycos and Yahoo, and pull out a limited list of the most likely sites.

www.homefair.com is primarily a real estate mall, but does include city cost-of-living info plus a quick-and-easy salary calculator.

www.movecentral.com a relocation mall with contacts information for much of what you need at a new location, including real estate companies, insurance companies, telephone service, schools, veterinarians, appliance stores.

www.moving-guide.com is a directory of moving companies and other moving services worldwide. Focused mainly on moving companies, and offers a nice variety of movers who specialize in everything from small homes to grand pianos. It partners with apartment rental and real estate sites to make finding other information easy.

www.relocationcentral.com is a complete source of relocation information, including state directories for everything from apartments to churches to utilities.

www.runzheimer.com is a fee subscription site where they posts their cost-of-living survey results and other proprietary data. This company has been in the business of evaluating new locations for major corporation site decisions, so their information has good depth, but is very business oriented.

www.virtualrelocation.com lists over 500 U.S. cities, with comparative data for real estate prices and taxes.

www.yahoo.com huge site where you can look up anything, but the quality of the information for someone moving gets much better when you click into their city section. There is vast information on cost-of-living, typical salaries, school spending, crime and air pollution.

Consumer Information Center information brochures Pueblo CO 81009 www.pueblo.gsa.gov brochures fixing up your home and How to Finance

www.MovingCentral.com offers much helpful information and their "Before You Move service to change all addresses for you with from their one central registration. This will mean advertisers following you, but the work savings is worth it.

FOLLOW THE YELLOW PAGE ROAD

Our favorite source of information is the yellow pages. In fact, as far as we're concerned, yellow pages, white pages, blue, green, and pink pages, telephone directories of all colors come way out in front of sliced bread as the most fantastic unsung invention of the twentieth century.

Tip: To obtain standard telephone books for your destination location, call your local telephone service representative. You may want to order both the white and yellow pages, because you'll want to be able to look up individuals as well as businesses, and most split telephone directories put the government agencies in the white pages. Your phone company will bill you directly.

If it can't supply a telephone book for the community you want, call (800) 848-8000 for Pacific Bell Telephone's nationwide service. It can ship you any city directory within twenty-four hours.

Charges from either your own company or Pac Bell usually run between $20 and $75 per city set (you can order just white or yellow), plus $4.50 shipping.

*A more economical way to get telephone book infor-
mation is to check your local libraries. They carry most
major city telephone books, and you can write down
names or photocopy important pages. Or ask friends in
the new location if they can ship you an extra set or last
year's edition.*

Once you've got the telephone book, browse the table of
contents. Check special sections for maps detailing transportation and other key points. Find the items of most interest to
you. Pay particular attention to the following categories.

Education—Children. If you're putting a child into a new
school system, finding the right place is one of the first, and
most crucial, steps of the move. Look for the government agency
listings, and focus on those that can help you find special classes
or sports programs that your child needs. Poll your new location contacts on what schools are generally good, but the agencies are the place to go to get school evaluations.

For school comparative test results, call the State Board of
Education. Ask to speak with the department head of the state-
wide school testing service. If the receptionist says there is no
such service, ask to speak with a parent education coordinator,
or someone else who can help you evaluate schools for the particular age group you're interested in.

You need to find out if the state administers comparative
tests (California and New York do, for example), what the tests
are called, and what state office gives out the information.

If you draw a blank, browse both the state and the local
government sections under "Schools," looking for more info
sources. Sometimes it's advisable to research information for
children older than your child. A state office for college admis-
sion standards or a bank making student loans, for example,
may give you the most concise list of secondary education tests,
who administers them, and which schools do best.

Don't stop browsing the Education/School sections once
you've found testing information. These lists contain all kinds
of contacts that will help you in your search for other programs—day care facilities, school handicapped assistance, bi-
lingual education, home teaching, parent education, alternative
schools—the bigger the community, the longer the list.

Education—Adult. Obviously, if you're attending a college or university in your new location, you'll be contacting it directly, but take time to glance through the education listings in the government pages of the telephone book, too. Here's where you can find the offices that arrange for grants and loans, or keep information on residence requirements for state education subsidies, community colleges, scholarships, and the like. These sources also will be able to provide you with lists of the other schools in the area that might offer difficult-to-find specialist courses that your own university doesn't provide, or night courses, if you're working and going to school at the same time.

Health. Ask the local Environmental Protection Agency for a list of smog zones pollen counts per area and/or noise pollution areas. Check to see if the yellow pages Hospital section includes an area listing or a map with hospitals pinpointed.

If you have special health needs, check our Contact Directory for Family and Health Services, the yellow pages under "Associations and Organizations" for contacts and the Internet for information and contacts. You may want to check with the weather bureau for a monthly tabulation of weather patterns, but probably this information will be included in the Chamber of Commerce info packet.

If you're moving abroad, write to destination hospitals or clinics that advertise international service, and ask what programs they offer. If your company or the U.S. Embassy has sent you any information regarding international health clinics, write to them as well.

Insurance. You'll have to change many of your insurance policies in the destination location. Call the destination State Department of Insurance, and ask if it has a list of companies with the fewest complaints. Also, ask for minimum insurance requirements, how long you have to reside in the state before you must change insurance policies, and other pertinent questions.

 Tip: Property insurance companies in your new location may be able to tell you about which communities have particular problems with floods, mudslides, and fire storms. Occasionally you learn of serious area handicaps when interviewing insurance people. A friend, for

example, found it is very difficult and expensive to get wind insurance in South Florida.

Entertainment. Today's telephone books often include a special listing of local theaters, restaurants, sports arenas, parks, zoos, shopping centers, museums, and libraries. Sometimes they also have locator maps and a calendar of events. If they don't have a special section, check the local government pages for libraries, parks, and museums and look up your particular interests under their yellow page listings. Many successful "fixer-upper" entrepreneurs have based their purchase decisions on the number of espresso bars and bookstores in a neighborhood.

Public Transportation, Zip and Area Code Information. Often telephone books have the best maps of freeways and public transportation that you'll find. You'll want to know where the airport is, both for convenience and to be aware of which communities have noise problems. The telephone directory maps also may locate area codes and zip codes—an invaluable aid when you want to know where a service vendor with an interesting ad might be found.

Utilities. Call to find out basic rates and special services. Jot down key telephone numbers in your new home telephone book. Put rate information into your "Monthly Budget Estimator" (Appendix D).

Taxes. Contact both local and state offices, and ask for both current and pending assessments. Again, fill in the blanks on your "Monthly Budget Estimator."

Home-Finding Agencies. Check the yellow pages under "Real Estate," "Rental Agencies," "Roommate Referral Services," "Relocation Assistance," and the like. Some yellow pages now offer guides arranged by specialty, which is a big help.

The yellow page search usually is more fruitful for us when we're looking to find a home than when we were looking to sell one. When the new neighborhood is a good distance away, we haven't gotten our bearings, selected a neighborhood, or wandered around looking for signs—yellow pages to the rescue!

Check for companies that specialize in the service you're looking for and coordinate with listings from newspaper ads.

Furnished Rentals. Look through "Hotel" listings for apartment hotels, weekly rates, and other notations indicating that the establishment caters to relocating people. You also may find economic accommodations under a "Boarding house" classification, although, budget-wise, the cheapest place probably will be the sublet ads in the newspaper. Since you may need to stay in a place for several weeks while house-hunting, see if you can find a furnished rental in a neighborhood that might fit your final needs.

Jobs. Employment and temporary agencies offer a convenient way to support yourself when you first arrive in a new community. Again, the yellow pages are starting to list agencies by specialty.

Libraries. Check your destination telephone book for the local library Information Service Desk and/or the Business Section. Ask for the names of:

√ *The local paper with the most help wanted ads.*
√ *The local paper with the most real estate sale and rental listings.*
√ *The best local business newspapers.*
√ *Any local kids' and/or parents' publications. (Also see Appendix C for this information.)*
√ *Any local publications specializing in your trade or profession.*
√ *A list of neighborhood or weekly newspapers.*
√ *Local "advertisers"—the freebie weeklies that run lots of private party want ads, plus local household appliance, car dealer, closeout, and bargain ads.*

Search the yellow pages for other listings that may be fruitful. Call the most important ones to obtain a limited subscription or sample copies.

THE NEWSPAPER CHECKLIST

If you've got plenty of time for your research, opt for a limited Saturday or Sunday subscription, then browse an occasional weekday paper from your local library or large newsstands. Special sections in weekday papers are rich with information on neighborhood and community activities.

The best job and real estate want ads usually appear only in the Saturday or Sunday paper. When you call the subscription department, ask which day has the most want ads, and whether you can subscribe for that day only, if there's a big difference in cost between full week and Saturday- or Sunday-only service.

> *Tip:* Be clear that you must have the classified section. Many large metropolitan newspapers ordinarily send out-of-town subscribers reduced editions without the local ads, unless you specifically order the "Metro" or "City" edition.

If you have a limited time to do your research, you may be able to find concentrated information in your current library's microfiche record of publications. Otherwise call the newspaper directly to find out if it has a library or is available online.

Job and Business Info. The want ads offer direct contacts, of course, but they also give other valuable information. As a group, want ads can tell you about general job availability and some of the wages and salaries that are paid locally.

Coverage of local business news in your field offers a gold mine of info for anyone going into a new area, particularly job hunters, as the names of people mounting new projects in your field are the best ones to check for new job openings. New people hired from outside a firm also usually hire new staff of their own.

Other items to look out for are any references to local trade groups or professional organizations. Even if you can't make a meeting, getting their information will give you names and telephone numbers of contacts who can tell you about your field — and maybe come up with just the right job opening, to boot.

Tip: *The Wall Street Journal* publishes the *National Business Employment Weekly,* (800) JOB-HUNT, listing managerial and sales positions, both nationwide and abroad. Pick it up on the newsstand, or three-month subscriptions are available. Check Appendix C, under "Job Hunt, Business, and Entrepreneur Services," for other employment publications specializing in particular fields; and the Network of City Business Journals, (800) 433-4565, with more than sixty-five local papers, and for associations/organizations that may have local newsletters and/or job bank services in your destination location.

Neighborhood Coverage. Articles give background information on where the "in" parties are held, which neighborhoods are going through the most change, having the most crime problems, and the like. Be sure to check the Business and Real Estate sections for information on new developments, new highways, and public transportation projects. Stick these articles in the research section of your accordion folder.

Calendars of Events. Usually at least the Business, Entertainment, and Social sections have once-a-week calendars, which will give invaluable listings on reaching local organizations you'll want to tap now and/or join later. Also look for calendars of children's events, sports events, education series, and volunteer events.

Home-finding. Newspapers are the number-one source of rents and/or home prices, according to the IIP Frequent Mover Survey. Be aware that different publications have different headings. Some split rental listings between apartments and flats—a term for a total floor unit with a separate front door that I'd never heard of, growing up in Colorado. Others put condo and co-op rentals in a different section. Sublets may be listed under executive suites, short-term rentals, furnished rentals, or vacation rentals. Also look for rental referrals, roommate services, and boarding/rooming houses.

Browsing these newspaper information sources also tunes you in to local real estate area maps, whether Saturday or Sunday is the traditional open house day, and which rental or real estate agencies seem to have the most listings. Again, put this info into your "Neighborhood" folder.

Home Fairs, Expos, and Seminars. Most communities have these two or three times a year. If you don't see any ads, the easiest way to find out about them is by calling a local newspaper city desk or ad manager, and asking for the dates. Fairs and seminars can be an invaluable help if you're moving to a community nearby or if you can schedule your home-finding trip to coincide.

Cost of Living. Automobile and furniture ads will help you get a fix on what to expect for those expenses in your new location. We've saved money by leaving large appliances and furniture behind on most of our moves, and buying replacements in the new location.

 Tip: Buying replacements in your new location will be absolutely essential if you're moving abroad. American appliances use different electrical power than do those in most other countries, you won't have any repairpeople who can fix your model, and, besides, shipping heavy things is ridiculously expensive.

TREASURE HUNT HELPERS

Numerous other places can provide you with vital information. Besides your current library and the destination Chamber of Commerce, the destination tourist bureau and local real estate agencies are good sources of information. Write the state or local Economic Development Agency on your business letterhead for entrepreneurial information.

Check travel books for temperature and weather charts and lists of fun things to do. Go over information in the latest almanac for important history and demographic information. Check Appendix C to find out where to obtain local real estate/rental photo advertiser magazines showing homes for sale and/or for rent.

 Tip: If you're moving with children, enlist their help with research. They can write to the Chamber of Commerce for an information packet and help peer over maps to find schools, parks, and libraries. By assigning your kids some responsibilities, everything will get done faster and they'll feel more comfortable about moving.

OVERSEAS OPTIONS

Whether you're moving abroad, or moving to the United States, you should start the paperwork early by contacting your passport office. Your travel agent usually can help with applications for temporary entry papers, tourist visas, and/or medical certificates for the countries where they're needed. A tourist visa usually runs out after 90 to 180 days. If you're going for a longer period, paperwork is more complicated, and you have to make a formal application to the target country's embassy or consulate. In most cases, you need to be prepared to show officially approved employment or a private source of income.

Requirements vary, as does processing time. Start the process twelve to eighteen months in advance if at all possible.

Tip: When moving abroad, make sure you have a U.S. checking account at an international bank that has offices in your destination country. Ask your current institution if it has branches or cooperative agreements there. If not, try CitiBank's Personal Banking for Overseas program at (212) 307-8511, or check with Bank of America, (800) 822-2222, or American Express, (800) 221-7282. Make sure to get a PIN number with four digits or less. Some international machines, particularly in Europe, won't accept longer access codes.

Large companies that want employees to transfer overseas work hard to assemble information packages and provide orientation sessions that will help the whole family settle in.

If you've decided to move abroad to study, find work on your own, or work for a smaller company that doesn't offer much orientation help, you need to prepare yourself for the language and cultural changes on your own. Take classes. Read travel books on the location and general "how-to's," such as Kepler and Gaither's *Americans Abroad*. Check your local phone book to see if the country you're headed for has a consulate program of films or music, where you can meet people and discuss lifestyles. Another culture-rich information source may be a church in your current area with a large ethnic congregation.

To get a good start toward answering the practical questions about budgeting, schools, and neighborhoods, try the U.S. Embassy or Consulate in the city you've targeted. When we moved to Europe, we weren't sure whether we wanted to go to Paris or Rome. We wrote embassies in both places. From France we got a brief note from a French secretary saying they had no information on rents and neighborhoods. From Italy we got a long, friendly letter. We loved Italy.

DOLLAR BASICS—DECIDING WHAT TO SPEND

Market values—home prices or rent—is the obvious number-one item to be researched when you're relocating. Among respondents to our lip Frequent Mover Survey, 67 percent ranked this item as the most important thing to investigate when selecting a home. Difficulty in finding an affordable home was also ranked by more people as the biggest problem encountered.

The most common advice is to set a dollar limit on what you're going to spend on housing, then stick to it. Sandra Fisher, a job-hunting respondent, even advised setting a housing budget, then cutting it in half. "Never assume you'll get a job quickly and your savings only need to stretch over four to six weeks," she explains.

Whatever you've personally budgeted, you'll find landlords want to verify that you make three to four times what you spend on rent. Lenders have a more complicated formula. Check Appendix D, "Loan Qualification Worksheet," for the numbers.

DETERMINING MARKET VALUE

The appraiser's big three—every home searcher, whether you're looking to buy or rent, runs into the same basic market value components an appraiser looks at—size, condition, location.

Size

Appraisers always measure the size of a home carefully. Banks know each extra square foot counts. Although rarely measured separately, cubic feet also makes a difference in how we perceive a home—witness the big success of cathedral ceilings and loft living.

Determining size needs ahead of time involves several checks. Be very clear on how many bedrooms, bathrooms, and garage spaces you need, as well as whether you want a formal dining room, an eat-in kitchen, and/or a family room.

Get a retractable tape measure at least twenty-five feet long, and measure the main rooms and that stretch of wall that houses your treasured cherrywood sideboard. Jot down specifics on the "Home Evaluator" in Appendix A. Be sure to calculate any requirements for wide doors or other access.

Be aware that unusual home-size requirements will influence what architectural design and neighborhoods you'll want to look at. Although all areas have homes of varying sizes, you'll find few three (plus)- bedroom apartments and even fewer one-bedroom homes. If your family is looking for a home at either end of the size spectrum, be sure to tell your rental or real estate agent on your initial call.

For one-bedroom homes, you'll probably be better off in older existing neighborhoods, where enterprising individuals have built individual one-bedrooms. Otherwise, look for a condo or co-op.

For large apartments, you'll find the best selection is with buildings constructed either during the past ten years or before 1940. The emphasis from the '40s through the '70s was on studios and one- or two-bedroom apartments. Three bedroom-plus sizes were thought to be exclusively for homeowners.

If your size requirements are even more unusual, your research will have to be even more resourceful. Friends of ours are do-it-yourself airplane builders, and they managed to find a subdivision with hangars and runways. You can fill almost any requirement, if you have patience.

Condition

When appraisers think condition, they're not only thinking leaking roofs and sagging floors, they're also thinking how well a floor plan works and how modern and usable a kitchen may be. Start your thinking about these items by looking around you. What do you like and not like about your current home?

What do you value about the fireplace, the use of openness or privacy, the garden?

What kind of basic condition the family is willing to live with is, of course, something you need to agree on ahead of time, because needed repairs will have a big impact on your neighborhood selection as well as price.

No matter whether you've opted for "brand new" or a "fixer-upper" or somewhere in between, look for a solid basic construction. We've redone many a kitchen and bath and even re-done several homes from basement to roof. The homes that have given us the most trouble are the ones with poor initial construction. (Or a bad floor plan: more about that in a minute.)

Poor construction invariably starts with a bad foundation—an expensive and difficult item to fix. Topping this problem with substandard framing (irregular spacing between the studs and joists, substandard building materials, etc.), and the project jumps into the prohibitively expensive-to-fix category.

Then there's the drab home that needs no more "fixing" than a coat of paint to make it shine. This is the gem professional renovators salivate over, because it often gets ignored by the general market and sells for a bargain price.

The Gold-Plated Bathroom. The overimproved property is at the opposite end of the condition spectrum from the fixer-upper. Over improvement can happen in any neighborhood; in fact, it's the neighborhood that determines whether an appraiser will designate the home "over" improved. Having a swimming pool is de rigueur in some communities but an "over" improvement in others. Ditto a second story, a three-car garage, and a gourmet kitchen. Adding a turret and a stone facade to a thirty-year-old row house is probably the ultimate example we've seen.

Owners are usually loath to part with overimproved homes. They often over price. It may be a long time before they accept not many row house buyers want a turret and they are unlikely to get a much higher price than the rest of the neighborhood. When reality sinks in, they may drop their price suddenly and precipitously.

To find this type of bargain while you're combing the ads to set up your home-hunting trip, look for those touting "Unique Features! .... Unusual Floor Plan! .... Biggest House on the

Hill!" Let agents know you appreciate the "Out of the Ordinary!" The results can be wacky . . . or the best buy on the market.

Something Old, Something New, Something Do-it-Yourself. This is another toughie needing careful advance decision. If you want something "so new the paint isn't even *dry,* " and your significant other wants something "with character and a story to tell," flipping a coin over how to spend the next five to seven years may be the only way to solve the conflict. Here are some considerations to keep in mind:

New Homes. A brand-new home has the peculiarly thrilling smell of new wood, new paint, new lives. Most builders give you color and finishing selections. The yard is graded for good drainage. The neighborhood is filling with families about the same size as yours that are also newcomers, looking to make friends.

But remember, new homes are never perfect. Just like new cars, they need some "breaking in" before you get the glitches out. If you've bought from a reputable builder, you've got someone on hand to fix problems. In any case, insist on going through the "Home Evaluator" in Appendix A and having a thorough home inspection before you sign your contract.

Try not to be one of the first home buyers in a new development. These unlucky souls are the ones destined to run the complete gamut of short-term problems, from improper utility installations to roof tiles overlapping up instead of down—a wonderful way to add excitement to a party held in honor of the arrival of the rainy season.

If you're buying before the home is complete, expect a builder to take anywhere from two to four weeks longer than promised to finish it for you. If you're having a new home built to custom specs, expect build-out from permit plan submission to final inspections to take anywhere from nine to eighteen months.

Existing Homes. We love existing homes. They seem to have more personality and often are built with better soundproofing, higher ceilings, and more detail work than any brand-new home of a similar size that we could afford. We also like to remodel. People who don't can find places where owners have already upgraded the plumbing and the wiring and installed kitchens and baths worthy of a magazine cover.

You have to expect to deal with more long-term problems, however. Home warranties on existing appliances and systems usually run out more quickly on existing homes than on new ones, and every now and then something needs to be fixed that has no replacement part, so you have to either figure out a creative alternative or tear everything out and start from scratch.

SFRs and Other Options. Year after year, National Association of Realtors surveys find the traditional single family residence (SFR) still tops the charts. A detached home, in fact, has been the choice of over 75 percent of the buyers, even for singles. As a result of this preference, no matter what the market, an SFR is worth more per square foot than the comparable townhome, condo, co-op, or duplex/triplex.

Because of the savings, include an evaluation of these options as you're putting together a picture of your dream home. Weigh price against the extra responsibilities of co-owning a duplex or acting as a landlord. Consider the wisdom of one of our Minnesota survey respondents who rejoices in condo living every November as the snow starts to pile up.

Floor Plan. A convenient floor plan can help make a small home livable. Conversely, a clumsy floor plan can make a home with plenty of rooms a disaster. San Francisco is cursed with numerous homes laid out on a "railway-flat" style, where you must go through the living room and the dining room (and sometimes even bedrooms) to get to the kitchen. Another ridiculous older design common throughout the West has a perfectly useless "sunroom" off a bedroom. While it can work as a hobby room or a temporary nursery, its isolation is always a problem.

Modern developers still often put laundry facilities in impossible places, or proudly present "open design" homes with high ceilings and no doors between rooms, which can result in humongous energy bills.

Floor plan is not something you can investigate long distance, but write down what's important to you now. That way, when you start actual viewings, the only homes on your short list will be the ones featuring that essential mudroom where Junior can strip off his rain gear before going inside.

Style. This one can be a marriage killer. Price usually is dictated by pocketbook. Floor plan and needs for hobby space and more windows can be accommodated. But style? "He wants a Victorian, I have to have something modern with big windows." "I love that soft, Santa Fe look, he wants brick." "She's fallen in love with the view from this apartment, but I'm not moving into a place where there's no molding on the walls and the fireplace has fake logs." Real estate agents hear variations on this song every day. Work out your differences now, in the abstract. You'll cut your looking time in half.

Landscaping. Most of our lives, we haven't had landscaping, we've had a deck. At one point we had a five- by five-foot lightwell we dubbed our "atrium." Painted white, planted with container flowers and a tiny, never-used birdbath, it satisfied our underwhelming need for our own patch of green.

Being such cityphiles, it therefore came as no surprise to us that gardens and yards ranked below having lots of closet space on the priority lists of our lip Frequent Mover Survey. However, some people are absolutely passionate about having a garden, and if you're moving with a family, this is an item that needs to be discussed with all members. Children, particularly, need to be aware if you're considering no-yard living.

Now that you've had some time to think about size and the many aspects of home condition that are important to you, go over the "Home Evaluator" in Appendix A and highlight those items. And if you're still not sure about any of them, spend some time at open houses in your present location. Browsing what's in the market will help you firm up these decisions before you make your home-hunting trip.

Location, Location, Location

While an appraiser is concerned with all three components of market value—size, condition, and location—the greatest of these, as real estate agents are fond of saying, is location, location, location.

Again, begin your process of evaluation by reviewing the neighborhood where you're currently living and filling in a photocopy of the "Neighborhood Evaluator" in Appendix A. What things do you like? Will you try to duplicate your current neighborhood, will you look for something very different, or will you improve one aspect but keep everything else very much the same? Grading your existing neighborhood will help focus your energies on the things that are most important in your search. From there, start evaluating prospective neighborhoods.

Location has a number of factors that are easily researched ahead of time. Again, preplanning will save you significant time and hassle later on. Here are five specific things to look for and where to find your clues.

Schools and Other Children's Amenities. These are an important part of the neighborhood preselection process. Consciously, we look for good schools, because they mean opportunity for our children. They also, of course, mean a neighborhood of concerned parents (like us), who'll make for good adult friendships.

Schools can be pinpointed initially on one of your maps. Then you have to find out more about which ones are best for your child when you're calling education authorities. Zoos and parks are also easy to locate on maps. The challenging things to find ahead of time are the day care facilities and the neighborhoods that have great children's clubs such as Scouts, Young Achievers, 4-H, or Campfire Girls.

Check with the leader of activities your child is already enjoying to find out if there's a way to get lists of clubs elsewhere. Look through the destination yellow page listings for "Associations," "Organizations," and "Churches," or write headquarters of specific groups as found in our Appendix C. Children's amenities are particularly important when you're targeting neighborhoods, because children will make friends more easily if there are many things to do within walking distance.

Adult Friendship Opportunities. You also need to pinpoint things for you to do ahead of time, because they're an important part of selecting a location. Ask your contacts and business colleagues where they live and why. Check your maps for churches, community centers, tennis courts, and golf courses. Have children in mind as much as yourself when you look through yellow page listings and Appendix C directory.

Tip: Making friends has been found to be a major reason for corporate transferees to feel the move is successful. Be sure to put some thought into finding a neighborhood offering you the opportunities you want to make new friends for yourself and your children.

Commute and Public Transport Accessibility. These concerns affect us daily. When you're identifying neighborhoods, look out for hidden transport problems—the neighborhood with an easy off ramp but no on ramp, for example, or an area like Weehawken, New Jersey, which seems very close to a metro railway stop on the regular street map but actually involves maneuvering twenty blocks around a cliff.

Crime Rates. Although these don't turn up on maps, articles detailing high- and low-crime neighborhoods often appear in newspapers. You may be able to get a copy of crime rate statistics from a real estate or rental agency or the local police community relations officer. Don't just look for numbers, however. Ask people if they know about any problems, and, if so, what happened. Your new community may have an entirely different definition of crime than you do.

The Intangible Value Indicators. Whether you're buying or renting, as soon as you start investigating more than one neighborhood, you'll find the exact same home costs more in one place than in another. At first this may seem arbitrary—particularly when the two places are only blocks apart, in the same school district, and served by the same transportation system.

Don't be fooled by newcomer's naivete. As Megan Walker, one of our respondents who's lived abroad, admonished, "Don't do anything the local people don't do. There's usually a good reason for everything."

The locals usually have good reason for their neighborhood pricing. Often these reasons are rooted in the deep-seated emotional needs for privacy and tribal identity. Understand these needs. Add whichever ones appeal to you to your own list of "have to haves." You'll find there is near-universal agreement that satisfying these primeval needs is worth every cent of what it costs. Since these factors also will play an important part in resale value, home purchasers should pay particular attention.

The Five Intangible Neighborhood Value Indicators

"Water Interest" Items. A hundred years ago, industry claimed most waterside locations. Much of the nation's supplies arrived by boat, and nobody paid attention to the human predilection to living close to water, anyway. Today, shipping has largely been replaced by air transport and trucking, and dock after dock is being turned into luxury housing. Away from the major rivers, lakes, and oceans, luxury housing often comes with streams or ponds. If a developer can't find a stream or a pond, a man-made "water-interest item" becomes part of the design.

This is an easy factor to see on your map, but steer clear of waterside developments still surrounded by railway tracks. Such neighborhoods may seem charming at the outset, but the tracks will oppress residents, even if they are no longer in use.

Hills and Views. Look for topographic altitude notations on your map, and/or areas with lots of curving streets. The Greeks, the Romans, and the Chinese all built their villas and castles on hilltops, and it wasn't just for the view. Such locations were easier to defend, and as long as they were built on bedrock, not shale, they were less likely to be destroyed by earthquakes and floods. They were also cooler in the summer and less prone to malaria.

We've harnessed flooding rivers, drained the malaria swamps, and invented air-conditioning, but the traditional love of hillside living persists, and people are willing to pay for the privilege. Payment goes up with a view. A home in San Francisco's Pacific Heights is worth $100,000 more if it offers a panoramic view of the Golden Gate Bridge, and an apartment with a view can command $300 more a month than its twin on the other side of the building.

Luxury Zoning. Look for curving streets, "water-interest items," and lots of green area. A neighborhood that's been zoned, designed, and built for high-priced homes will have large lots and expansive floor plans. Check newspaper ads for new developments that have a community clubhouse, a golf course, tennis courts, and other facilities. Such communities usually also require that all property owners adhere to community rules, which can include restrictions on what color you can paint your exterior and where you can park your vehicles.

Zoning is the legal manifestation of human tribalism. We love living with others who are similar to us. Coming home to a neighborhood of similar dwellings soothes the inner psyche with the feeling of belonging. The design trend is away from walls and gates isolating a single-strata neighborhood, but it's not clear how successful the new integrated and "self-sustaining" communities are going to be. We've definitely agreed we like individuality in each home, of course, but anybody wanting to plonk a college dorm or a fast food joint in the midst of an existing quiet family neighborhood is not going to be welcomed.

Trees. Another one of those subtle appeals to ancient sensibilities. Trees give privacy. Trees cut noise. The more trees, particularly well-established ones, the more appeal. Developers understand this. They dot their front yards with newly planted saplings and, in more upscale communities, keep as many established trees as possible when they lay out the streets and pinpoint where homes can be built. Determining from afar how leafy green an area will be is difficult, but scan the real estate and rental photo magazine advertisers for neighborhoods depicted as full of established greenery.

North End of a Community. The most mysterious of values. Developers have noted the northerly path of luxury development from Dallas to Chicago. The northern part of each separate community is where the dollars are—north San Mateo is more valuable than its southern streets and, as you go north into San Francisco, there's a trough of lower values, before higher values cluster in the northern part of the city.

Investigate this value factor when you're trying to determine which neighborhood will grow the fastest in value. Don't simply assume the path of luxury is headed north. Doublecheck by counting the number of luxury developments springing up in the different directions, and go with the local trend.

THE THREE MAPS YOU ABSOLUTELY MUST HAVE

Now that you have a picture of what elements your dream home and neighborhood will have, how do you pinpoint which areas to go home shopping in before you actually arrive in a new location?

Even if you are getting extensive information on neighborhoods from your company, or you already live in a neighborhood close by, you'll need to become *very* familiar with three different types of maps. They will save you from the dilemma of one family we worked with that had inadvertently moved out of their son's school district, although they were only a few blocks away from their old home.

Rental / Home Price Neighborhood Keys

Whether you're renting or buying, you'll need to know how rental and real estate agents designate each neighborhood. In most cities, this information is very easy to come by, because newspapers feature neighborhood-keyed maps, and both rentals and sales are listed by these location keys.

 Tip: Newspapers that sort their ads by rent or price make it more difficult to get oriented to a new community. If the first local paper you browse uses this practice, try hard to find a competitor that doesn't.

Area Map with Transportation

You'll need this for an overview of which communities make for easy commutes. In some places people commute only by car; others have extensive bus and/or rail or subway systems. Check your yellow pages for transport maps. The State Highway Department may be able to tell you where to get the most detailed transport maps.

Be sure to get a copy of public transportation time schedules as well as the map. You'll find that some communities have much faster and/or more frequent service than others. As environmental concerns continue to impact auto traffic, these public transportation systems will become more and more important.

Detailed Area Map with Facilities

We all want to be close to some local facilities. Good schools are crucial to parents. It's vital to research not only which schools fit your child's needs the best but also exact boundary demarcations.

Other requirements that may turn up on your list? Being within easy walking distance to a college or university; being in the catchment area of a hospital or a church; living in the same neighborhood as a relative, friend, or work colleague; being only five minutes away from shopping or entertainment.

Whatever your specific needs are, locate them on a map that identifies all streets, one-way markings and barrierlike freeways, ditches, and railroad tracks. This map also needs an easy-to-read index. When you go on your house-hunting rounds, you want to be able to look up addresses quickly and easily.

Tip: Several sites on the web like www.geocities.com and www.mapquest.com can help you enormously with maps for routes to your new location and maps of different neighborhoods.

Other people prefer larger, bound maps like the Thomas Bros. Guides (between $10 and $35 per area), because they lie flat easily and have big print. They're currently available only for California, Seattle, Portland, and Phoenix. You can get them at many bookstores or call (800) 899-MAPS. Rand McNally makes the widest variety of maps—look for their Flash Maps for ease of use. They're available in bookstores nationwide, or call (800) 323-4070. If your local bookstores don't seem to have good detail maps of your new location, you can also check the destination yellow pages for a bookstore that specializes in maps.

When you're evaluating several maps, look for the publication date to get the most updated information on roads in new subdivisions. Sometimes map makers put a new date on a map without updating, however, so it's also a good idea to look at each rendition of an outlying area you're interested in and choose the map that has the most detail.

CUSTOMIZING YOUR MAPS

Once you've assembled your maps, the best way to use the information they give you is to customize them. Start with the Rental/ Homes for Sale Key Map. Usually this is printed in the newspaper in the same section as the "for sale" or "for rent" ads, with the boundaries for each neighborhood standing out clearly.

From the information you've assembled, locate which neighborhoods have your essential requirements. Cross out any areas that present big commute problems. Circle schools and parks. Identify libraries and town centers, which often house lots of community activities and are particularly good sources for children's groups.

Don't forget to mark shopping centers. Consider eliminating neighborhoods lacking good shopping facilities. We usually look for areas with bookstores and neighborhood restaurants, which offer relaxed opportunities to make friends. When renting, we always check out the Laundromat situation.

With your neighborhood selection now narrowed down to five or six, jot down the high and low rents and/or prices in those sections. Color in the ones that meet all your criteria with a highlighter. It's a good idea to outline those neighborhoods in a highlighter on your detail map too, so that when you start looking for specific addresses, you can tell immediately if you're in the right place.

Now, as you're making contacts with friends, references, and colleagues, ask about your selected neighborhoods, specifically, to doublecheck that they will work for you. As soon as you set the dates for your home-hunting trip (see Chapter 8), make viewing appointments in the selected areas.

finding the new Homestead

TRIED AND TRUE METHODS FOR FINDING THE PERFECT RENTAL

Temporary Quarters

Finding a place to hang your hat, while you look for a long term rental or a place to buy, is an important first step to settling in. Again, there's a lot you can do beforehand to smooth the process. Investigate contact possibilities. Find out if Uncle Harold or Friend Susan has an extra bedroom to rent and/or check out the various possibilities outlined in Chapter 3.

However you set up your temporary quarters, try to make sure you can stay there comfortably for two to three months. Although we've helped people find a home via the "one-week blitz trip" mapped out in Chapter 9, it's not easy. The National Association of Realtors has found that home buyers take an average of five to ten weeks to find a home, and going through the escrow process will add another four to six weeks.

Give yourself two to three months' temporary living quarters when looking for a great long term rental as well. You're much less likely to squish into something ridiculously inappropriate if you aren't pressured to make a decision under a tight deadline.

Long Term Rentals

The tried and true method for finding a long   term rental is driving around looking for signs. Although this may seem terribly old fashioned and time consuming to the computer oriented, not to mention impossible to do ahead of time, a majority of renters and a high number of purchasers swear by it because it avoids later disappointments when a place you've found through an ad turns out to be in a neighborhood that doesn't look inviting or a building that doesn't please.

This doesn't mean you can't narrow down your search, and even find a place, long distance. You'll be balancing rent affordability against a number of factors. Here are some considerations to keep in mind.

Location. Look over your customized maps just to be sure you haven't forgotten something. Location will be the biggest contributor to enjoying your new home, so it deserves lots of careful planning.

Soft Market Bargains. Get market savvy. Is the newspaper full of "One Month Free" offers? Are managers offering "No Deposit" specials? Are there many apartments where pets are welcome? If so, it's a soft rental market, and tenants with good credit can find very good deals. If, instead, there are few newspaper ads over one inch long and pets are usually disdained, you won't find many below market rent deals.

Style. Modern vs. traditional, large complex vs. small building, professional vs. mom-and-pop management. If you want a large, modern, high end complex, the real estate/rental photo magazine advertisers we list under "Home Buying, Renting, and Auxiliary Services" in Appendix C will have a good selection.

If, on the other hand, you want something secluded, friendly, and managed by an owner living next door, check rental agencies, particularly the ones that sell lists of addresses from landlords. Your best way to search these rentals, however, is via signs on buildings.

Call ads that seem interesting, and get specifics on the accommodations. If there aren't many opportunities to bargain, and you like the big and modern complexes, often you can sign yourself into an apartment before you arrive. Just remember—never sign a lease for longer than three months sight unseen.

If you want to bargain hunt, or you love the smaller, more casual buildings, a final decision will have to wait till you've arrived at your destination. Take the time to set up viewing appointments the week before the homehunting trip, however. Preset appointments will give you a better start on orientation.

 Tip: For the economy minded apartment seeker, check the local college or university Student Center for listings of apartments according to size and cost. Some colleges only make these available to their students, but it's worth a try, especially if you plan on taking extension courses there.

RENTAL AGENTS, BUYER'S AGENTS, AND OTHER HELPFUL SOULS

In order to hit the ground running on a homehunting trip, you need to have found an agent to help you already. If you're either a buyer or a renter, this means back to your contacts, the want ads and the yellow pages, calling and interviewing. But don't start galloping off in six directions. The first thing to do is to survey what types of agents are available, evaluate what kind you want, then start calling.

Rental Agent

Most residential real estate agencies have someone who handles rentals. These people also are trained to help you get oriented in a new community, to know the schools and the commutes, and to give good advice on what rents to expect for mid to upper range rentals. Usually calling want ads of interesting places will put you in touch with the rental agents who specialize in the kind of property you're looking for. Another source are the "Rental Referral Services" in the yellow pages, which often sell lists and can be a good source of smaller mom-and-pop properties. Many times you don't have to pay a fee, the landlord does.

No Agent

This idea appeals to buyers wishing to save money. The possibility should be explored if you:

√ *Have plenty of time to spend on your home search.*
√ *Love to shop.*
√ *Feel comfortable negotiating directly.*
√ *Understand the local real estate and finance market.*

In any other case, we recommend working with agents in purchasing a home. The question of which agent, however, has gotten much more complex in the last few years with the introduction of the "buyer's agent."

Traditional Agent vs. Buyer's Agent

The concept of the buyer's agent has been rumbling through the real estate brokerage world for over a decade, has been vigorously supported and attacked therein, but has just begun to make itself known to the general public.

Warning: *This concept may seem inconsequential at the outset, but it turns out to be important in practice.*

Traditionally, an agent contracts with the seller to perform the service of marketing a property. Their agreement is spelled out in a "listing," which typically stipulates that the agent will be paid only if a sale is accomplished within a certain period of time. The agent's payment is a commission, based on a percentage of the sale price. It also is usually agreed that the commission can be split with another agent, who works with the buyer. This agent is legally dubbed a "subagent," although the term is rarely used in conversation.

The subagent, however, *still owes primary allegiance to the seller, not the buyer.* This is legally true, even though, in reality, most agents feel they represent "the deal" rather than any of the people involved.

Negotiations are supposed to be played like a game of poker. Each party reveals concessions one at a time, and never tips the remaining contents of the hand to the opposing team. This leads to conflicts when an agent mentions a seller's unofficial rock bottom price or a buyer's pressing need to wrap up a decision before tomorrow morning's flight out. Suits have been filed and won against agents who had released inside information. Laws regarding agent representation have been clarified.

Lawyers have wanted to change the law so that real estate companies would be restricted to representing only the buyers or only the sellers, just as legal firms may represent only one party in litigation. But attorneys get paid, no matter who wins. Agents get paid only when both parties win and the deal gets done. So far, most legislation that's been introduced simply requires that an agent disclose to everyone which party she works for.

This means you, as a buyer, have a choice as to whether you will work with the traditional seller's subagent *or* with the emerging buyer's agent. From either type agent, you should expect professional help in evaluating neighborhoods, assistance in selecting property inspectors and title and escrow facilitators, information on the lending market, and guidance on the escrow process. Both kinds of agents also may offer insurance plans that will pay your mortgage if you lose your job and other incentives, such as free trips or presents.

There are some basic service differences, however, so here are some of the arguments for each possibility.

Traditional Agent / Subagent: Pro

√   *Paid via seller's commission—never the buyer's responsibility.*

√   *Does not require a contract with you, which allows you to work with many agents and/or directly with sellers in buying your home.*

√   *May work better with traditional seller's listing agents, who sometimes refuse to work with a buyer's agent, because they don't want to split their commission with a declared adversary.*

The trend is toward more cooperation with buyer's agents, but it took till the mid-90s before the concept was formally recognized by the National Association of Realtors.

√   *Cooperation with the sellers may be better when the market is hot, homes are selling quickly, and seller's agents are firmly in the driver's seat. Buyers maneuvering through a hot market need to work out a very specific routine with any agent, so that the fast paced, multiple offer/counter-*

offer dance can be played as adroitly as possible. See Chapter 6 for more insights on hot markets.

√   *May act as a "dual" agent—as the seller's listing agent as well as the person working with you. Although this situation is rife with conflict of interest possibilities, it can make for a quick, easy deal, because negotiations don't have to go through so many different people.*

√   *May have better access to "insider" deals with a seller's agent who has low priced listings that sell quickly within the same agency. In contrast, many buyer's agents work in companies that do not do any listing.*

Traditional Agent / Subagent: Con

√   *Is legally required to work for the highest price.*

√   *Is legally required to give first affiliation to the seller. This means that although an agent has to give you all physical information about the property, she is restricted from giving you information about the seller that might adversely affect the price.*

This is a big change from the past, when agents were very cavalier about sharing "seller motivation" insights with buyers and "buyer motivation" tips with sellers. The new legal clarifications have made unauthorized discussions about a seller's problems—impending divorce, purchase of another house, and so on—a litigation issue. In contrast, today's subagent still can tell a seller about shared confidences from a buyer's personal situation that may make her willing to pay more, as long as the buyer was notified in the beginning of the agent's allegiance to the seller. In such cases, the buyer has no legal recourse.

Result—if you don't want sellers holding out for a higher price because they know more about you than you want them to, don't have a subagent help you find financing or discuss any other personal situation with her.

√   *Some legal beagles insist that this affiliation to the seller extends to a subagent's not being able to assist with a number of other vital buyer services—for example, she can't give you neighborhood comparable sales numbers, can't tell you how long the home has been on the market, can't vigorously negotiate on the buyer's behalf.*

This interpretation is a gray area. Policies vary from city to city and from company to company. Talk to prospective agents about how they'll represent you. Ask what their policies are about agent representation of sellers and buyers. If you feel you'll get the representation you want but you're uncomfortable with some items, be sure to get copies of their policies in writing.

Buyer's Agent: Pro

√ *Has clearly defined duty to act on the buyer's behalf at all times. Can be confided in about finances and any other personal complication that may affect a deal. If the impending sale of your previous residence is hung up because the buyers can't get as much financing as they need, your buyer's agent might know another lender, for example. Or she might be able to negotiate a lower down payment on your new house, so that you can help the buyers of your old house with a second loan.*

√ *Orchestrating a sale and purchase is complex, and the more your team members are clearly on your side, the more you can use their expertise.*

√ *Will put less house-by-house pressure on you, because you have agreed to have her represent you, no matter what home you find.*

√ *Could offer a full range of "one stop shopping" services— a data bank of consultants and inspectors to help you and a computerized loan organization (CLO) system to bring you a wide variety of loan programs and online electronic application and approval.*

Tip: *Traditional agents can offer these services as well. Just remember to be careful not to disclose any personal or financial information you don't want a seller to know.*

Buyer's Agent: Con

√ *Requires a contract limiting you to working only through her.*

√ *Often requires an upfront retainer of anywhere from $50 to $500. This fee usually is refunded upon payment of commission on the purchase. Sometimes you, as the buyer, also are required to make up any difference between the commission paid by the seller and an amount you and the buyer's agent agreed upon.*

A few buyer's agents are moving to have the buyer pay a set fee, which is deducted from the purchase price. Such direct buyer payment breaks the final bond between the agent and a higher purchase price, but it is difficult to add the fee to the purchase price financed by the lender and therefore your cash closing costs are higher. Also, check with your tax advisor as to whether paying a buyer's agent is tax deductible.

√ *May not be able to get you into best bargain deals during a hot market, when seller's agents may subtly steer sellers away from a buyer represented by a "hired gun."*

√ *May limit your home selection because of legal restrictions on showing you homes listed by their company, since the company may be prohibited from having primary affiliation with both seller and buyer.*

√ *May also have legal restrictions on showing you a home that they have shown before to another buyer, because the first buyer's rights take precedence over yours.*

Our recommendation? If you feel comfortable with the purchase process, go with the traditional agent and subagent scenario. The flexibility will give you the opportunity to browse more neighborhoods and get market input from more people. We're infirmation freaks, and more input makes us more satisfied with our choice.

If you don't feel confident, and/or you're short on time and/or you don't like shopping, see about signing a representation contract with a buyer's agent. Interview several agents following our Appendix A, "Buyer's Real Estate Agent Evaluator," for market savvy, helpfulness, and service options. Check the yellow pages for firms that advertise that they do buyer's representation.

Usually local Century 21, RE/MAX, and ERA agencies have buyer's agents. One of Century 21s' trainers, Judy Bittner, says her relocation specialists often go so far as to get their buyer's children into the right school and hold a "Getting to Know New Neighbors" housewarming party.

For nationwide specialists, check our list in the Contact Directory (Appendix C) or contact the Real Estate Buyers Agent Council (REBAC), which is affiliated with the National Association of Realtors with more than 24,000 members in the US and Canada. They can be reached at 800 646-6224 or www.REBAC.net. For buyer's agents who work exclusively with buyers, contact the National Association of Exclusive Buyer Agents at 800 986-2322 or www.naeba.org.

If there are a number of buyer's agent services in your area, you should be able to find a buyer's agent who will do just the job you want. If not, or if you find a traditional subagent with a good reputation whom you really trust, go with your gut. But keep your head about revealing any negotiating weaknesses to anyone but a buyer's agent.

Discount Agent

Both traditional subagents and buyer's agents can offer commission discounts or other incentives to have you work with them. These policies are often advertised in the telephone book or in the real estate/rental photo magazine advertisers.

As we've mentioned earlier, if you or a member of your family (including either parent) have been officers in the Armed Forces, you can join USAA (800) 582-8722. In conjunction with the consulting firm, PHH Fantus, USAA has a MoversAdvantage program that provides you with a relocation consultant for free, plus a real estate agent bonus. However you find an agent, be sure to interview several and take notes on your "Buyer's Real Estate Agent Evaluator" in Appendix A.

MOUNTING A NO FEAR ATTACK ON FINANCING

The Myths of Mortgage

Buying a home is not just about picking out a neighborhood and liking the bricks and mortar, it's about money. We all understand this, but we still are shocked when we realize that it's not the house that's going to be that mythical "biggest purchase in a lifetime, it's the mortgage. It turns out that each of us will pay more money in interest to our friendly lender than we will have paid to buy the house.

A second myth is that the sequence of events should run:

1.   *Find a house.*
2.   *Negotiate the price.*
3.   *Find a loan.*

We advise the reverse. Decide on a loan with a monthly payment that works for your budget, then go looking for a home in the price range that matches your financing.

Going at it this way saves time, particularly since you can do everything ahead of time by mail. With the local newspaper real estate section in hand, you can interview your list of prospective lenders by telephone now. This means that you can select a program and a loan advisor you like and that works for your budget *before* you do your homehunting trip.

Getting Preapproved

Getting financing in hand is particularly helpful because you can get the lender to preapprove you for a specific loan amount. This approach not only makes your homehunting trip easier, it provides a good negotiating tool with a seller, because your offer includes the ability to close quickly.

Tip: *When getting lenders to preapprove you, have them review your written application and give you the maximum amount they'll finance in writing. Don't settle for just a quick telephone prequalification with no review of your credit and income. You don't want the lender dragging its feet when you're ready to take out the loan.*

Regardless of a written preapproval, you still must make your contract contingent upon getting your mortgage. Otherwise, rising interest rates, a low appraisal, or an unethical lender can still leave you without your loan . . . and a seller who can sue you for breach of contract.

Choices, Choices, Choices

Choosing a loan today is no easy task. Since adjustable rates were introduced over ten years ago, your monthly payment is only one of several variables that can make the difference between your best deal and your worst nightmare. Here are some terms to know to keep the latter from happening.

Rates. Every lender touts the best rates it can, and newspapers often publish grids showing which lender offers which rate. Use the "Loan Payment Calculator for each $1,000 of Loan" from Appendix D to calculate what a rate means to you in dollar amounts.

Loan Programs. Many of today's mortgage brokers offer a wide selection of lenders, each offering varying loan programs with different rates, origination fees, down payment requirements, and speed of processing. A good broker can shop loan programs for you on her computer just like a travel agent can shop for the cheapest and most convenient airline ticket. These agents can save you much time and worry, but be careful of low interest loan offers that are too good to be true. Bait-and-switch deals often get canceled two days before you're ready to close escrow. Either find a mortgage broker through a referral, or get the names and telephone numbers of three or four previous customers, then check to find out if they'd use the broker again, and why.

Length of Loan. Lenders often offer much better rates for loans lasting only five to ten years. These loans, obviously, can put you in a bad position when they have to be refinanced.

Other low rates may be offered on fifteen-year amortized loans that turn out to have a high monthly payment amount with twice as much money going toward the principal than with a standard thirty-year amortization. Be sure you read all the fine print under the claims for very low rates.

Documentation. Most lenders will send you an application package with a checklist of the documentation needed from you, such as the completed loan application and the credit check forms.

Often, particularly if you're self employed or have been working for two years or less, they'll want other forms after they've reviewed your initial package. These may include a "letter of explanation" (needed if you've had one or two late payments on credit cards) and a "gift letter verification" (needed if your parents are giving you the cash for the down payment).

Turnaround Time. Lenders should be able to tell you their "turnaround time," that is, the number of days it takes to process your application, obtain an appraisal, and fund the loan. They start counting from the day they receive your *complete* package of documentation. Usually, they'll take thirty to forty-five days to fund. Some have developed fast track programs and say they've cut turnaround time to two weeks, but incomplete information from you or one of your information verification sources can ruin the schedule.

> **Warning:** *If a lender tells you it's "a little behind" on appraisals, this almost always means trouble. Your close may be delayed forty-five to sixty days. Mount a twice-a-week checkin schedule with your lender and orchestrate the rest of your escrow checkoff items (see Appendix B) accordingly.*

Be particularly careful if you're in both sale and purchase transactions concurrently. As soon as you send in the application, call and ask if it's complete. Ask how long it will be before the lender can give you the formal commitment letter stating that it will give you a specific amount against a specific property on a specific date and at a specific rate. Doublecheck how long after that before it can fund.

Ratios. The amount of money you'll get as a loan is based on two ratios: loan to value ratio and buyer's income ratio.

The "loan to value" ratio is the maximum loan amount expressed as a percentage of the property value. It can range between 70 percent and 90 percent, depending on the loan program, and is crucial if you don't have very much money for the down payment.

The "buyer's income ratio" once was based on a simple formula. You were supposed to be able to borrow three times as much as your gross annual income.

With wildly fluctuating loan interest rates and much of the population into binge-purge consumer credit cycles, lenders found the old formula didn't work. Today's requirements are more complex. To find out how much loan the bank believes you can afford, fill in the "Loan Qualification Worksheet" in Appendix D.

Adjustable Loans. Payments on these loan programs adjust periodically, according to the ups and downs of a base rate. Typically your monthly payment amount will change once every six or twelve months. Because you're sharing the risk of rising rates with the lender, the starting interest rate is lower than with a standard fixed rate loan.

To evaluate, ask what your "maximum payment scenario" would be if rates skyrocket. (See the "Loan Evaluator" in Appendix A for the formula.) Tell your loan advisor you want the highest amount you'll be paying for the next five years if rates go back to 15 percent. She'll complain this is unlikely. That's true, but you need the maximum payment scenario in order to compare the different loans on an equal basis.

Another item to doublecheck with adjustable loans is the use of a "teaser" rate, which is in effect only for the first few months of payment. This makes the loan look good on first evaluation but can mean that outrageous charges run up quickly.

Loan Caps. Adjustable loans should have "maximum amount caps" on payments and life of the loan.

Payment caps are the maximum payment increase you can experience at each adjustment period. Typically they range from .5 to 2 percent.

The life cap is the maximum payment you'll have, no matter what, for the life of the loan. It currently varies between 5 and 7 percent above the initial start rate.

Negative Amortization. Despite having the lowest payment cap, negative amortization loans are the worst of the adjustable loan programs. They keep your payments low by adding rising interest due back into the loan amount. You end up paying interest on interest. We've had these kinds of loan programs several times and hated them, but sometimes they're the only kind of loan offered.

Below Market Rate Loans

The most consistent source of below market financing is the existing owner. Check "Fast Move, Soft Market Options" in Chapter 6 for suggestions, including seller carrybacks and lease options.

The seller is not your only option, however. Numerous special programs are available if you have the time to search them out. They currently include:

√   The VA program, *the oldest and most easily obtained, so long as you're a veteran. It offers both a lower down payment and a lower interest rate.*

√   The Parent Power program, *currently available only from Merrill Lynch. It finances up to 100 percent of the price if your parents cosign.*

√   The Work Perk program *includes both lower rates and lower required down payment when your employer cosigns for you. This is offered nationwide but must be arranged through your employer. If your employer hasn't started a Work Perk program but might be willing to help, call the Economic Development Agency in the state capital to find out what might be possible.* Local subsidies *are available in several states and many communities. Call the local mayor's office, Housing Office, and Economic Development Agency.*

√   First time homebuyer programs, *usually administered by local housing authorities.*

√   A rate list *from numerous specialists, local and nationwide lenders is available on web sites listed in our Contact Directory.*

Savvy Loan Shopping

Start calling likely lenders. Ask your real estate agent, your title company, your lawyer, and your friends and relatives who they recommend as a lender or mortgage broker. Check the local paper's real estate section for ads and lists.

Review the "Loan Evaluator," the "Loan Qualification Worksheet" and the "Loan Payment Calculator" in Appendixes A and D. The more familiar you are with how they work, the more self assured you can be during the interviews. Remember, loan advisors will be working for you. The only way they make money is when you take a loan with them.

LITTLE DETAILS TO SELL YOURSELF TO PROSPECTIVE LANDLORDS AND LENDERS

Whether you're looking for a rental or a lender, there are a number of things you can do ahead of time to make yourself more "bankable." The first one is to pull your own credit report. Check our Contact Directory for web services that will obtain a credit report for you or try to all Equifax (CBI) at (800) 685-1111 or Experian (TRW) at (800) 682-7654 (these line are often busy for hours, so the services are helpful). Review the report carefully, to be sure there are no inaccuracies. Include a copy of it with your loan or apartment application.

Another important item will be referral letters. See the sample "Personal/Business Referral Letter" in Appendix E. These are particularly helpful if you can find someone in your destination location to write them. An old friend from college may be well known to the local bank manager. Utilities and other services are always happy to see recommendations from your current providers, and these letters can mean a lower deposit when you start setting up your household.

Landlords are interested in children and pets. Take pictures, and write up a "resume" describing how they behave. Pet information should include health records as well as any references from existing landlords. You may want to check with your SPCA or the American Kennel Club for obedience classes and/or Pet Good Citizen Tests. Adding these pieces of information to your application will make you less of an unknown to the people you'll be meeting who will be making important decisions on your credibility. They can pay for themselves many times over.

CUTTING VEHICLE RED TAPE

Relocating a car is one of the "little details" of moving that drives everybody nuts. During the last decade, the loudest shrieks were heard in California, where owners of cars not meeting emission standards could face stiff fines and/or requirements for hundreds of dollars of retrofitting for cars that had no problem qualifying for registration elsewhere.

During the 1990s, the federal government and other states are also coming up with stricter emissions laws, and more and more standard cars are being manufactured to meet them. Nevertheless, take the time to contact your destination's State Motor Vehicle office and get a copy of what's required now. If your present vehicle doesn't qualify easily, you'll be far better off selling it in your present location and buying a used car that already meets the new state's requirements when you get there.

Tip: *If your car has developed rust from "snow state salt," you'll have particular problems selling in "sun states." Giving the car away to a needy organization may make sense tax wise, and it's a fast solution to the nonqualifying or heavily used vehicle problem. Check with the Volunteers of America or the Kidney Foundation.*

Vehicle Requirements

Some states and countries have pamphlets detailing their requirements. If they don't, your "What and When Required" questions should include:

√ *What tests are required: Emissions? Oil? Brake? Steering? Lights? Other?*

√ *When are tests necessary: Upon moving into the state? Annually? Upon sale? Other?*

√ *How much does testing usually cost? Does the tester perform any repairs necessary, or do you have it done someplace else? Are there limits on how much repairs can cost? Does the state have a list of licensed mechanics?*

√ *If you're buying a car from a private party, are other tests required besides the ones required when you buy from a used car dealer?*

√ *Are there significant tax breaks between vehicle types and ages? Are there additional local vehicle taxes and/or parking fees, and, if so, what departments should be contacted? Note: Often states don't have all this information, but counties do. Since local vehicle tax and parking fees can vary by several hundred dollars a year, and since higher local tax often goes hand in hand with higher insurance rates, this can be important for your community budget research.*

√ *How, where, and what does it cost to obtain a new driver's license and vehicle registration plates?*

√ *Is any significant new legislation coming up that will make some models obsolete? If something on your car will have to be changed radically in six months, again you should consider selling or giving it away.*

Overseas Considerations

If you're moving abroad, even if you're moving to the country where your automobile was built, don't assume you can drive it once you get there and have no problems getting things fixed, if they break. Every country has different emissions and other requirements, and we've run into problems getting an export version of a VW fixed in Germany. Call the consulate, the importer, or a freight forwarding company that specializes in automobiles to find out if your vehicle is destination compatible. Check requirements for both driver's license and vehicle plates at the same time.

NINE

The New Nest

THE ONE-WEEK HOMEHUNTING BLITZ TRIP

In the past, companies usually figured a transferring family would need between two and three weeks to find a home in an unfamiliar location. Following the "Restructured 1990s," however, homehunting trips are being cut back like everything else. Here's how to set a doable schedule for a one-week homehunting blitz, despite the National Association of Realtors' findings that the average home search takes eight weeks of looking.

If you have more than a week for your homehunting trip, you've scheduled yourself into an alternative move, or you're shopping for a new place in a location close to where you now live, spread the following itinerary out. Our recommendation is to do each of the scheduled days a weekend at a time, so that you have the rest of the week to absorb what you've found out, and you can call for more information as you need it. Don't forget to give yourself a seven-week decision deadline, so that two months from now, you'll be in contract and working to buy your home.

Advance Reconnaissance

We've already outlined your plan-ahead strategy in Chapter 7. A vital element for a homehunting blitz trip is to have already selected a rental or real estate agent to help you. In a one-week trip, you'll find it impossible to interview agents and do reference checking, yet these advisors will be *invaluable* in making your hunt successful. Get them in place in advance.

 Tip: *If you've signed a contract with a buyer's agent, one thing she already should have sent you is a copy of the purchase agreement form that's standard for the area. If not, have her leave it at your hotel for browsing your first evening. Being familiar with the contract will make it easier to formulate your offer.*

Narrow your choices to a maximum of three neighborhoods and one size and style of home. Be explicit with your agent about what you want and how much you can spend.

Be sure to take your maps, your existing home measurements and tape measure, your evaluation sheets and research, and your camera or camcorder. Wear comfortable clothes and walking shoes. Don't worry about impressing lenders or landlords with high heels or a suit and tie.

Try not to take your children along on a short homehunting trip. You'll need to focus your full concentration on research. Do remember their "have to haven's" as you take notes and pictures so they can help with the final decision making when you get back home.

Scheduling Specifics

Day 1: Orientation. Time your trip so that Day 1 is the day *before* the traditional "open house" day for your new community. Stay in your first choice of the neighborhoods you'll be exploring.

Call your agent and confirm your schedule of viewings for the next few days. Never schedule to view more than eight homes per day. Information overload is a decision killer. Paring your choices down with advance research is the only way to conduct a blitz trip.

If you're not driving your own car, rent one and drive the main streets of the three neighborhoods you've selected. Do this without your agent, so that you can get the feel of people better. Talk to everybody you meet about the neighborhoods you've selected and what's happening with both jobs and the local housing economy. Ask these questions, even if you already have a job and/or you're looking to live in a short term rental. You may find some crucial fact that will change your moving plans entirely. At the end of the day, rank the three neighborhoods, so that you can focus your hunt on the first one or two.

How to Succeed at Effective Hanging Around

A homehunting trip is a sociology crash course. Even if' your investigation is centered on a neighborhood only six blocks away, you'll want to know ahead of time whether you and your family will fit in and enjoy life there.

From Day One, look around you. Pay attention to the cars people drive and how well the lawns and homes are kept. Note who's on the streets during the day. A dearth is a sign of young singles/ couples; lots of children or retirees are indications of other age/ work groups.

If you're looking for neighborhood camaraderie, look for backyard barbecues, Little League team posters, basketball hoops, and children playing hopscotch or jump rope. Note whether people wear the kind of clothes you like to wear.

Check main street corners for local weekly newspapers full of local information and perhaps an ad for just the home you want. Go inside libraries and supermarkets and look at community display boards for babysitter and day care information. Stop at schools and churches and ask people about the neighborhood. If there's a community center or club house, have lunch there, talk to people, and look for club and sports activity notices. Keep a "smile log" of friendly things that appeal to you in the different locations.

Day 2: Open House Tour Day. If you're renting, your rental agent may just give you a list and some keys. If you're buying, your agent will probably chauffeur. No matter who is driving, as you're going from one place to the next, be sure to fill in both your "Home" and "Neighborhood" evaluators (Appendix A) with at least:

1. The address, a brief physical description, and your gut reactions to both the home and the immediate neighborhood.

2. Pictures of the front and one or two of your "have to have's," whether it's the kitchen or the garden or the airplane-sized garage or whatever.

3. Neighborhood impressions. Look at the surrounding streets as well as the specific block. If one of the advantages of the area is a community center, a resident's clubhouse, and/or tennis or golf facilities, drive by these places and take pictures as well. If it's a new development, stop in homes that are at various stages of buildout to check the quality of foundation and framing, and chat with the carpenters and electricians about how everything is going.

4. Take time to talk to the people you see on the street. Strike up conversations about the weather or how to get to a specific location. Mention you may move there. Ask what they do and don't like about their neighborhood. If you have friends or relatives in the neighborhood, get together with them and find out more about the area.

More "Hanging Around" Tips: Look for people who enjoy the same level of friendliness as you do. Different locales have very different ways of socializing. A salesman friend of ours from the East Coast, for example, remembers the first encounter with his prospective father-in-law, a Colorado rancher. Determined to make friends, the Easterner launched a half hour of pleasantries about clear skies and the mountains, to which his new acquaintance finally muttered, "You know, son, out West . . . men don't *talk* so much."

Day 3: Regroup. Have breakfast in a different neighborhood cafe Review the list of homes you're scheduled to view now in light of what you've decided about neighborhoods, and make sure *only* the most likely candidates remain on the calendar.

Even with the best agent in the world, you may not be able to get inside of all the places you want to see. Go ahead and drive by any exceptionally eligible listings so that you can decide if tile facade or the street will veto the possibility at the outset.

At the end of the day, evaluate. Have you seen one or two homes that fit your requirements? Are you ready to sign a lease or make a purchase offer? Review your notes, your research, and your current ads. If you're not ready to settle for a place you've already seen, schedule viewings for Day 4. If you're looking in a new subdivision, find out as much as you can about the builder/developer.

Keep asking everybody questions.

Day 4: Viewings, Final Round. By now you should have at least driven by all the candidates in your top neighborhoods that fit your price and size range. This is the day to catch up with those that looked interesting but you couldn't get into or to go back through your short list of two possibilities. If you've already made a decision, skip this step and get into negotiating. You can use the extra time later to get inspection contractors lined up.

Day 5: Decision Day. Now is *not* the time to crowd your mind with additional viewings. Instead, move heaven and earth to get back through the home you've selected, looking for physical defects, and visualizing how your furniture and lifestyle are going to fit. Take more pictures. Draw a rough diagram of the home, with taped or paced-off measurements.

Review the lease or the purchase agreement. Discuss with your agent or landlord what kind of offer you should make. Fill in a rough draft of your contract carefully, asking questions about anything you don't understand.

Don't be shy about negotiating with an agent or landlord. Ask how she would structure the best deal, then ask what other scenarios might work better. If you're buying, give yourself some room to negotiate on both price and terms—you need the owners to counter with their preferred scenario before you decide what things you're willing to cut the most.

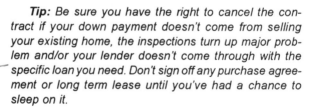

Tip: Be sure you have the right to cancel the contract if your down payment doesn't come from selling your existing home, the inspections turn up major problem and/or your lender doesn't come through with the specific loan you need. Don't sign off any purchase agreement or long term lease until you've had a chance to sleep on it.

Day 6: Lease/Offer Day. Always something of an anticlimax. No matter how much you've decided to go with the landlord or seller's wishes, no matter how carefully you've documented your own creditworthiness, it's very rare to have a landlord or a seller sign off immediately.

Don't be insulted when you're told they're going to pull another credit report and recheck your references. After all, you'd do exactly the same thing if the tables were turned, right? Use as much of this day for doublechecking your decision as possible. Interview property inspection people. Talk to more people about the neighborhood. If there's any chance the landlord or the seller might not accept you, explore your alternatives for another rental or purchase.

Day 7: Back Up and CYA (Cover Your Aspirations). By now the landlord or seller should have given you a response. If you haven't gotten your number-one choice, or if your deal still may fall through for some reason, check out two or three other places and make a backup offer contingent on your not getting your first choice.

Tip: Landlords or sellers will rarely review (much less accept) a "second choice" offer, so you'll have to take copies of their rent application or purchase agreement with you to send back to them if your first choice isn't successful.

Another tactic is to make your offer or rent application contingent upon something else—a friend's viewing or your lawyer's review, for example—which allows you to bow out more graciously than stating up front you really prefer someplace else. This is a particularly advisable route if you feel the two choices are very close, and you may end up going with the second one, anyway.

Whatever you do, make certain that you have an "exit" clause completely under your control—not the landlord's or seller's. And have the courtesy to cancel any pending rent applications or purchase contracts as soon as you know your preferred deal is going to happen.

Once you've secured a backup position, you need to follow up on practical details, as described later in this chapter. Check with your agent and your loan advisor as to how long escrow will take to close, and find out if you need to schedule yourself into interim housing.

CREDIT RECORD REDOX

If you have time for a more protracted home search, here are further game plans for fine tuned negotiating and bargain hunting. Your first step in bargain hunting, whether you're buying or renting, is to be certain your credit is in great shape. To obtain and review a current copy of your credit report, go online to www.quicken.com or www.banxquote.com for multiple reports (you pay by credit card. Or you can go direct by contacting your local Experian (was TRW) office or call its national phone number, (800) 682-7654 or the webpage, www.experian.com or Equifax (was CBI) is at www.equifax.com or (800) 685-1111

Tip: If you have credit problems that need repair, contact the Consumer Credit Counseling Service (CCCS) nearest you and find out what you can do before you homeshop. That service can help you avoid credit repair agency scams from companies charging upfront fees and then not doing anything.

In many cities, you can find the CCCS in the local white pages, or call (800) 388-CCCS. This national non-profit organization offers a full program of classes, individual counseling, budget setting, and credit negotiating assistance for little or no fee. In addition, it acts as an information clearinghouse for local rent share/rent subsidy programs and first time homebuyer financing.

NEGOTIATING
THE SUPERSWEET RENTAL DEAL

Few books have been written about negotiating great rental deals, but it can be done. To be done well, it takes as much strategy as negotiating a higher salary or buying a car at a good price or getting a below-market financing deal from a home seller.

Soft-Market Guidelines

Be aware of the market. Savvy renters know when ads proclaim "One Month Free Rent! .... $399 Moves You In!" and "Our Loss Is Your Gain!" that a creditworthy tenant can find a really good deal with a little shopping around. Evaluating which is really the *best* deal, though—ahh, that's the rub....

Obviously you need to find which neighborhoods to look in, and, also obviously, you need to inspect the various offerings physically to cross off any complex infested by cockroaches of the six- or the two-legged variety.

Other than these on-the-ground inquiries, look at neighborhood economics. Are the rental bargains a result of developers having glutted the area with apartment buildings, or is the neighborhood or the local economy in decline? If the neighborhood and the economy are strong, there probably will be other apartment buildings going up, even with rent bargains. If the neighborhood looks questionable or there's rising unemployment as well as rising apartment vacancy, you may want to rethink the move.

Do your personal budget and set priorities. This involves adding all the deposit and rent money needed to cover the length of time you estimate your budget is in trouble. Figure how much you can pay first, then negotiate a deal that meets this goal. If you've just started a job and you're counting every penny, negotiate first for a low deposit, then for a low rent. If you haven't got a job and figure you may have to live off savings for some time to come, negotiate for the best rent/deposit "all-in" deal. If you're a desirable tenant with a good credit report, be sure the prospective landlord knows about your record. As they say, "If you've got it, flaunt it."

The state of the economy will color your decision on whether you want to go with a month-to-month lease or lock in your current rent on a long-lease basis. If you figure there will be an abundance of apartments and/or the economy will be down for months to *come,* don't tie yourself up with a long term *commitment.* After all, rents may be even better down the road.

On the other hand, if you think the economy will be looking better soon, and/or your job situation will be fairly secure, strike your best bargain and lock in a six- or twelve-month lease.

Regular Market Guidelines

Now, let's say it's not a soft rental market. Landlords are not advertising fabulous deals—the smaller ones aren't even advertising at all, they just put a sign in the window. Is bargain hunting limited to round after round of dialing phone numbers, hoping one or two will come down a little bit on their rent?

Nope.

Do your budget just the same. Arm yourself with your latest credit check and your letters of recommendation. Start looking for the same bargains a budget-minded home purchaser does—fixer-uppers, up-and-coming neighborhoods, and so on. Browse the pages that follow, then dc) your on-the-ground search. When you've found a gem, sit down with the landlord, give her your budget, and explain how you intend to do one or more of the following:

√ *Pay a lower rent initially, then go up 10 to 1 5 percent in three to six months. (Be specific about your plans—and be realistic.)*

√ *Put down a full deposit in three to six months. (Ditto above plan description.)*

√ *Add value to your tenure by doing repairs, helping with janitorial or other needed tasks.*

You'll have to talk to more landlords than you will during a soft rental market, but bargain rent is worth the hunt.

DOWN-AND-DIRTY BARGAIN HUNTING FOR RENTERS AND BUYERS

Before you go bargain hunting, review the family's original "plan ahead" list regarding acceptable compromises on the components of market value. Now that your househunting is turning up real choices, evaluate them against what you've already decided works for you.

The Far-Out Fixer-Upper

If they have the choice, investors usually prefer finding a fixer-upper in a solid neighborhood rather than a solid home in an up-and-coming neighborhood. You can quantify the risk of how much a renovation is going to cost vs. what it will sell for in the current market. Nobody can quantify the risk of how long a neighborhood will take to turn into a silk purse—how much it will sell for in five or six years.

Another attraction of fixers, no matter where they're located, is that your own vision—and sweat, tears, and bloody knuckles—creates a wonderful home that you can enjoy before you enjoy your profit. A home can be the ultimate of "having your cake and eating it too."

We've done this, and we, our pocketbook, and our marriage have been stronger for it, but do remember—the sweat, tears, and bloody knuckles part *always* lasts longer and hurts more than planned. As a wise and pregnant friend once said, "Temporary is such a long time, when you're in it."

Now you've been warned, what to look for?

Step back from the attraction of the poor little house nestled into an overgrown garden that sighs softly, "I need you," as you walk through. To evaluate whether this is a good monetary deal, review the "Fixer-Upper Budget Estimator" in Appendix D, and remember the appraiser's Big Three:

√ Size
√ Condition
√ Location

Molly South, the legendary investment property guru of the Bass Brothers' organization, loves to tell the story of how she and her partner, Robert Moore, found their first big success. They arrived in a strange city at about nine o'clock one evening. It was pouring rain and they missed meeting the real estate person who was going to show them the property. They drove to the location anyway and sloshed around, looking and puzzling over several structural challenges, including an improperly built breakwater that was letting the ocean pound an unprotected side of the building.

They turned and looked at each other and smiled, "This is it," they said in unison. The reason for their exuberant (albeit dripping) evaluation?

√ *They knew the project was big enough to offer them economy-of-scale management. (Size)*

√ *They figured the physical problems looked worse than they actually were and could be fixed at a reasonable cost. Meanwhile, the basic layout would work, (Condition)*

√ *The property was enticingly perched in an upscale, water-oriented (obviously) community where no competitor was ever going to be able to build next door. (Location)*

They bought the property and rehabbed it. It is now Pier 39 in San Francisco, one of the world's best-known tourist attractions and shopping centers.

The middle-class options—the areas with good schools and lots of established working people of all ages—are the blue-chip rehab investments. We don't recommend exclusive neighborhoods, even though the renovators who've made the biggest bucks have often worked there. Unfortunately, these are the people who've also lost the biggest bucks in the recession. Taking the risk of renovating a mansion, unless you can afford to live there and support it yourself, is foolhardy, unless the economy is very good.

The Overimproved Home

The flip side of the poor condition home is the overimproved "Best House on the Block!" Owners have lavished attention on this home. If other homes on the block have one fireplace, this one has two. It not only has a gourmet kitchen, it has a large add-on pantry and a wine cellar.

Like an overindulged child, this house often has problems in the outside world. When it goes up for sale, the owners want profit on every pound of pennies they poured into it. When nobody comes forward at their price, they become insulted and do one of two things:

√ *Burrow in and stay where they are.*

√ *Accept what the market dictates or take a liking to a simpatico buyer and lower their price, often to the point where it becomes the "Best Bargain on the Block."*

Your job as a bargain hunter is to find an owner going into the latter mode of operation. It helps if you are a sympathetic buyer who appreciates the "out-of-the-ordinary" items they've added, while negotiating a good price and terms. These homes sometimes work very well for a caring renter, who's willing and able to trade upkeep work on a home that doesn't sell for reduced rent.

Whatever deal you negotiate, check the condition of an over-improved home carefully. Most probably maintenance has been superb, but occasionally you run into a handyperson with more ideas than skill who has casually removed a load-bearing wall to make the dining room bigger.

The New Built

Developments. The ultimate in good condition (usually), newly built homes can be hard to find at bargain prices. But builders do have "closeout" sales. In soft markets, they even hold auctions. Another good deal may be found by buying the model home and temporarily leasing it back to the builder for the first six months to a year. As this gives the builder more money to buildout other homes, she often will give a particularly good price on a show model.

Don't be timid about giving a builder a lowball offer, no matter what the situation. You won't insult the salesperson. She's not a homeowner who only has one home to sell. It's just business.

Be wary of a builder in financial trouble who'll accept just about any offer you come up with, however. This is likely to mean shortcuts have been taken in building materials and workmanship, and nobody will be around to carry out the warranty next year when the roof starts to leak. A half-finished development that's orphaned from its developer quickly loses value.

Whatever the deal being offered, inspect the prospective home carefully. Quality construction turns up in smoothly opening drawers and doors, larger-than-average rooms, lights in unusual but helpful corners and cupboards. Builders often will gussy up showplace areas with stone tile and brass-plated fixtures, but the basic structure is what will count in the years ahead.

Sometimes a builder won't budge in price but is perfectly happy to negotiate on options—superior-grade tile, carpet, and appliances, a fireplace or a deck. This may be the best deal for you, because it keeps the value of the neighborhood high for future buyers and appraisers.

Custom Built. Having a home built to your specifications can do serious damage to the pocketbook. Look for owner-builder classes or clubs, where you can find reliable contractors, who like working with individuals. Check home improvement and decorating magazines for companies that sell plans and kits that can be customized economically.

And spend a lot of time planning before you get to the architect's drawing stage. Don't start pulling down walls you decide don't look right, like Bugsy Siegel inventing Las Vegas. Remember the carpenter's motto: "Measure twice, cut once."

"Up-and-Coming" Neighborhoods

If you're looking for bargains and/or steep appreciation, you'll want to investigate the "up-and-coming" neighborhoods touted so invitingly in every agent's song and story. Up-and-coming neighborhoods are supposed to appreciate faster than the surrounding areas, because the character is changing.

We recommend investing in up-and-coming neighborhoods only in an area you know well, where you've been able to watch changes over a period of years. Check for basic economic reasons behind the renovated facades and cheery gardens.

In general, the current move back to the cities has been driven by the baby boom bulge of young singles with good, city-center jobs, an interest in city center theater and music events, and a disinterest in spending time and money on a commute. It's followed an ebb on city living created by families that wanted more space, parent-oriented schools, and lots of child activities in the community.

Some city centers have flowered much more radiantly than others and continue to attract enthusiastic new homeowners and tenants even in the family oriented times. These blossomings haven't "just happened." They cluster around the magnet of good culture centers, community-oriented universities, and/or good, fast public transit. As energy costs and commute times rise, communities oriented toward city center and public transport continue to grow in value.

Whether you're willing to put in some sweat equity on a fixer-upper in this kind of area or you buy a home that's already rennovated, you still should be able to hum that investor's

classic, "I Bought Cheap and Sold Dear." But don't start to
negotiate until you've gone over every possible thing that could
go wrong.

The Savvy Investor's Neighborhood

The homeowner/investor who made money through the real
estate recession of the 1990s didn't do it with just a smile and a
paint job. Everyone had to work hard to keep properties viable
during lean times. And they'll all tell you their most important
skill is selecting the right deal in the first place. Here are things
to watch out for.

The No-Nos. Slums and serious downward trends are
graphic and easy to pick out. A seedy look with unkempt yards
and dead and dying vehicles strewn about is a sure sign of
problems. Lots of adults hanging around during the day indi-
cates joblessness. Muscle cars cruising the streets can mean
drugs. The most worrisome sign of all is newly boarded up
homes. If those homes could have been sold or rented at all,
they would have somebody in them. These neighborhoods are
headed in the wrong direction. Don't join them.

The Maybe's. A few homes that were obviously boarded
up a long time ago with others sporting new faces and nice
curtains may indicate a neighborhood turning around.

> *Tip: Always drive around any up-and-coming neigh-
> borhood you're seriously considering at night. Make sure
> the nice curtains go with a nice interior and nice cars
> bringing nice working people home. You don't need a
> flock of brand new Buicks and Lincolns, unless that's what
> you yourself drive. An up-and-coming neighborhood usu-
> ally is populated with midpriced cars two to five years
> old.*
>
> *But if the redone facades hide an empty interior or a
> down-and-out rental, if the landscaping was profession-
> ally installed and never touched again, you've got an area
> that's attracted speculators but no real people. You need
> real people to create a livable neighborhood.*

The Yes-Yes's. Look for the neighborhoods with a budding
cultural life. Count the number of espresso bars, bookstores,
and young artists, who are often the first to note an upward

neighborhood trend. An impending city hall zoning change, such as the one that turned the Westwood section of Wiltshire Boulevard in Los Angeles into an area of glittering posh condominium towers, can do it. Massive community projects to tear out rail yards or rehabilitate beach areas are often, but unfortunately not always, successful. Historically, the most positive and significant neighborhood changes seem to have been a combination of intelligently run public effort and well-chosen developers.

Auctions

Those who belong to A.A. (Auction Aficionados) swear by this route to great bargains. They also exercise great discipline. The mark of the amateur is to get caught up in crowd frenzy and bid more than market value.

Auctions are popular in soft markets. If you see many advertised, owners are trying every method they can to sell. Call the auctioneers and get their brochures. If a preliminary look at the list shows interesting addresses, check out the auction house reputation before you trek out to view the properties. Call the Better Business Bureau for any complaint record. You don't want to lose a hunk of cash that supposedly was going to be your bargain down payment to a slick telephone operation that heads for the Bahamas right after the auction.

Assuming the company checks out and you like the property, make sure you completely understand the bidding process. Know what rights you have (if any) to back out of the deal if property inspections or the bank appraisal turns up unforeseen problems. Set your absolute maximum bid and stick with it, no matter how tempted you are to go up "just a little bit higher."

Probates, Foreclosures, and Corporate-Owned Properties

These are usually thought of as strictly buying territory, but they also can work for renters. We have one friend who lived for free as a caretaker for five years in a home going through probate and other legal tie-ups. Lenders and corporations owning transferee's properties often look for renters in a soft market and will trade lower rent for upkeep work, for showing the property, and for being ready to move if a buyer comes along.

If you're a bargain-hunting buyer, you should put these homes on your must-view list, but remember, like most bargains, you make up in price by having to spend extra time and effort. Sometimes, particularly in soft markets, you'll see newspaper ads telling you where to get lists of these properties, but usually they have to be dug out of court records and careful interviewing of hard-to-find people such as corporate relocation property managers and bank REO (Real Estate Owned) officers.

To find these bargains, check the property listings first. They should give contact information. Otherwise ask the courthouse recorder where to find the official publication of record newspaper for foreclosures and probates. Sometimes these sources list the people in charge, but not always. Call the company, and ask for the relocation department or the REO department, and go from there.

Even when you get contacts and property address lists, often it's difficult to impossible to inspect the property. Then the people managing have no authority to negotiate. Then the negotiators can't give any other price than the one an appraiser came up with three years ago. Then you have to fill out 6,000 forms. Then you can't get a loan, because the new lender's appraiser can't get in to do an appraisal either.

Don't spend much time on these properties unless:

√ *You love playing three-dimensional chess and swimming with the sharks.*
√ *You want to buy more than one and can amortize the time and energy invested over several deals.*
√ *You know property and can judge condition, neighborhood, and market value well enough to be sure what your maximum offer should be.*
√ *You can negotiate a price at least 30 percent lower than market comparables.*

Owner Motivators

All the preceding information doesn't mean that you can't find motivated owners looking to either sell or rent. Today's probate executors often seem much more focused and property oriented than they were in years past when all energies seemed to go into legal fees or family politics. Corporate relocation departments have adopted new kinds of property sale and rental strategies. Lenders are hiring brokers to push both rentals and sales and mounting auctions to move their backlog of foreclosed properties.

But the most motivated owner is still the individual, and the individual is almost always trying to balance out the problem of price vs. time and energy spent. An ad that reads "Quick Close Needed" is an ad that should lead you to an owner who'll cut price if you can guarantee a quick close or agree to a no-hassle rental.

Other motivators are personal. Life changes frequently make a seller want to get away from a property. A divorce, a new baby, a job transfer, a parent who needs help in another community. All these can mean good prices or rentals. Behind the obvious motivators often are even more powerful psychological ones. A family feud can turn owners against a place they once loved. A vacation can make people feel they *must* make that move to Hawaii.

It's hard to research owners' motivations. Often you never meet face-to-face. Whether you're looking to rent or to buy, the way to reap these bargains is to keep making below-market offers. Once you get a yes, you still must do a thorough physical inspection and comparable search before you can complete the deal and enjoy the fruits of your labor.

RENTER'S FOLLOW-UP STRATEGIES

Move-in Challenges

Renters often find move-in time is less than copasetic. We've run into everything from the appearance of an army of cockroaches to being switched into an apartment vastly different from and inferior to the one first viewed.

If you go through a formal move-in walk-through with the landlord, most of these problems can be sorted out then. If not, and the people before you have left a horrible mess or there's any other serious problem, contact your landlord *immediately.*

You have a choice. Either require someone else to come do the cleanup, or tell your landlord that you'll be willing to take care of the mess in exchange for a reduction in the next month's rent. We recommend the latter, because we usually do a better job than the landlord's people. Also a quicker job. Most land-lords should be willing to agree to pay for your doing the work, because it also guarantees you'll leave the apartment in good condition at the end of your lease or forfeit your cleaning deposit.

Photograph any major problems as proof of the amount of work needed. Keep track of the hours you spend, so you don't end up selling yourself short.

Also, if you're doing repairs or painting, be sure to keep receipts. Landlords might not agree to pay you for your labor, since they believe it's your choice to make these adjustments to your living situation, but they should agree in advance to reimburse you for materials that improve their building. Don't propose any new decor involving black, chartreuse, or hot pink, however.

Getting Insured

The landlord's insurance only covers the building and liability outside your unit, so you need to get renter's insurance to cover your belongings. With most large insurance companies, this is fairly easy. Annual premiums run around $200 for $25,000 coverage of fire, theft, vandalism, and water damage plus $100,000 liability if someone is hurt while visiting you or your sink runs over and you damage the ceiling below. Many insurance companies advise $300,000 of liability, due to the rise of lawsuits. Extra insurance for hurricanes, earthquakes, and the like also are available for small additional premiums.

Check into discounts for having a smoke detector, a security system, or if you're a nonsmoker.

BUYER'S FOLLOW-UP STRATEGIES

Calling in the Cavalry—Prepurchase Property Inspections

Real estate agents have grumbled loudly about the proliferation of property inspections over the last decade. Inspections can kill deals and devastate sellers. And they don't do much for agent morale either.

But because they help buyers avoid problems, they're generally considered to be good for buyers, except that they lengthen the process and can add many hundreds of dollars to your purchasing costs.

Inspections come in an amazing array of types. Some of them are simply reviewing pieces of paper, but most involve physically walking through the property. Start by reading the "Seller's Property Disclosure Form" (see sample in Appendix E) to determine which inspections are going to be essential for your deal. If you get copies of existing insurance, warranties, and/or the home plans, check them too.

If you don't get a property disclosure from the seller, consider photocopying the one in Appendix E and asking the seller to fill it in. Otherwise, check with your agent and ask which inspections are customary and advisable. Here are some of the most important inspections.

Destination Services and Prepurchase Appraisal. If you're transferring with a corporation that may have to help you with selling this home down the road, it is going to be very cautious about the purchase. Many now require prepurchase appraisals, which can add several weeks to your escrow period.

The Basics: Flood/Avalanche, Fire, Wind, and Earthquake. Oddly enough, finding out about these potentially devastating risks is often the most difficult task. It usually involves time-consuming assembling of documents that you have to review yourself. You can get hold of flood and topographic maps from the U.S. Department of the Interior/Geological Survey Office to check hillside stability and earthquake sensitivity. Your lender probably will require flood insurance if you're in a danger area.

Check whether an area is particularly prone to avalanches, tornadoes, hurricanes, or fire storms by going over your newspaper research. Follow up by interviewing insurance people and the locals.

Tip: If the area is prone to drought, like most of the West, beware of a neighborhood with trees and bushes growing right up to the house, and narrow, winding roads that can prevent fire engine access to the area. These factors all-to-often combine into firestorms that not only burn homes to the ground but sear out the plumbing and leave cars in small, melted piles.

The General Contractor's Field: Pest, Water, Foundation, Roof, Appliances, Electric, and Plumbing. Many contractors who do these inspections are separately licensed. However, often you can get a general contractor or licensed home inspection person to do all the inspections together, except for pest infestation. Since termites or rot can destroy foundation and framing, almost all buyers insist on having the pest inspection done, even if they don't bring in an outside expert for the others.

The sellers may already have paid for some of these inspections. If so, and if you feel comfortable with the results, it's one less expense you have to shoulder.

> √ *Important: Try to accompany the inspectors as they go through the home, so you can see actual problems, ask questions, and take notes as they're discovered. If you can't make it, send a trusted friend. These inspections can open further price negotiations with the seller.*
> √ *They can indicate problems that can cost thousands of dollars to fix. Don't treat them casually.*

The Environment: Radon, Asbestos, Lead, Electromagnetic Fields (EMF's), Buried Fuel Tanks, Well Water, Septic Tank. As buyers become more environmentally aware, real estate agents are seeing deals unravel because of inspections that turn up totally unexpected environmental problems.

Again these inspectors are often separately licensed, and it's difficult to organize the whole flock to do separate examinations. And they're even more expensive—often running more than two or three times the cost of traditional general contractor inspections. Again, evaluate what you need by checking the "Seller's Property Disclosure," reviewing your research, and interviewing to find out what problems are prevalent in your area.

If hazards turn up, you've got to think about abatement. Abatement is a grizzly word that always reminds us of a scene from Kafka because environmental solutions don't seem to be evolving nearly as fast as environmental problems. Getting the work done can cost months of searching for a qualified, reasonably priced contractor and thousands of dollars. Obviously, it's better to get these problems dealt with now instead of later.

The Survey. Unless you're buying a farm or a country cottage, your city or county should have a map of your lot showing boundaries. If your community does not have these records, or if the records are old and suspect, or if there's a driveway or another area on the property that seems to be shared by a neighbor, it's a good idea to get a survey. We know of more than one case where even a portion of the house was on somebody else's land.

The Vital Paper Search: Title, Building and Use Permits, Zoning, Future Use. An essential tool to smoothing the paper search should be your escrow holding company. Shop a couple of these to find out rates, and get recommendations about service. This company is responsible for holding your earnest money deposit as well as facilitating the escrow process. *Never* pick one with a sloppy reputation just because it happens to have the lowest fees.

> *Tip:* Ask your title company to put your good-faith deposit in an interest-bearing account, where you collect the interest. When you're checking title company rates, ask if you can get a discount if you refinance within the next few years and buy another title insurance policy from them.

Fortunately, the paper investigations involved with purchasing are less time consuming than checking physical soundness. They are, however, just as important.

You absolutely must review the title report and the report from the city zoning and/or building department. The title report affirms that there is no long-lost relative who shares in the title or a contractor who never removed a claim (i.e., the "cloud" of a mechanic's lien) against the house.

The zoning/building reports affirm that the property doesn't have any infractions against it. Be wary of a building having a permit variance—it might be three stories high in a two-story zone. Check with authorities whether the variance might expire, or whether you're prohibited from rebuilding three stories if the house is destroyed by fire or some other catastrophe.

Future use is more difficult to determine, as a freeway project, or any other grand scheme, probably is not recorded yet. Ask the people at zoning if they've heard of anything pending, and check your newspaper article research.

Home Warranty Contracts. If the seller does not provide a home warranty, you can buy one yourself. Often home warranty companies will write a policy on a home being sold without an inspection. They typically cost between $200 to $400 for a year's service contract on your appliances and major systems—plumbing, heating, electrical, and hot water.

Review competing policies for clauses that cover preexisting conditions that were not known to the sellers and existing wiring and plumbing that may not be up to current building codes. Check to find out if there are additional per-call service fees. Get client references, and find out if they perform their service well.

Preclose Walk-Through. You, the agents, and the seller have worked hard to solve all the presale problems. You've stayed up all night filling out papers for the lender. You've held your breath worrying over things that might go wrong so long, you've turned blue. Now why walk through the property one more time before the close?

You don't have to. For most of the homes we've bought, we've skipped this inspection. But we buy fixer quality, not pristine, so we expect a contractor's mess a week after we take over. If there are removable things in the house that really make a difference to you—the dining room chandelier is a favorite—you should have put them in the contract and you should do the final walk-through.

Advanced Negotiations and Alternative Financing Tactics

Although deals do come together smoothly with an initial offer, most of the time the seller wants a different scenario and issues a counteroffer. Your hard choices may start here or later, after the inspections turn up a problem or the down payment you were expecting from the sale of your old house doesn't come through. Here are some strategies to use when the crunch comes.

Problem: The house you're buying turns out to have a serious foundation problem, which the sellers are willing to have fixed, but it will take as much as four months to have the work done. You have to move before that.

Strategy: Talk with the contractor and see how firm she is with her bid. It's a good idea to get a second and perhaps a third bid. If you feel comfortable with having the work done after you move in, get the seller to put funds to pay for the work into the escrow, go ahead and close, then oversee the work after you move in. You'll get better work from the contractors, because they know you're going to be around to see the job holds up well.

> *Tip: The means of paying for any major work will be a key issue. The contractor's costs should not go on the purchase agreement as a direct price reduction. It should be a "deferred maintenance holdback" set up in escrow. This way it can be funded with the cash from your own down payment and from the monies the bank loans. After the close, the holdback will be used for the repairs only.*
>
> *The lender will want to know how this agreement is working and may factor the repair into their appraisal. Often it requires the escrow holdback to be under its control and the contractor payment to be held back until it has inspected the work. The lender may take extra time to close your loan if the work comes as a surprise. You may even have to get another lender. Get your lender's reactions as quickly as possible.*
>
> *(There is more about this technique in "To Fix or Not to Fix" in Chapter 6.)*

Problem: You're scheduled to move in three weeks. The buyers of your Old Home notify you they won't be able to go through with their deal because their own home sale has fallen through. You don't have enough for your own down payment without their paying you.

Strategy 1: See if your buyers can get a short term bridge loan from either their existing bank or the lender that has okayed them for the purchase of your home. They should check with their employer. Often companies can help with a bridge loan to tide employees over till they find another buyer.

Strategy 2: Another option would be for you to extend a short term second to your buyers. Make sure they have some down payment—most lenders advise at least 5 percent of the purchase price.

If your buyer can't (or won't) make this arrangement, nullify that contract, put your place up for sale again, and investigate your own bridge loan possibilities.

Problem: Loan rates just went up, and you no longer qualify for the amount needed to buy your home.

Strategy 1: If the seller doesn't need immediate cash, ask her to do an installment sale, carrying back an 80 percent loan on the property at a lower rate than what the bank wants to charge you. This should still give the seller more than she'd get if she put the money into a CD.

Strategy 2: Ask the seller to give you a lease option. That way, you can go ahead and move in, and agree to go forward with the purchase within one or two years. You will have to guarantee that it' you don't qualify by then, you'll help present the home to other buyers.

If the seller trusts you and doesn't need your cash in order to go into her own new home, this is a hassle-free option for her, but it can present other problems. Read Robert Bruss's minibook, *How Home Sellers, Buyers, and Realty Agents Can Profit from Lease Options* ($4; Tribune Publishing Company; 75 East Amelia Street, Orlando, FL 32801) before proceeding.

Problem: You'd been told you could get a 95 percent loan-to-value loan, but the lender has changed its policy and no longer offers this kind of loan.

Strategy 1: See if you can borrow the extra down payment amount from the seller. If not, try friends or relatives. If not, see if you can find a mortgage broker or investment company that specializes in equity sharing. Get a copy of the Anderson/Lamb book, *Equity Sharing: Profiting from Joint Home Buying* (Contemporary Books; 180 North Michigan Avenue, Chicago, IL 60601), and investigate the possibility of setting up your own equity share partnership with an investor.

Strategy 2: Ask the seller for an installment sale—see above.

Problem: Your bank notifies you that the credit problem you had two years ago disqualifies you from getting your loan.

Strategy 1: Be sure to get your notification in writing, as the lender's letter may help you get the credit reporting company to clear your problem.

Be aware that lenders are forbidden by law to decline your application due to discrimination or neighborhood "redlining." If you suspect a lender might be violating equal opportunity lending laws, do *not* let it subtly force you to withdraw your application without its written notice.

You'll need to apply to another lender as quickly as possible. Check with mortgage brokers who can shop a number of lenders. Tell them up front about the problem you've had with the original lender. They may be able to find you a lender that caters to individuals with lower credit. These lenders will have higher rates and fees.

Strategy 2: Ask the seller for an installment sale—see above.

Buyer's Remorse

No matter how perfect your prospective home may be, no matter how uneventful the inspections go, there will come a time when your blood runs cold, your feet turn to ice, and nothing about the decision seems right. Sudden terror is good. It keeps us from stepping out of airplanes without parachutes and other stupid acts.

However, it can be strongly irrational. Distract yourself for at least an hour, better twenty-four, with something you enjoy. Then take another look at those pictures and the research and numbers. If you still feel there's some reason you *absolutely should not* go forward, don't.

Most of us find, however, that anxiety about buying has either disappeared or has brought some forgotten problem to the fore that can be dealt with on a conscious level.

The most common anxiety is fear of having paid too much. If you did a thorough job of your research on the market values, check those notes now. If you didn't do your research, mount a blitz of visiting every comparable home on the market that you can find. If your market analysis supports your choice but doesn't point to the most fantastic deal of the century, don't worry. Unlike automobiles and prom dresses, homes have *always* appreciated for people living in them longer than five years.

As real estate columnist Raymond Brown has observed, people who worry that the best time to buy was in the past don't stop to look at the numbers. The price your neighbor paid seven years ago looks absurdly cheap in today's numbers, even with two or three intervening years of recession. The same will be true seven years from now about your own home.

Making Your Close Happen

As soon as your offer has been accepted, read through the "Escrow Timetable and Checklist" in Appendix B. Fill in the calendar deadline dates according to your own contract.

> √ **Warning:** Be sure to conduct inspections and sign off on contingencies in writing by the deadlines stipulated. Otherwise, you can lose your right to terminate the contract because something is unacceptable to you, or you may find the contract has been terminated automatically and someone else is in line to buy the home you want.
>
> √ We try to get documents reviewed and inspections completed several days in advance of deadlines, so that if some problem turns up, there's time to negotiate a solution before we have to irrevocably accept the situation or terminate the contract. Otherwise, negotiate with the seller for an extension rather than an acceptance or termination.

Don't let your vigilance waiver as you get to the point where the lender and title company are sending you final documents. There can be *substantial* mistakes in how the numbers have been calculated. We once received loan closing papers that gave us $25,000 less than what we were supposed to get, and the loan officer was away on vacation. It took nearly a week of telephoning to get our loan documents rewritten. We almost always win a few concessions from the title company on excess documentation charges that can add up to several hundred dollars.

Never sign off on loan documents and closing instructions without reviewing and asking questions about anything wrong or written in indecipherable legalese. Give yourself at least twenty-four hours to be sure you don't miss anything. Review with a lawyer, if you feel unsure.

WHAT TO DO IF YOU START WORK TOMORROW AND YOU STILL DON'T HAVE A NEW HOME

Once in a while a done deal unravels at the last minute. You may have found a perfect place, but the owners suddenly have to postpone their move for a month. Or the roommate you were moving in with suddenly can't do it. Or nothing you've seen comes anywhere near fitting your "have to have's."

Bummer, big time, as they say. Particularly if the missing "have to have" is a home within budget. Particularly if another "have to have" is a move-in deadline with a countdown in hours, not days or weeks.

Evaluate whether you can stay where you are for another month or two while you sort out the problem. Of course, if the furniture is already en route or the job you're starting is farther than a two-hour commute, this option doesn't compute.

Solve problems other than housing first, because they will impact your budget and, therefore, your housing choices. Call the moving company. Ask how long delivery can be delayed for free. (This seems to vary from shipment to shipment.)

Find out if there is any free storage, or how much it will cost, but don't order it until you evaluate unfurnished interim locations. Storage can run you as much as renting a small apartment. So what if it's crammed to the rafters? Your monthly bank balance will be healthier and you've got your things where you can get at them.

A call to your new boss explaining the problem may get you a week to ten-day reprieve. Be diplomatic about this suggestion. You don't want to sound like you're not gung-ho about your new position. It may be that you already know you're scheduled for a crucial meeting three hours after you find your desk, and there's no way you can arrive at another date. In that case, call your boss anyway, and tell her what a heroic effort you're making to get there.

The easiest option for solving a temporary glitch is to start calling the executive suite people in the yellow pages under "Hotels" or "Apartments." Or check the newspaper for furnished apartments, short term or vacation package stays, which often are cheaper than executive suites.

Tip: If you don't have the local yellow pages or news-paper on hand, check the Internet for sites—www.rentnet.com or www.crscorphousing.com both have lists, but your local newspaper might be better. Or call the National Interim Housing Network at (800) 742-6446. It will put you in touch with local sources that specialize in short term rentals.

If budget constraints prohibit the furnished short term rental, check the "Sublets," "Roommates Wanted," "Boardinghouses," and "Rooms for Rent" newspaper sections. And call back the local contacts you've made, explain your problem, and tell them you're looking for a house-sit or short term rental. Be observant and creative. We've found that, both in Italy and in Hong Kong, the cheapest, cleanest, safest place to stay for a short while is a brothel. In countries where brothels are legal and monitored by health authorities, this works for couples who don't mind curious stares.

The axiom is that we're all only six phone calls away from any contact we need. Finding an emergency home isn't easy, but all we really have to do is make six calls . . . well, maybe sixteen.

TEN

Moving Company Tips and Traps

THE TWO BASIC QUESTIONS

Your moving strategy can run a wide gamut of challenges. You may decide to throw out all existing furniture and most of your clothes, dishes, and linens, stuff your three best outfits, your collection of rare kitchen gadgets, and your jewelry in a suitcase, and whiz off in your car.

Another time you may be concerned about dozens of antiques including a priceless family harpsichord that has to be hoisted out of a Queen Anne turret.

What you want in either case are the tools to make your move as simple and economical as possible, given the things that are most important to you. Move planning involves two basic questions:

> 1. Should you use a moving company, do it yourself, or send things through an alternative shipper?
> 2. Approximately how much is it going to cost?

In Appendixes A and B, we've provided a "Moving Company/ Options Evaluator" and the "Steiners Furniture Checklist." These will help you organize your research so you can come up with a clear-cut choice on how you're going to orchestrate your move and who's going to help.

CALCULATING COSTS WITH STEINERS FURNITURE CHECKLIST

Most estimates of moving costs are based on the amount your household goods weigh. How are ordinary people supposed to know how much their furniture weighs? Well, sometimes a receptionist will be helpful and mention the common industry rule of thumb that says an average room runs between 1,000 and 1,500 pounds.

With this information, you can count your rooms. Don't include halls and bathrooms, include kitchens and laundry as one room if appliances are going, and decide what to count as far as basement and garage are concerned. This makes an average two-bedroom home come to a five-room count: bedroom, bedroom, living room, kitchen, dining room. That's between 5,000 and 8,000 pounds, depending on how much heavy furniture and how many books you have. With this ballpark weight figure, you can gather price differentials between moving companies and move-it-yourself alternatives.

The room count approximation, however, doesn't help with trying to decide whether the sofa set or the washer/dryer is worth moving. Look over the "Steiners Furniture Checklist" in Appendix B. We've developed it from a combination of the Pentagon's standard list and furniture mail order catalog weights. It will give you a guide to how much average pieces of furniture weigh and what size truck the do-it-yourself move will take, based on the company's vehicle size guide. (See "How Much Stuff" later this chapter.)

We recommend you go through your house room by room with the "Steiners Furniture Checklist," and note each piece. Don't forget to go through the attic, the basement, and other hiding places.

Even if you already know for certain that you're not taking the sofa, put it on the list anyway, and mark it for sale or donation. This way, you'll have a master plan of what you're doing with the entire house, a tool that will become invaluable as you progress through the decisions that have to be made.

Fill out the checklist carefully, then review it with the rest of the family. You may find the dilapidated family room chair is actually somebody's favorite reading nook and should be taken with you, no matter how much it costs.

Listing cubic footage and dimensions on the form also will help you think through how much space your furniture will take up in your new home.

DECIDING WHAT TO LEAVE BEHIND

Paul Evans, an Atlas estimator who's been in the moving business for years, says the best advice he'd give his sister if she were moving long distance is to weed out mercilessly. Things you don't use or poorly made furniture has no place on a van that's costing you a dollar a pound to get there. Here are two different ways to tackle the task.

The One-Fell-Swoop (Clyde's) Method

Schedule the garage sale for weekend after next. Place the ad. Go through the entire house filling in the "Steiners Furniture Checklist" and carting all "sale" items down to the garage. Take a couple of breathers to scout other garage sales and bone up on market values.

The advantage to this system is that everything gets done quickly. The disadvantage is that it takes enormous energy, and you risk making a mistake.

The Sneak-Up-on-'Em-in-Small-Forays (Shari's) Method

Do your weeding in spurts, filling in the "Steiners Furniture Checklist" room by room, but not deciding everything's fate at once. Take out the most obvious eyesores first, then sort through the more beautiful and beloved stuff as you find out more about what the move is going to cost you. Sell items individually in newspaper ads or give them away.

The advantage to this system is that it doesn't wear you out as much and you can be certain that everything on the "sale" list really should be there. The disadvantage is that you may not be done by M Day.

Tip: *Expensive furniture and high-end appliances are difficult to sell at a good price in a garage sale. Sell such pieces ahead of time through newspaper want ads or— if you have a number of items—get bids from several antique dealers.*

Medium- to low-end appliances and plants do fairly well because they are sold at garage sales often, so knowledgeable people look for them there. Expect to get about half what you paid for an appliance and between a buck and $15 per plant. If you've got expensive appliances or rare cattleyas that should go higher, advertise them separately under "Household Furniture" in the newspaper to get the specialist buyer.

Sadly, books, magazines, and newspapers, the beauty and bane of the Steiner existence, don't do well in a garage sale. We interrogate friends and relatives to find recipients of these items, but the best bet seems to be the library or church that has an annual benefit bazaar.

Tip: *Don't have a toy sale unless your child is at least a junior or senior in high school. Often children are frightened and confused by a move and will suddenly cling to that worn but winning lovey you thought they forgot three years ago. Let the children know that all the familiar toys and clothes are coming along, and they'll get to unpack them and enjoy them in the new home. You always can weed out things next year, after they've settled into their new environment.*

The Household Hazardous Waste Hurdle

As landfills have gotten scarce and people have become aware of how easy it is to contaminate groundwater, communities everywhere have instituted strict prohibitions against allowing hazardous wastes into regular household garbage or the city sewer systems. This presents a problem to the moving householder, particularly if you've just repainted everything to make the home look better for prospective buyers. The list is long and includes hairspray as well as drain-cleaning chemicals. In Appendix B, we provide a "Household Hazardous Waste

Checklist" of things you're not supposed to toss into regular garbage.

Almost every home has one or more of the items listed. If you are having movers come in and pack, you'll find they won't box these things, as it's illegal for them to be in vans because of fire and/or spillage dangers. You should have the same inhibitions about carting these things around with your furniture in a do-it-yourself truck.

To get rid of them, include unopened cans in the garage sale and/or ask friends if they want anything. Check your telephone government pages for your city's hazardous waste collection or recycling programs, and/or your yellow pages for ads about local dumps. There should be a specific day for appointment pickup by the city, or one of the dumps should offer a special program.

WHAT'S MOVING GOING TO COST?

Let's get back to our two big questions—whether to move it yourself or use a moving company and how much it's going to cost. Every now and then an industry goes through sweeping changes. This happened when AT&T broke up into the Baby Bells, when the end of the Cold War put the missile industry out of work, and when the national Household Goods Act was passed. The Household Goods Act didn't make nearly as many headlines, but it is vital to anyone who's moving between states. It gave the public two big benefits:

1. *The right to negotiate discounts on the rates.*
2. *The right to binding (guaranteed) estimates.*

Unfortunately, national deregulation did nothing for rates on *intrastate* moves (those within one state). These are still usually set by state law, and often no discounting or binding rates are allowed.

THE FIVE ELEMENTS OF COST

The five essential elements in answering the cost question are:

√ *How much stuff you're moving.*
√ *How far you're moving.*

√ *How tricky your things are.*
√ *How tricky your locations are.*
√ *How much physical work is involved.*

Here's how they interact, even if you're doing a local move, and the company charges by the hour.

How Much Stuff

Obviously, if you only have a car trunk full of belongings to take with you, you won't be reading this chapter. The following insights are directed to the rest of us.

Go back to your "Steiners Furniture Checklist." Add up everything you're definitely taking. If you have heavy items on the "maybe" column, mark them with your highlighter, so that when you're talking to movers, you can ask specifically what it will cost to include the extra pounds.

 Tip: Because the rate per hundred pounds is range-bracketed and goes down as your load gets bigger, you may be able to ship pieces "free," if inclusion puts you in a cheaper bracket. Ask for range rates and breakpoints. When you're negotiating your final discount, ask if you can trade any leftover excess furniture allowance for something else you need, such as a short stint in storage.

Besides giving you a telephone quote based on estimated weight, moving companies will send an estimator to walk through your home, tell you how much she believes your things will weigh, and give you a written binding estimate of how much the company will charge.

Your do-it-yourself costs are easier to calculate. Van rental companies offer free guides for the size vehicle you need depending on the size of your home. Their guidelines:

√ *A trailer for a studio to a small one-bedroom apartment.*
√ *A twelve-foot van for a large one-bedroom or a small two-bed-room.*
√ *A fourteen-foot van for an average two-bedroom apartment.*
√ *A seventeen-foot van for a two-bedroom house.*
√ *A twenty-four-foot van for a three-bedroom house.*

√ *A twenty-six-foot van for a five-bedroom house.*

If you're moving yourself, try not to underestimate the size of the van needed. If you underestimate, you'll have to go back and rent another trailer to supplement your original vehicle.

Overestimating, however, is also a problem. Besides having to pay more for the vehicle, the load is more prone to shifting and breakage if it's too loosely packed.

How Far You're Moving

Get a map or an atlas and add up how many miles you'll be moving. Don't try to get it down to the last half mile. None of the moving companies will agree with your precise numbers, anyway. However, their basic rate is usually based on a dollar rate per thousand pounds per mile, so you'll need mileage to calculate the cost.

If you rent a truck, of course, you'll need mileage to figure both the rental and the gas cost. Knowing the distance also will tell you what kind of a drive you'll personally be looking at if you opt for doing it yourself.

 Tip: *Rental agencies figure bigger trucks get between five and eight miles to the gallon. Be sure to ask each company you talk with what to expect in the vehicle you need.*

The moving company cost for the distance you're moving is influenced by *location* as well as miles. The factor here is the industry's definition of what is considered "local," "*intrastate*" or "interstate."

Local moves are usually defined as less than 150 miles away and not crossing a state line. They are only lightly regulated, and their competitiveness is determined by how many companies there are in your hometown going after your business. They typically charge by the hour.

As we've already mentioned, *intrastate* moving companies are usually governed by the Department of Transport or the Public Utilities Commission (PUC) in each individual state, and rates often are set by law.

Interstate moving companies are no longer governed federally (the Interstate Commerce Commission (ICC) was dissolved in the late 90s). Since the Household Goods Act, however, *interstate* movers can, and usually do, offer discount rates. Ask them what their tariff is (it may vary from company to company), whether their tariff is due for a change (like auto dealerships, they know when rates are going up in advance), and—most important—what their discounts are.

Discounts vary enormously. In competitive times, corporate contracts for shipping more than a hundred households annually have inspired moving companies to quote discounts over 65 percent. Human resource managers, however, advise that going with bids much below the competition is asking for trouble. Lowball offers can mean more additional charges later, · poor service, excessive breakage, and/or no insurance reimbursement.

Tricky Stuff

Everybody knows that a grand piano is going to be expensive to move and should not be put on a rental truck by a ninety-five-pound weakling. There may be any number of other items in your household that need advance planning and may give pause to do-it-yourself plans. As you're getting your bearings right now, here's a quick list of articles most likely to give trouble:

√ *Pianos of all kinds, harps, organs, bass violas, tubas, large drum sets, and the like. Even with carrying cases, your musical instruments can have serious problems in transport.*

√ *Antiques or artwork bigger than you can easily carry.*

√ *Antique clocks with detachable pendulums.*

√ *A very valuable and/or an extra-large wine collection.*

√ *A rare plant collection.*

√ *Extra vehicles, including lawn tractors and snowmobiles.*

√ *Boats, airplanes.*

√ *Horses and farm animals.*

√ *Pool table (particularly if it has a slate top).*

√ *Spa or hot tub.*

√ *Chest freezer and contents.*

Items like these will need special handling no matter who moves you. If you're having a company do it, speak with your estimator when she's going through your home to find out how she'll handle it. Ask her to break out how much this item and its insurance will cost separately. Try to take anything manageable with you in the car, or you may opt to ship things an alternative way.

> *Tip:* A few moving companies have on-board electric generators and will move freezers with the contents. These companies are usually more expensive than their competitors, but if you've got nearly 500 pounds of venison, as one Colorado respondent to our survey had, you don't mind the cost. You may want to investigate a refrigerated truck or other alternative shippers for this one item.

If you're moving yourself, get help on difficult items from specialists. Check the phone book. Look for piano movers or packing companies specializing in crating and shipping antiques and/ or art work.

Tricky Locations

This will also mean extra dollars, no matter what. It will also mean more wear and tear on your back if you're doing it on your own. Don't forget to tell estimators what kind of location you have at *both* ends of the move.

A number of location factors trigger add-on fees in the moving industry.

Stairs. How many, how high, and are there any turns? Those of us who have stairs get so used to them, we don't previsualize the problems involved. Measure your furniture, and plan how you'll maneuver large pieces through the stair obstacles that stand between their current and future resting places.

Cranes, Hoists, Rigs. You'll need some sort of special apparatus for any item that needs to be taken out of an upper-floor window because it's too unwieldy to make it down the stairs. If you live in a large complex, check with building management. It may have a hoist or crane permanently set up to deal with this problem. Otherwise, ask your van rental agency, look up "Crane/ Hoist Companies" in the yellow pages or look up hourly movers, who will probably be needed as extra help, anyway.

 Tip: We lived for six years in a three-story home that reminded us of a New England farmhouse. When we went to move our furniture out, we discovered that the charming entrance arch we built after we moved in would no longer accommodate the sofa . . . or the breakfront . . . or the desk.

Our do-it-yourself Moving Day got postponed while we rushed around looking for a crane or a hoist. After hearing several staggering rental rates, we finally found an enterprising hourly mover who helped us devise a rig/ small hoist/slide system that worked via the old-fashioned elbow grease plus creativity principle.

Our advice? Don't wait till M Day to solve these problems.

Elevators. Companies often charge more for elevators than they do for a straight flight of stairs, because elevators take longer. Unlike stairs, however, the charge is usually the same whether you're on the second floor or the 12th.

Excess Distance. (Usually this means more than seventy-five feet, but ask.) This is often caused by a street too narrow, too winding, or too steep to park the truck at your front door. Some locations are tucked away on such winding roads, the movers have to hire a small truck to shuttle everything up to the door from the bottom of the hill.

Urban Surcharge. Some companies charge extra for pick-ups and/or deliveries in and out of urban areas, where traffic delays can add significant time to the move.

Physical Work Involved

This factor includes special services, such as disconnecting and connecting appliances, as well as whether the movers have to work overtime (or on the weekend) or need extra helpers at the destination end.

· You should know that once the boxes are packed, moving companies figure that loading 1,000 pounds of furniture into a truck will, on average, take an hour to move the items plus two extra hours inside the truck making certain that boxes won't shift and that heavy items are on the bottom and distributed on both sides of the van.

WEIGHING MOVE-IT-YOURSELF OPTIONS

Be realistic about the comparable savings of moving it yourself. Compare: a 1,000-mile interstate move for a 6,000-pound load (typical for a small household) can cost approximately $2,000 for a do-it-yourself move (without extra labor help) and approximately $4,000 for a moving company.

If you simply can't afford having movers do it, then that's that. If you've got the money, but you've also got the brawn and the inclination to do it yourself, then there are a couple of items other than cost that you should consider in the equation.

Doing it Yourself: Pro

√ You handle your own things.
√ You have more control over pickup and delivery dates.
√ Your things get there when you do.
√ You save money.

Doing It Yourself: Con

√ You'll have no damage and breakage insurance, unless you have an accident.
√ You have to do a lot of heavy lifting.
√ You have to drive a truck. Today's rental vans offer power steering and automatic transmission, but they're slow, clumsy on turns, and can make a terrible mess of the motel marquee if you happen to drive under a low one.
√ You have to do a lot more organizing getting the truck, packing items, tow apparatus, insurance, and any special permits needed. (Check with the agency about what's needed.)
√ To save on per-day costs, you should unpack the truck within twenty-four hours of your arrival.
√ Last-minute problems, such as having to hire unloading help at the delivery site or getting the wrong size truck and having to go back and rent an add-on trailer, can cut your savings.

Selection Criteria

You can find move-it-yourself rental companies in the yellow pages under several categories, with the biggest listing under "Truck Rental." Look for ones with binding estimates, no return charges, easy driving features, power tailgate lifts, and other items detailed later in this chapter and on the "Moving Company/Options Evaluator" in Appendix A.

For long-distance moves, you'll probably be limited to the Big Four companies—U-Haul (they created this market), Ryder (they're going after this market), Hertz/Penske, and Budget/Sears—because these big nationals have the best one-way rental offers.

MOVING COMPANY PROFILES

Most long-distance moves are done through a local agent for one of the big national van lines. Here are insights on programs from some of the best known, plus info from both our IIP Frequent Mover Survey and an insightful, copyrighted, *Consumer Reports* poll of over 22,000 of their readers who had recently moved.

Tip: Check with the Consumer Reports *article reprint service to find out what their latest report may be. They can be reached at (800) 766-9988 for hardcopies, or if you're a subscriber, you can get it from their website at www.consumerreports.org.*

Allied

Allied vies with United and North American as the biggest carrier. *Consumer Reports* ranked them midpoint in satisfaction, and 22 percent of their respondents reported inaccurate estimates.

Arpin

This is one of the smaller lines, and it's customer oriented. *CR* reports 77 percent satisfaction, and 4 percent inaccurate estimates, but they performed the fewest moves on the survey. No one in the IIP Frequent Mover Survey reported using Arpin.

Atlas

Atlas has a big network with good customer satisfaction ratings. Only 3 percent of *CR* respondents reported inaccurate estimates. A large portion of their business is corporate relocation. They are not as likely to provide binding estimates or accept credit cards as some of the other lines. They have a referral and discount coupon arrangement with the Century 21 real estate network and may discount their tariff even more if competition is stiff in your area.

Bekins

Although Bekins has now topped the IIP Frequent Mover Survey on customer satisfaction two years running, it did not do as well on the *CR* poll. For small extra fees, Bekins offers relocation assistance through an affiliated company, extra unpacking, and performance guarantees.

Mayflower

This company has a customer financing plan, the Mayflower Card, and also accepts credit cards. It supplies helpful information and appealing literature for children. It did not do well on customer satisfaction surveys and had 40 percent reporting inaccurate estimates in the *CR* survey.

North American

North American has very good free information packets for children and teenagers and information packets on several states. It provides a clear packing brochure with photographs. While it rated low on satisfaction and received the worst rating (46 percent) on inaccurate estimates, it now offers not-to-exceed binding estimates. North American accepts credit cards, or you can sign up for credit from the company.

United

United has aggressive agents with good follow-up plus the biggest information packets on all phases of moving. It reports that its Betty Malone relocation services, which provide free information on many locations, both nationally and internationally, is used by nearly 100,000 people a year. United does extensive office relocation as well as homes. It did well on customer satisfaction but tended to have inaccurate estimates.

Wheaton

This is another small network that has a good customer service record with only 3 percent of *CR* respondents reporting inaccurate estimates.

SELECTION INTERVIEWING TIPS

The "Moving Company/Options Evaluator" in Appendix A covers the major questions you need to ask both the moving and move-it-yourself companies you're evaluating. Here are some interviewing tips.

General Impression

You need to know the company's reputation and whether it has a customer service "attitude." Take notes on how friendly people are and how quickly they follow up with helpful information. If they don't listen to your needs now, when they're trying to get your business, how about later, if there's a problem?

Getting actual references and checking complaint records is important. Despite the fact that most interstate companies act as agents for the big national van lines, the local company can be much better or much worse than the network as a whole. Companies should be happy to give you references, and list their professional affiliations. It's a good idea to check these, as well as call the Better Business Bureau.

Rates

Rates include charges for shipping plus packing and any other services. Surcharges can be sneaky. Overtime charges, for example, have caused many customer complaints, because the movers were the ones who stood around not doing anything until they kicked into overtime. Henry P. Costantino, a relocation expert who wrote the very thorough *Moving? Don't Be Taken for an Expensive Ride,* points out that the drivers and loaders often work on commission, and they are very aware of the charges they rack up.

Do-it-yourself extra charges also are easy to overlook. Don't forget you may need to have a towing device for your personal vehicle(s). Ask the company whether the states you're going through have permit fees and taxes that need to be paid. You need to add in your personal hotel and labor charges to the overall cost, but don't forget also to deduct the labor and time needed to oversee a moving company operation. And, of course, deduct the costs of the family trip that will have to be made to the new location, no matter what. The "Moving Company/Options Evaluator" in Appendix A lists these items to track costs.

Packing Charges

Evaluate packing charges against the hassle of doing it yourself, whether you're having a moving company do the shipping or not. We've always done all our packing ourselves, but a number of the IIP Frequent Mover Survey respondents reported they prefer splitting duties up—doing their own unbreakables, such as books, clothes, and linens, and having the mover doing the fragile items.

Note that some do-it-yourself companies offer helpers to come in on an hourly basis and do as much of the packing and lugging as you want. Also, check yellow page and advertiser ads for movers that will work freelance.

Payment Policy

Paying for the move can present a problem. Moving companies have long taken the concept cash on delivery literally. Not for them are the profligate wonders of credit cards. People who move are obviously not to be trusted. (To be fair, most credit cards can't shoulder a big moving bill that runs over $5,000. People who move also are usually moving bank accounts, and our checks *are* more likely to have problems than normal.)

Fortunately, van lines are now changing this policy, so look for a company that accepts cards or is willing to make credit arrangements. If you must pay on delivery, a certified check from your bank, which must be cosigned by you as well as the driver, is the safest way to carry the funds.

Important Services

The most important of services are frequent and flexible service and the ability to transport your things directly to their destination. A company must be registered separately in each state where it does business. If it isn't registered for direct transport to your destination state or if you're not going on a frequently traveled route, the mover may arrange to relay your shipment to another vehicle. Relaying doubles the chances of loss, damage, and delays.

Occasionally you'll need specialist services for transporting valuables or a piano or whatever. Go over the list and add your own requirements.

Estimating Policy

Estimates should be free. Do-it-yourself companies give you written commitments, based on the size vehicle you're ordering. (Of course, you still may have a size inaccuracy.)

Moving companies can issue three different types—the (nonbinding) estimate, the binding estimate, and the not-to-exceed binding estimate.

The (nonbinding) estimate, which is all you can get in some *intrastate* situations, is not guaranteed. You do not know the real cost until after the truck is loaded and weighed.

Although the van lines industry reports that nonbinding estimates are still the most common, we don't recommend this method. Moving survey respondents reported that charges above the estimate could run more than 20 percent.

There may be a significant difference between what you estimate your things will weigh from the "Steiners Furniture Checklist" and what a moving company estimator gives you. If all the estimators come up with about the same amounts, you probably have nonstandard items.

If you live in a state where it's illegal to give binding estimates on *intrastate* moves or a location where you can't find a moving company that will give them, be sure to attend *both* before-and-after weighings, as is your legal right. You need to know how much the truck weighs before your things are loaded in order to calculate your household's weight.

We recommend using a binding estimate. With this method, estimators list all the items to be shipped and all the services you require on the estimate form, then mark it as a binding price. Have them itemize each charge, so that if you want to delete or add something, it's easy for you to know the cost. Changes go on a written addendum—the change order they must fill out and you both sign *prior* to the move.

The estimators also must write down how long the price is in effect, usually sixty days. If they are due for a tariff increase, be sure that you move before then or that they'll guarantee in writing to hold the price till you move.

A third type of estimate gives you the best of all worlds: a not-to-exceed estimate. The movers give you a binding estimate, then weigh the vehicle and *reduce* the price if the weight is less than anticipated. Ask all movers you interview if they offer this service.

Discounts

Moving midmonth instead of the first or last week of the month can save you money. So can moving midweek instead of on the weekend. Even bigger dollar savings can be achieved by moving your date forward or backward a few weeks into a different season. Most areas' heavy seasonal activity is between May 1 and September 31, but the pattern is reversed in sun states such as Arizona and Florida.

Check ads and the yellow pages for companies that specialize in frequently used routes. (Washington/NYC has almost become a shuttle.) If you're moving from a popular area to a less popular one (from Miami Beach to Detroit, for example) you should get a discount, because movers are likely to get a full load on the return trip.

Look for companies with no overtime charges and/or delivery and performance guarantees. As companies are becoming more quality conscious, some are offering partial refunds if you experience poor service. Some also offer special rates for particular groups, such as senior citizens.

Finally, face-to-face negotiating tactics will pay off, particularly with moving company estimators. Do-it-yourself companies seem less likely to offer anything other than company-wide seasonal or area discounts, although Budget currently is offering discount coupons available through real estate agents nationwide.

Timeframe

The number of days you'll need to reserve ahead and the time involved between pickup and delivery will vary by season. If your moving date is flexible, get information about seasonal and/or midweek/midmonth differences.

Movers need to stay flexible about pickup and delivery dates because they usually are filling their truck with several households' worth of goods. A few (particularly Bekins) will designate exact dates, but they often have a surcharge for this service.

Even after contracting to do your move within a range of dates, the movers can give you a call and tell you they've been delayed and must reschedule. According to the Better Business Bureau, you have no legal recourse for the inconvenience, unless the you can prove they did not "exercise reasonable diligence."

Be warned, however. If *you* are more than two hours late meeting them for the delivery, they have the right to put your things in storage, and you'll run up stiff storage and redelivery charges.

Insurance—Moving Companies

All companies include a basic insurance in their basic rate. This only covers 60 cents per pound, however, so you'll probably want more coverage.

Check with your existing insurers to find out what's already covered—usually fire, theft, and water damage for the move. Ask if they supply extra coverage for accidents and/or storage. Add-ons to your existing policy may be cheaper than the insurance the moving company sells, particularly for high-value items such as computers, furs, art, and antiques.

Your extra premium insurance choices with a moving company are either depreciated coverage, which will get you a used refrigerator more or less the same age as your existing one, or full-value coverage, which will get you new replacements. The latter, of course, costs more. Ask about these coverages and charges when you're doing your initial telephone interviewing, so that when you get to the point where the mover is writing up the estimate or order for service, you can fill in exactly what you want.

Be particularly careful researching how the mover covers high-value items. Most are reluctant to ship jewelry, won't write extra insurance for collectibles such as stamps or coins, and will cover only written appraisal value for art and antiques. If your homeowner's policy won't cover these things, consider taking them with you or shipping them via an alternative.

Insurance—Move-it-Yourself

A big difference between this insurance and the one given by movers is that move-it-yourself companies *don't insure against any kind of shipping and handling damage* unless you have an accident. Neither does your household insurance. You're just as liable for a plate being broken if you pack badly and hit a bumpy road as you would be if you tripped as you were bringing the turkey to the table.

Rental agencies do offer personal accident and cargo insurance and physical damage waiver policies. They will itemize these rates, which are based on value and number of days covered, for you in their estimates. Again, check to find out if your existing household and/or car insurance already will cover these items or can cover them for a lower premium than the rental agency offers. Be aware that if you're driving a larger vehicle with six or more "wheels on the road," your regular noncommercial vehicle insurance probably won't suffice.

Storage in Transit (SIT)

Neither our respondents nor Consumer Reports advises storing furniture because the damages double, and it's more difficult to get insurance to cover the problem. If you have to store before moving into your next home, ask all moving companies if they have any free storage period.

Ask your moving company about the difference between its SIT and any permanent storage it may offer. Permanent storage often is more expensive, and the mover's transit insurance doesn't usually cover it at all. Try to visit the storage facilities to see if they are well tended, and find out how difficult and costly it is to retrieve one box (last year's tax records, for example), out of storage.

Alternative Shippers

Alternative shippers are included on your "Moving Company/Options Evaluator" (Appendix A) so that one list covers all possibilities. This makes comparing the cost of shipping some items with a moving company and some with air freight or regular mail easy.

NAILING DOWN THE BEST CONTRACT

Evaluate the Market

If you're moving on a frequently traveled route and you can be flexible on move dates, you should be able to negotiate quite a good discount, particularly in the highly competitive market of the 1990s. If you're moving from one small town to another and there are only a few companies competing for your business, negotiations will be more difficult.

 Tip: If you're moving in an area flanked by major destination cities or on a frequently traveled route, you may be able to find a freight consolidator going to the large destination city who'll pick up your load at a good discount. Go to the library and check that city's yellow pages.

Don't Lose Your Cool

Be friendly, but make sure you get *itemized* estimates, with each service fee broken out separately, so that negotiations can be both on an overall and a specific basis.

The Power of Reputation

Always let an estimator know that you're going to check their company's references, claims record, and general reputation thoroughly. If you have a policy of writing companies either to praise or complain about specific service, talk about that too.

The Power of Competition

Always explain that you're getting more than one estimate. Some moxie people headed for an interstate transfer have had an "estimating party," with all the movers going through at once. Ask each interstate mover what its regular tariff is, then what its discount policy is. Then ask to have their BLD (bottom-line discount).

Don't just accept the first estimate. Compare the estimates from all the companies, and call back the top two. Explain their estimate is "In the running, but . . ." Estimators usually are paid by commission. They spend years figuring out how to get you to pay the highest price. The more you negotiate, the better off your pocketbook will be.

You also may want items taken off or added to the estimate. Get all changes in writing on an addendum form you and the company both sign before Moving Day. The actual truckers cannot make changes, and movers sometimes use *any* changes to nullify your carefully negotiated binding estimate. Plan accordingly.

No-Nos
Don't ever sign anything blank, and don't sign the company's order for service or addendum forms until you've reviewed all the estimates and discussed *and written in* the concessions.

Ending on the Upbeat
Even after you've signed the order for service, you may cancel the move for any reason. You are not bound to perform the move with the company until you sign the bill of lading at your home the day the movers arrive.

ALTERNATIVE SHIPPING POSSIBILITIES

There are lots of circumstances where alternative shippers come in handy. One is when you don't have many things, but you don't want to cart some of the valuable ones across the country in the back seat of your car. Others are when you **can't** get everything into the van; or when you're having the movers do it all, but you want to save money on those twenty shelves of impossible to replace books.

To find the wide array of services open to you, ask contacts for recommendations, and check the Internet (particularly www.moverquotes.com), the yellow pages, want ads, and Appendix C. Here is a summary of what to look for.

Air Cargo

If you have something large, fragile, and/or valuable, and the trip involves several nights' stay en route, air cargo may be a big blessing. Consider particularly for pets, jewelry, and other valuables you don't want to be secreting in and out of hotel rooms en route.

Tip: If one member of your family is flying, she may be able to take valuables and pets as excess baggage.

Auto Transport

These folks arrange for someone to drive your car across country, ship it by rail, or whatever you wish. A must to investigate for overseas moves if you have to take your car. Look under "Transport" in your local newspaper and advertiser want ads for car drive away services.

*Check Out : www.iyoupack.com ; 1-877- YOU-PACK
website # 1-800-355-1696   968-7225*

Freight Consolidating

Ever get stuck behind a truck in traffic and find yourself trying to figure out what the LTL sign stands for? It's "less than load," and it means that, with these folks' help, you can get your moving bill down to less than lavish proportions by combining your load with others going in the same direction.

To find them, check the "Freight" and "Trucking" listings in the yellow pages. Look for "piggyback" services as well as LTL. Also look under "Transport" in your local newspaper and advertiser want ads.

Some people have had good luck finding freight consolidators by advertising in the Personals that they want to put together a full load. Other people like to check the local university's bulletin boards for ride-share information.

> must be out of state, 500 miles or more, 28' trailer 5' minimum

Freight Forwarding

These are the big ocean and rail shippers that are essential for international moving. Dealing with them directly can save

*Another : Movex self service moving 1-800-876-6839
you load, we drive)*

Also : Help-U-Move + ValueMoves on Realtor . Com site

money on long, large shipments, but be sure you hire one with a reputable customs brokering service, or your things can get badly hung up at one border or another.

Mailing Services

Mailing services are typically good only for small things, but they'll box and ship books and other UPS and U.S. Mail/Parcel Post things for you.

Packaging Services

Packaging services have more facilities for handling large things than mailing service companies do. They usually offer a pickup "curbside shipping" service as well as packing and crate building.

Packing and Crating Services

Packing and crating services are an old-fashioned yellow page category that today includes the full range of packaging and shipping services as well as the original crate building specialists. These vendors can help you with musical instruments, antiques, artwork, electronics, and other "difficult" items.

Rail Companies

It used to be that traveling by train with your belongings going as excess *baggage* was cheaper than traveling by air with extra *luggage*. In the States, this is no longer true, so long as you can get yourself an airline ticket during a sale. Passenger luggage maximums on coast-to-coast routes are currently 150 pounds for rail, 210 for air; cargo runs $296 per 1,000 pounds for rail, $210 for air.

Neither service will guarantee that all pieces in large shipments will arrive at the same time you do. Amtrak rail is particularly hostile to the idea and refuses to ship anything electrical or fragile. Southern Pacific even refuses to ship anything less than a full carload.

Steamships and Freighters

Talk to ship brokers and consolidators about handling single-household shipments. Several people we've talked with took a much more ingenious approach: They moved abroad via a freighter, taking their core household with them as a mix of luggage and freight. For faraway locations such as Australia and Europe, this may be a great way to save money.

 Tip: Finding a freighter that stops at your destination, takes passengers one-way, and will carry individual loads isn't easy. Try an online specialist like www.tcpltd.com (which also does cruises) or talk to a travel specialist. Carolyn Rasmussen of Carolyn's Cruises says she's booked trips for years and can tell you quickly what's possible on routes and rates. Currently it's impossible to go one-way between American cities, she says. For out-of-the-country trips, you get 40 cubic feet/350 pounds free luggage allowance. You can call Carolyn's Cruises at (800) 292-3265.

Use a freight forwarding or packing and crating service to organize getting your things dockside and getting them picked up at the other end. Then add suntan oil and yachting whites to your "Take-It-With-Me" list.

Trucking

Look for the "less than load," "small load," or "piggyback" trucking services. Other truckers usually are not interested in single-household shipments.

United Parcel Service (UPS) Ground

UPS is good for shipping smaller personal items and clothes. When Donna G. Albrecht, a well-traveled interviewee, was returning to California from her mother's funeral in Florida, she went to UPS to ship home some family heirlooms. "I found that for a small extra charge, they guaranteed my package would ride in front at all times under the driver's vigilance and arrive in perfect condition," she comments. This may be a precious find for people puzzling over how to ship computer disks and tapes in hot weather.

U.S. Third-Class Mail and Parcel Post

Third-class rates for your books and magazines used to be highly recommended, but stabilized freight rates and rising postal charges have changed that. Shipping small things by mail is economical for international as well as Stateside moves, but for anything except books, you may have to stand around customs for hours, as individual parcels not vouched for by a moving company or freight forwarder are suspect.

Be sure to clearly mark any books as such. Other small things shipped internationally should be marked "No Commercial Value." Talk with someone at a packaging service or the post office about the forms needed and the best ways to ship to an individual location.

ELEVEN

How to Arrive with Your Aunt Sally's Teapot and Your Sanity Intact

PACKING STRATEGIES

Pack Kids and Pets First

No matter how you go about getting all your things into boxes, onto a truck, and into your new home, keep one thing in mind. Preteens can be a big help with advance operations, but *they should be with a friend or a sitter on Moving Day.* Ditto your pets.

Both invariably get hyperactive because of the commotion and the sense of big change in the air. At best they get in the way, cause delays and mistakes. At worst they can get into poisons or dangerous equipment, trip a trucker carrying something heavy, or wander off and get lost.

Tip: Be sensitive to your children's fears about the move. Reassure them that you will be back to get them before you leave and that you won't go off without them.

The Moving Company Does It

If you're having a moving company do your packing as well as moving, prepare for a blitz. Have everything organized ahead of time—all items not going with them isolated, all appliances moving with you unhooked, clean, dry, aired out, and containing a sock full of baking soda to absorb smells on the trip.

Packers are told to pack *everything,* so wastebaskets, ashtrays, and food containers must be empty.

Even with professional packers, you can't escape the responsibility of overseeing final checkout. As Kay Cooperman, one of our respondents, commented, "I'd been told they'd clean up after they loaded everything. They took off with my cleaning supplies and the vacuum cleaner, but left fingerprints on the woodwork, dirt from outside all over the carpet, and dust where the large pieces of furniture used to be. And they forgot to pack the things in one closet."

Ask to review the moving company's "Household Goods Descriptive Inventory" while the movers are setting up, so that you can go over the abbreviations used (B=Bent, S=Scratched, T=Torn, and 1=Arm, 4=Front, 10=Top, etc.). As your mover loads things into the truck, each piece will be tagged with a number, then notations on scratches, tears, and dents go onto the form with the corresponding number. Inspect the furniture with the mover. If there's just one scratch on a tabletop, don't settle for "Item #36—S,10." Write in "Item #36—S, 2 inches, 10, on corner." That way, if a new scratch appears all across the top, you can claim damages.

Packing-It-Yourself Options

There are two other options—doing all the packing yourself or packing just the soft goods and the durables and leaving the breakables for the movers.

The advantages of doing your own packing are:

√ *You may take better care of your things.* Consumer Reports *respondents reported 32 percent who packed themselves had breakage problems, but 55 percent had breakage when they had the movers do it.*

√ *You save the packing charges, which can add up to a third of the overall moving cost.*

√ *Even if you leave some items for the movers, it's easier to keep your things organized when you pack and mark boxes yourself.*

The disadvantages are the time it takes and the fact that making a moving company insurance claim on breakage with goods you pack yourself is more difficult.

Packing is an organization challenge. On the one hand, you want to pack as much as possible ahead of moving week. On the other hand, you may still be having prospective purchasers or friends coming through, so you don't want boxes all over the house. Besides, things invariably get packed that you need the next day.

We've developed the following Steiner Smooth Move System, with lots of suggestions from friends, clients, and our survey respondents.

Packing Materials

The most economical source of supplies for packing materials is a specialty shipping and packaging material store.

Tip: *If you don't have a discount source in your area, and you're looking to buy boxes and other staples in twenty-five-piece lots, call Bradley's at (800) 621-7864 for a catalog.*

It has almost everything—boxes and plastic bags, in various sizes, bungee stretch cords to secure padding, rolls of thirty-six-inch corrugated wrapping material for padding, storage tubes for posters. Its prices are about half what a moving company charges. While Bradley's can't supply some things—wardrobe, dishpack, and mirror boxes, a few tools—otherwise, it's a big help.

Box Collecting. Start collecting boxes as soon as you decide to move. The penultimate find is somebody down the street moving in. Drop by and ask owners if they'd like your help in getting rid of boxes. We usually offer to buy the wardrobe and mirror/picture boxes that are in good shape for half price and cart everything away. If you happen to hit one or more of these treasures several months before you start packing, fold the boxes fiat and store in the attic or garage.

Check local stores. Furniture boxes are often too big to handle, but sometimes lamp departments or stores have good sizes.

Liquor stores have the best, sturdiest, most consistently sized boxes. They come complete with handy cardboard dividers for glasses and small items. Having boxes mostly the same size makes packing the truck much easier. Ask what days the store unpacks wines, and arrive yourself to break them open, so the lids are intact. The store usually slits lids, because it's faster. If someone breaks open boxes for you, tip or do something to show appreciation.

> **Tip:** Andy Smitters, one of our frequent mover respondents, advises checking boxes you pick up on the street carefully. Turn them upside-down and thump them before putting in your trunk, as they can hide some unwelcome insects.

Other sources to check are box manufacturers (in the yellow pages, under "Boxes") or packaging stores. Office supply store boxes aren't good, because they come with separate lids, which are likely to pop off, even when carefully taped.

Moving and move-it-yourself companies tend to be the most expensive box source, but their boxes are sturdy, standard size, and easy to handle. Their wardrobe, dishpack, and mirror boxes are particularly useful. Sometimes local movers will sell secondhand boxes, and some moving companies have a box supply outside their warehouse for anyone to pick up. Ask all the companies you interview. If you can find one that rents or sells seconds, it also may pick up your boxes after you've unpacked for free.

Personal Resource Packing Materials. Use your own sheets, towels, clothes, and air-popped popcorn for wrapping and cushioning as much as possible. You can use old newspapers, but they may leave ink on everything. Ask your newspaper production office if it's using the new soybean inks that don't stain as badly as the old kind. Protect against ink by putting items in plastic bags before wrapping. We recommend using old newspaper for the bottom cushioning covered with a layer of clean unprinted newsprint between it and your things.

Bargain Packing Materials. Find out the most economical source of unprinted newsprint, which IIP Frequent Mover Survey respondents liked best for packing breakables. Besides checking with newspapers themselves, look for paper wholesalers listed in the yellow pages under "Paper Products." Query suppliers of restaurant/butcher wrappings as well as newspaper suppliers.

Shredded paper also may be a packing option. Look under "Paper Shredding" in the yellow pages or ask local government and business offices what they do with theirs.

Padding. Hoard any covers or blankets you don't mind tearing to serve as padding for large furniture pieces. Ask friends and relatives if they have any of these things they were thinking of giving away.

You can buy Bubble Pack and Plastic Popcorn from moving and packing retailers, but we don't recommend it because it's expensive and it pollutes the environment.

These retailers also sell wide corrugated wrapping material for padding, but this is not as easy to bend around corners as woven padding. Look for blankets and covers secondhand at a thrift shop.

Strapping/Banding. You can tie padding on with rope, tape it with sealing tape, or secure it with long bungee cords. If you've got numerous large pieces that need padding, you may want to get the bungees for speed and safety. These can be bought at a notion's wholesaler.

 Tip: Never tie, tape, or cord furniture without padding, as the tape can leave marks and the tape or rope can cut into the finish. Always use extra pieces of cardboard to insulate the furniture from the rope at the corners. If you're shipping something with fragile legs, nest a padded box inside the legs to brace them and use tape, not rope or cord, to secure the outer padding.

Plastic Bags. Get plastic bags in various sizes. If you're going to need them to protect against old newspaper ink, you'll need lots. If you're using clean newsprint, get a good supply anyway, as plastic bags are great for storing desk, drawer, and cupboard items plus holding mounting screws from furniture you disassemble. Once you've collected items in a bag, tuck a slip of paper identifying the contents into it. Tape it shut, then tape it inside the drawer or to the underside of the furniture so it will be handy when you unpack.

Labels. All labels should be the easily removable type, but never put them on polished furniture, anyway. Order labels with your name and new address and telephone number or a contact number, if you don't have a destination address yet.

Get small, self-stick, colored labels; tie-on labels; tape; twine; and fine-tipped, nonpermanent, black marking pens. Stock up on garage sale marking items at the same time. Packaging and office supply stores have a good variety of these products. Some of the larger moving companies include free labels with their estimator information packets.

Designate a label color for each room—for example, Kitchen= Yellow, Living Room—Red—so that boxes will be easy to place in the new home.

If you're using moving company boxes, just stick a colored label on the printed area and write next to it the room location, the contents, and any special instructions, such as "Fragile," "This Side Up," "Take It with Me." (See the "Take-It-with-Me Tote" section later in this chapter.) Tie-on labels (look for the elastic, slip-on ties) go on non-boxed items that can't have sticky labels.

Tools. An automatic, hand-held tape dispenser is invaluable when you're packing lots of boxes. Ditto a razor-point utility knife at unpacking time.

ORGANIZATION

General Guidelines

Pack and mark boxes with contents and room as you go, so that unpacking is easier. Except for wardrobe and dishpacks, boxes should be packed to weigh no more than forty pounds. Heavier boxes are difficult to manage and can burst open en route. If you're packing heavy items, weigh them on a bathroom scale to check as you go.

Work Assignments

Each family member should pack a different room. Children should be responsible for their own things as much as possible. Tape and label boxes for the younger ones, and show them how to pack heaviest items in the bottom. Often children are excellent helpers who can help pack adults' clothes and household soft goods in other parts of the house.

Pacing Yourself

Do one area at a time. That way, you and your fellow packers will all have manageable, one-evening-at-a-time projects.

If you're having a weekend moving party, calculate how many boxes you'll be packing, then figure the number of helping hands to invite. According to the Atlas moving expert, Paul Evans, professional movers pack an average of four to ten boxes an hour, depending on whether they're working on unbreakables or on lamps or dishes. They estimate each worker can do fifty to sixty boxes a day. Don't expect you and your untrained helpers to do better than that, even when you're willing to work a longer day.

Priorities

Start cleaning, sorting, and packing from the back of closets and drawers. Work on a card table you can cart from room to room as you go. Tape a piece of plastic over it to protect from dirt and ink stains.

Clean everything out of each space, keep a large plastic bag for throwing away the hopeless stuff, and put the remainder in three containers—"Sale," "Shipping," and "Take-It-with-Me."

Don't get so absorbed in packing that you forget other duties. If you're selling and buying homes, check with your agents regularly to be sure both escrow timetables are moving according to schedule. (See the sample in Appendix B.) If you're renting, verify your move-out/move-in dates with both your landlords.

Check your Chapter 13 timetable for important items that may be overlooked. If you're moving out of or into a highrise, make elevator reservations. Make easy-to-execute appointments to give up your keys after you've got your things out and to get your keys before you arrive at your new home.

Box Preparation

Tape the box bottom seam and sides. Your unpacking will go better if you mix different types of things from a single room rather than trying to put all the curtains in the same box. Label boxes on all four sides plus top and bottom with room, general contents, and special shipper notations. Your name and contact information only needs to go on one side.

Except for boxes holding soft goods, cushion every box with three or four inches of crumpled newspaper and a layer of clean newsprint. Place the heaviest items in next, surrounded snugly with crushed newsprint. Cushion between layers with more newsprint, and use a cardboard separator to make a flat surface.

Next do a layer of lighter items. Pack the top with another layer of cushioning that pushes against the lid as you close. When taped shut, the box should feel firm on all sides and should not bulge.

Self-Packing Containers

Use all container furniture—chests, drawers, hampers, the insides of any large appliances—to pack light, fragile items with sheets, clothes, and other soft goods. Then blanket and band the container. Never pack furniture with heavy, durable items, because tools, statues, bookends, and the like can break through furniture walls or pull a washing machine drum off its mounting.

If you're moving yourself, you may need to take the drawers or contents out of heavy armoires and chests before you start moving it downstairs and into the truck. Blanket the frame before carting to truck. On the truck, unblanket, replace the drawers, and then reblanket to protect it en route.

Heavy Items

Never pack breakables with heavy durables, such as tools, statues, or clocks. No matter how much packing materials or towels you put between them, the breakables get crushed. Use small boxes, otherwise they will be too heavy to work with. The general rule is, the heavier the item, the smaller the box.

Tools

Pack tools in their own carrying cases or inside a plastic bag with soft goods. As long as the soft goods won't get dirty, it's better to have boxes with a couple of heavy items packed at the bottom and light soft goods at the top. Be sure to rubber-band electrical cords, so they don't tangle.

If it's not too bulky, take the loaded tool box with you in the car, as this knocks weight off your load, and it will come in handy in the new house before the furniture arrives.

Breakables

Wrap fragile items in several sheets of cloth or paper. If you're doing plates or other articles all the same size, wrap them individually, nest three to five together for extra support, then wrap the bundle as a separate package before placing it in the box.

Save fragile items such as cups and glasses for top layers in dish boxes. They should be wrapped, nested, bundle-wrapped, and stacked rim side down. Crystal should be on the very top and wrapped individually in tissue paper—newsprint is too stiff.

Be sure to mark all dish and other breakable item boxes with "Fragile" and "This Side Up."

Flat Items

Pack dishes, records, and other flat items standing on their edge, as this distributes the weight better. Pack the bottom of the box with crumpled paper, and place a row of individually wrapped large platters and plates all the way across. Put in another layer of crumpled paper on top and then a cardboard separator. Repeat the same process with smaller plates on the next layer. All the plates should be standing vertically—large plates on the bottom, small plates on top—and if there's room, do another layer with cups. Cups should be packed standing on their rims.

Also pack books on edge. Alternate the spines, one facing up, one facing down. Stuff popcorn or newsprint into excess spaces to keep books from shifting. For shipping via third-class mail, books should be packed in small boxes by themselves.

As we mentioned, third class used to be the cheapest way to ship books, but now, with rising postage rates, you should investigate UPS and other alternative shippers. If you're moving long distance, it may be cheaper, but with short-distance moves, it may be more economical to ship these boxes with the moving company. Look into each option to see what's best for you.

Telephone Books

Telephone books need to be available as much as possible during the moving process. Take both your existing books and the destination books you've already obtained with you if you can. Otherwise, consider shipping them express or pack them in a well-marked carton that you can unpack early.

The new book will be important from your first day in your new home. The old book will be vital if your home hasn't sold and you have business to tend to. Or if school transcripts, doctors' records, and the like turn up missing a crucial page or signature. Or if you need to get in touch with neighbors who aren't in your personal address book.

Clocks

Pendulum clocks need to be disassembled and the weights packed separately. Heavy and antique clocks need very sturdy packing and are better crated. If you're unfamiliar with how to disassemble them, ask a specialist.

Clothing

Wardrobe boxes hold two feet of hanging clothes. Pack them with all hangers facing the same way and fairly tightly, so they wrinkle less. These boxes are wonderful for speedy packing and unpacking, but typically weigh over seventy pounds and are bulky to get on and off the truck.

Drapes and Curtains

We never seem to get the same size windows from one home to the next, so we leave current window *dressings* behind, and ask the owner of the next house to do the same. If you take them, try to have them cleaned the month before you move, then leave them on the hanger in the dry cleaning bag and pack them in with the clothes in the wardrobe box.

Carpets

Have these cleaned the month before as well, and ship in the dry cleaning bag.

Large Appliances

We don't recommend carting refrigerators and washer/dryers with you. Not only are they heavy to transport, often they don't fit or operate properly in the new location.

Tip: Be particularly careful about appliances requiring natural or LP gas or 220 volt hookup. American electrical appliances usually don't work abroad. You can use transformers and adapters for some electrical appliances, but they never work well. Razors and hair dryers, for example, always short out. One of our U.S. survey respondents living in England had the unpleasant experience with his American-made electric clipper that shorted out in the middle of a haircut.

If you just bought a luxury model appliance last year, and you *really* want to take it with you, contact the original vendor for shipping information, and how to block the motor and other movable parts with a brace. Your utility service may help with disconnect/connect procedures.

Small Appliances

Review their usefulness. If you haven't used an appliance in the last three months, sell it or give it away. Do not ship them abroad, as most don't work with overseas electrical services. If you are shipping, remember to brace movable parts and to fold up and rubber-band cords.

Electronic Equipment

The rules are the same as for small appliances, except that personal computers, CD players, and other digital equipment less than five years old may work abroad without problems. Check your user manual.

Tip: Computer floppy disks, music tapes, and other plastic items can be ruined in an uninsulated van on the road in summer heat. If this is a concern, talk to your mover about how to protect these articles and/or make other arrangements for shipping,

Before packing fragile equipment, remove any appendages, such as printer feeder trays, to pack separately. Brace and tape nonremovable items, such as record player arms. Place old disks inside disk drives to protect heads from bouncing. (Don't use disks that contain valuable information; a bouncing head can trash the information.)

Place each item inside a plastic bag before packing to prevent packing material dust from getting inside it. If you have original boxes and Styrofoam braces, use them; otherwise, use a box at least four inches larger all around than the item, put a layer of packing material in first, then the equipment. Place packing material gently into all the cracks and crannies. Cover with another layer of packing material, so that the item is well cushioned and the entire box is full, shut, taped, and marked.

Medicine and Food Containers

Use up all refrigerator foodstuffs ahead of time. With medicines and food staples, tape them shut and pack in plastic bags before wrapping and packing.

Plants

Again, we recommend not trying to ship plants. Moving companies *will not* ship except on local moves. If you're moving yourself and it's midwinter or midsummer, don't torture your green friends in an uninsulated vehicle. Try an air freight option.

If you're not going far and you're taking your plants with you, give the last watering at least twenty-four hours ahead of moving, Pack wet newspapers around the soil in the pot and tape it down to keep soil spillage to a minimum. Put them in a carefully marked "Load Last/Unload First" box.

If you have a valuable collection of plants to ship quite a distance, contact an insulated freight shipper or a packaging store. Many states and countries have restrictions on incoming plants because they may be invasive or harbor pests. Shippers should have these regulations on file, or contact your state agriculture agency.

VAN LOADING

Figure on at least three hours per 1,000 pounds as a goal time for yourself and your untrained helpers. The key job goes to the person inside the van, packing snugly with fragile articles on top. In estimating how long it's going to take and how many helpers you need, make certain you take into account the tricky stuff/ tricky location factors.

Carting your things onto the truck is tiring, and you'll need to take frequent breaks, even if you're used to working out. Take them . . . and while you're thinking sensibly, remember those health class admonishments advising you to crouch down when picking things up so that you use your leg muscles, not your back. Don't add a chiropractor's bill to the moving cost.

Moving is no longer the straight mule work it used to be. Do-it-yourself rental agencies will rent you dollies, hand trucks, and other helpful equipment, even if you're using a friend's van. Some trucks come with power-lift platforms and/or adjustable ramps that can be fed directly into the front door, eliminating the need of going up and down the porch stairs.

MY TAKE-IT-WITH-ME TOTE—A CHECKLIST

Must-Haves

All family members should each have their own prominently marked container for personal things they want with them on the moving trip. There also should be general containers where you include:

A money belt or money garter where you carry cash and credit cards to cover trip expenses. In a separate location, keep a coded list of credit cards and 800 numbers for reporting loss.

Your "Important Documents" accordion folder, which should contain:

The moving company binding estimate and any addenda, the order for service, and the bill of lading.

A certified check (needing your cosignature to cash) to pay movers if you haven't been able to arrange credit or credit card payment.

Travel tickets, reservations, passports and visas. School transcripts, insurance policies, doctors' records, all bank records, and other vital documentation.

Your "Neighborhood Information" folder, with articles and other research giving data that will make settling in easier and more fun.

Your personal telephone books for both old and new locations and both old and new city telephone books (if they're not too bulky).

Children's toys—a lovey friend and things to do on the trip. See "Avoiding the Kids' 'Are-We-There-Yet?' Dirge" later in this chapter

Pets' favorite toys, carrier, blanket, comb or brush, pooper scooper and Baggies, food and water dishes, food and can opener, and a supply of water. Unfamiliar water can cause problems for already stressed animals. Also, take paper towels and air freshener for accidents.

Always have any animal that is going to be let out of the car wear a collar or a harness that has *current* contact ID, and keep it on a leash.

Jewelry and other small valuables—questionable. Many movers will not ship small valuables (including such nonbreakable items as a stamp collection) with the furniture load. But there is always a danger of loss or theft if you take them with you on the road. Consider having them insured and shipped by air.

Traveling clothes and personal suitcase items, including enough for a few days after you arrive. Don't forget to include a first aid kit, any medicines or vitamins needed daily, and any current prescriptions, including eyeglass prescriptions. Somehow, in the rush of packing, our family always manages either to break or lose at least one pair of glasses.

If you're going to be on the road several days, or if you have some time at the new home before furniture arrives, take basic picnic supplies, including paper plates, cups and utensils, plastic bags, instant soup mixes, instant coffee or tea, and an electric coffee pot to heat water in.

Maybes

The following items may be too bulky to take with you. If so, consider purchasing them at your destination or shipping by air cargo or UPS ground if the bulk of your furniture won't be moved for a while. Your vacuum cleaner, mop and disinfectant, and some rudimentary tools to spruce up your new home before the furniture arrives. If you've planned some interior painting, wallpapering, or more extensive refurbishing, pack accordingly.

If it will take several days for the furniture to arrive, consider staying with friends or at a motel or hotel. Alternatively, take sleeping bags, rudimentary kitchen utensils, window coverings and thumbtacks, a telephone and a lamp or two. If you can squeeze in a card table, so much the better. If you're not shipping furniture until the house sells, plan to rent beds, chairs, and tables or pick some things up at a thrift shop or garage sale.

TRIP TIPS

Safety First

Traveling on strange roads, particularly in an unfamiliar rented vehicle, can wipe regular safety routines from our minds. Don't forget the following:

√ *Safety starts at home. Get your vehicle thoroughly inspected before you go. Be sure that tires are aligned and inflated properly, to help with fuel efficiency. If you're going to a colder climate, check antifreeze, oil weight, and snow tires or chains.*

√ *Have good maps of all the areas you're going through. If you're renting a vehicle, maps should be provided.*

√ *Plan your trip on the "beaten paths" rather than on isolated roads.*

√ *Check radio road reports periodically to avoid tie-ups. Never take small, backroad "shortcuts" late in the day or in stormy weather.*

√ *Be sure to wear your safety belts, including the lap belt, even with an air bag.*

√ Schedule to arrive at your stopovers before 5:00 p.m., so you're not maneuvering through other people's commutes and/or trying to read the map and find a motel after dark. If you have to drive long days, it's better to start in the pre-dawn dark than drive during the 5:00 p.m.-to-midnight peak accident hours.

√ When you park during the day, park in the shade to keep the car as cool as possible. When you park at night, park under a light to make the vehicle less vulnerable to thieves.

√ Lock your car, van, or truck doors at all times, including when you're in the vehicle. Be sure the trunk or back van door is always locked.

√ Don't pull over to help a stranded motorist. Call for help from the next telephone.

√ If your vehicle breaks down, pull over, put on the warning flashers, walk to the nearest telephone for help, then wait in a store where you can see the van or inside the vehicle itself until the garage repair person or the police arrive. Stay in your car and ask passing motorists to call for help rather than go off in their car with them.

√ If you're driving a van or truck, beware of low tree branches and overhanging signs.

√ When you go to your vehicle, don't unlock it until you've checked to be sure no one is in it.

Avoiding the Kids' "Are We There Yet?" Dirge

Traveling time passes slowly for a child. Get a travel game book, and have everybody pick one to play. Store up a surprise bag of fruit, crackers, and new puzzles, games, and coloring books to give out at certain hours. Make sure you have enough for every child to get the same item at the same time. Use a kitchen timer to provide fairness about sharing and/or announce "rest stop time."

Take card games and any board games with magnets or pegged pieces. Hand-held electronic games, personal radios, or stereos with headsets are a great way for everybody to "do their own thing." Take along talking books and old radio shows as well as music.

Older children should each get their own map, research the trip, and pick out a couple of interesting sights along the way, where you can stop and unwind for an hour or so. It's fun for everybody to switch seating, driver, and chief navigation officer duties.

Dr. Stevanne Auerbach, author of *The Toy Chest* and other parenting books, suggests encouraging a child to do a trip journal or picture book and to take along a pillow for each child to take naps.

Buy picnic food along the way and eat at picnic grounds, where pent-up energy can be released. Short hikes every once in a while are good ways to get a feel for the countryside you're traveling through. If the weather is bad, eat at food halls in large shopping centers, which usually have a covered play area nearby.

Before the movers arrive, vacuum and fix such things as broken electrical outlets that will be hard to reach after furniture is in place.

Go over your original furniture layout to confirm that everything will fit where you planned. Photocopy enough copies of the plan to have one taped to the doorway of each room, so that neither you nor the van people have a problem about which wall to place the breakfront against.

Finalize your arrangements to have pets and children out of the house while the movers are there. This is even more important if you're moving yourself, because your attention will be even more concentrated on the job at hand.

When the movers arrive at your new residence, go over items and the inventory form with the same diligence as you did when they left. If at all possible, have two people—one to direct where boxes and furniture go and one to check off items on the form. *Be sure that every item arrives.*

If you're having the movers unpack, watch carefully. You'll want to know if they're rough with boxes or if they drop the piano. When they're done, look over every item, and note any new dents, scratches, or rough treatment on the inventory form before signing. They should point out broken items they have found, and you may wish to photograph these.

 Tip: If the damage is small, ask the mover if the company will pay you now. It may prefer not to have a claim go against their company record.

If you're going to do the unpacking, check any piece of furniture where padding has slipped. Open any boxes that have been obviously crushed or damaged en route, observe any damage, and write it by the proper item number: "Item #34 received damaged. 7 broken china plates." Get the mover to initial this. If you've got a camera, take a picture of the problem.

Tip: *John Fristos, who headed the Interstate Commerce Commission Office of Compliance and Consumer Assistance when it was overseeing the household transportation industry, says that in the thirty-four year he worked with consumer complaints, the biggest problem in the industry was always unpaid damage and loss claims. He recommends inspecting the condition of your furniture, particularly valuable antiques, upon unloading. If you're not able to do that, it helps if you cross out the acknowledgment that "This is a true and complete list of the goods tendered and of the state of the goods received," on the inventory and write, "Subject to my final inspection of all items for concealed damage or loss" above your signature.*

Be sure that all copies of the inventory carry the same notations. Follow the procedures outlined in the next section on filing claims.

WHEN TO TIP

Movers are always being asked to do special favors for householders. They deserve a tip if they've driven extended periods to make your schedule; if they've kept your antique clock in the cab, so that it arrived in perfect condition; and especially if they've had to haul your 900 pound bowfronted chest of drawers through three rooms before you decided on its final resting place.

Let them know you appreciate their efforts. Tips in the neighborhood of $20 to $50 for the driver and $5 to $20 for the helpers are about right, depending on the service you've received.

UNPACKING AND CLAIMS
THAT GET RESULTS

We still haven't unpacked some boxes that were packed the move before last. This is not a recommended procedure, but we've never met anyone who succeeded in unpacking *everything* within the first month after arrival. Our major effort on arrival is to unpack major things so that the house is livable, then go after less essential things on a room-by-room basis.

 Tip: Consider disassembling the boxes, folding them flat, and keeping in the attic or garage for future use. The wardrobe containers may come in handy immediately for storing seasonal clothing. Or you may want to sell the boxes through an ad in the local advertiser.

Then there are always things that are destined for the back of closets and cupboards. Don't just shove them away. Even though you don't plan to use the china set till next Thanksgiving, you should open and go through any boxes with fragile items *within the first month after your arrival* to check for breakage.

If you find anything broken, photograph it and *leave it in the box, as is.* The moving company reserves the right to inspect the box and the way it was packed before recognizing a claim. ICC watchdog Fristos has advised that it helps to get a neighbor to testify as to having seen the problem in the box as soon after the move as possible.

Whether you noted damage on the mover's inventory or discovered it later, you have to get the claims forms from your moving company's destination office. Many companies allow you to file a claim on *inter*state, even without any notations on the inventory, for up to nine months from move-in day. If you were moving locally or *intra*state, you need to check local regulations.

File the pictures, forms, and other evidence with the local company, but be sure to *keep a copy yourself.* Include as much premove evidence—pictures, appraisals, purchase receipts— as possible. If you're filing a claim on an item you packed, you do best when the box was obviously crushed (another picture here) or you observed rough handling and noted it on the inventory form.

The company should give you a written response to your claim within 30 days and pay, deny, or make an adjusted offer to you within 120 days of filing. The van line should give a copy of a booklet, "Household Goods Dispute Settlement Program," when it gives you an estimate on an interstate move, and the company also will send you the forms for appeal upon request.

If you find you are not getting any satisfaction on a claim and the item was valuable enough to make it worthwhile, most moving company contracts allow you sue or take a complaint to Small Claims Court. Otherwise, you may want to contact the American Movers Conference at (703) 706-4978 or on the website at www.moving.org, for arbitration. Although this is industry-sponsored service is fairly new and untried, it is operated on an independent basis. For intrastate and local moves, look for the state transport or public utilities office. You also can contact the Better Business Bureau in regards to unethical practices.

TWELVE

Settling In

FIVE CALLS YOU ABSOLUTELY MUST MAKE WITHIN TWENTY-FOUR HOURS OF MOVING IN

Practically everybody we've talked to feels wiped out the morning after the movers leave. Often there's been a kink in arrangements—the electricity or telephone hasn't been turned on, the refrigerator got lost in transit, or whatever. But the reason for the big blah's is emotional. "Home" suddenly seems so intensely unfamiliar.

After turning on the utilities, make time to get connected with your new community. Prime the emotional pump. Build energy and enthusiasm and reach out with these first five calls to build your new buddy system.

Friend or Relative

We like to start with a no-risk call to someone who's been recommended by my fifth cousin. Unlike a work colleague or a neighbor, it won't matter if we break some social code we're unaware of.

Call, introduce yourself, explain you just moved in, and ask for information about where to get something newcomers need. A quest for a discount food or home remodeling store is a good ice breaker. If the contact is friendly, you'll be at the person's house for dinner tonight. If not, at least you'll have gotten a start on neighborhood orientation.

Church/Club or Charity

Call the main office and ask when the next meeting will be and to be put on the mailing list. Ask if there are informal get-togethers or committee meetings you can attend before the next meeting.

Kids' Club/Friend

Call contacts and ask about meeting dates and chauffeuring arrangements. Offer to help with anything the neighborhood needs, as this is a great way to make friends and get your bearings at the same time.

Family Activity

Take a break from arranging furniture and make reservations for some leisure activity this next weekend. Find ideas in the "Neighborhood Information" folder, which you assembled before your move. Pick out something that will be fun to do together. Try for an activity that's very different from what you've done in your old neighborhood—an ethnic festival, a river kayaking trip, a day at a theme park. Taking a tourist tour of your new hometown can be lots of fun.

Sports Facilities/Classes

Again, your "Neighborhood Folder" should have information on these activities. Pick something that will have you involved with your new neighbors in a joint activity on a regular basis.

CHILD CUSTOMIZING FROM DAY ONE

Your child's new room can be both a thrill and a terror to her. If she's happy planning her new nest, let her do her own unpacking and putting away. It doesn't matter how long it takes, so long as she puts her own stamp on each item.

If she's not happy with the move, share the unpacking with her. You do the pulling out of boxes, and let her do most of the putting away. If she seems to get tired, ask for her help with another room, and finish up her things later. She may need time for assimilation.

Tip: Dr. Stevanne Auerbach, child psychologist and expert on how children play, suggests that a child may enjoy having a photograph or drawing of her old room, either to help decorate the new one the same way or to have as a reminder.

It's important to clean a new house when you're moving in with young children. Even if the place is brand new, you'll want to take disinfectant to floors, handles, and other objects likely to be in baby's hands just before thumb-sucking time.

Be sure there are no dangerous chemicals or objects within a child's reach. White powder in corners or underneath sinks is suspicious. The previous owner may have mounted a poison attack on insects or rodents.

Put dummy plugs in electrical outlets and latches on cupboard doors. Make sure no door automatically locks as it shuts. Deactivate bathroom and bedroom locks that are easy to engage, leaving your unhappy child inadvertently locked in.

As soon as the furniture is in, put up stair gates and any other barriers needed to fence off "forbidden territory."

The yard and garage should be checked as well as the house. Even if your child doesn't play unattended very often, these areas are likely hideouts for forgotten paints, cleaners, weed killers, and sharp tools.

Have your child help in your danger-proofing efforts. Explain that you're doing all these things so no one in the family gets hurt. Emphasize that your efforts are for everybody, not just the kids. She'll enjoy being included as a guardian of the family's welfare, and if she finds dangerous articles on her own later, she'll point them out to you.

Megan Walker, one of our most articulate survey respondents, advises posting area emergency numbers near the phone the first day. Walk through the house with the children exploring nooks and crannies and secret places, and at the same time make sure everybody knows how to get out if there's a fire.

If you've moved to a country where water is suspect, explain cautions. Getting accustomed to prohibitions on water direct from the tap and always peeling fruit before eating may come as a surprise to children.

Have your child memorize her new address and phone number, and give her a card with this information to carry in her pocket. Include your work phone number and the number of a neighborhood friend, and help her memorize these as well.

Give her her own photocopy map of the local area to carry. Highlight your location on it. Make a game of remembering not only the street address but the names of cross streets and large streets nearby.

Teach a child to ask a store clerk for directions if she gets lost rather than stopping anyone—either adult or child—on the street. Better still, she should go to the nearest street corner to find out where she is, then call you collect on a pay telephone.

PET CUSTOMIZING TOO

Besides diffusing all of the preceding dangerous items for your pet, be sure to take time to set up her living area with familiar things and play with her in several different places both inside and outside the home. If she's going to be allowed to roam the neighborhood, don't let her go for at least two weeks. It's best to take her on little forays on a leash with you before you turn her loose. She'll need time to accustom herself to the smell and location of her new home.

AND THE FUN PART... CUSTOMIZING FOR YOU

The first week often is spent with bare-bones furniture while you wait for your stuff to arrive or find where to buy new things. Be sure to put up blinds and group whatever furniture bits and pieces you brought with you into a comfortable living area. If it's going to be a while before your things arrive, consider renting furniture or buying pieces from a thrift shop or from ads in the paper.

You should know how to turn gas, water, and electrical services off at the main switch, in case of a problem. Test water sprinklers and fireplaces even if it's not the right season.

Make sure that any gas equipment needing ventilation—heaters or hot water heaters—is vented properly to the outside. Carbon monoxide poisoning can be a real danger to your family and pets.

Try out hot and cold controls on showers—it's amazing how often they turn out to be backward from your old system. This is not a experiment you want to conduct while you or your child is in the shower, rapidly turning into a lobster.

We love to go shopping the first weekend to find a special rug or tablecloth or other item to fit the style of our new home. On our last move to California, we found a local glassblower who created a unique front hall vase for us.

Another project to get in hand as soon as possible is gardening. Nothing brings you closer to your new home than getting new seedlings to grow, even if your first efforts are limited to one flower box.

A BASIC KITCHEN STARTER KIT

Set up a working kitchen ASAP. Buy nonperishable staples: spices and condiments, cereal, and canned goods. Don't feel that you have to do a week's worth of shopping. That can be done later when you know more about which supermarkets are the good ones. However, you should pick up little extras, such as instant biscuits, or a fancy dessert, or a quick way to make the first meal emotionally satisfying.

Moving does take a lot out of you physically, so having vitamins, fruit that won't spoil quickly, like oranges and apples, or dried fruit, around for snacks, is a good idea. Getting used to your new kitchen may take a while, so have something on hand to quiet those hungry mouths while you're looking for the pilot light.

Dishes and Cookware

A shared meal makes for a good friendships. We like to have enough dishes, glasses, cups, and flatware to invite a couple of new friends and neighbors over for a spaghetti dinner or enough paper and plastic things to do a backyard wienie roast.

BARGAIN HUNTING

No matter how many of your things you're shipping, you'll need to get the lay of the shopping land quickly. Even if your new neighborhood is already familiar to you, ask your new neighbors where to shop. They may have horror stories about the supermarket you thought you'd use, or wonderful information about a small farmer's market that's open only one or two days a week. They're also likely to have tips on local discount outlets and the timing of big sales. Besides, asking advice pulls you into the friendship circle. Go through your "Neighborhood Folder" for snippets on this information and check bookstores for area bargain-hunting books too.

Most communities now have some of the national chain discounters and "big box" superstores. You may find these in newspapers and the yellow pages, but it's important to ask your contacts and neighbors. Sometimes these outlets are so well known, they don't advertise. If they're located in a community that's close but still outside your telephone book area, you may not find out about them unless you ask.

Catalogs

Another way to get good prices is to get on discount catalog mailing lists. Here are a few:

- √ *Book Passage, (800) 321-9785. Travel and language books.*
- √ *Catalogs, (561) 997-1221; 951 Broken Sound Parkway NW, Building 190, P.O. Box 5057, Boca Eaton, FL 33431-0857. This is a catalog of catalogs, including stained glass windows, antique clocks, and carpentry tools.*
- √ *Damark, (800) 827-6767. Don't go for its membership club; the basic catalog is just as good for closeouts on computers, home and office accessories, furnishings.*
- √ *Quill, 100 Schelter Road, Lincolnshire, IL 60069-3621, (909) 988-3200. Office products.*
- √ *J.C. Whitney & Co., 1917-19 Archer Avenue, P.O. Box 8410, Chicago, IL 60680 (312) 431-6102. Automotive parts and accessories.*

CHILD'S SCHOOL

Starting a new school presents more challenges and more personal risks than starting a new job. Even if you've moved halfway around the globe to take a new position, you know if it doesn't work out in six months, you can look for something else. You've changed jobs before, and you can do it again.

Your child is going into an environment she'll have no choice but to master. Although you may be able to arrange another school if this one doesn't work, she is not in control of this decision. Remember, her experience of dealing with change is less than yours. In her perspective, her new school is the world, and a year is forever.

Share your thoughts and feelings about your new life. Let her know you feel both exhilarated and fearful. Play storytelling games where you each describe the most wonderful and most awful new school and new job.

Get a list of other classmates and their parents' names and telephone numbers from the school as soon as possible. If your child already has started making friends, call their parents and see if you can chaperone a weekend trip to the zoo or some sports outing. If not, ask the teacher which children would be likely matches. Get the names of kids living near you who share your child's interests and activities.

Many schools assign a buddy to newcomers. Particularly in kindergarten, teachers make a point of helping children get to know each other.

Make a point to volunteer for parent/teacher assistant duties early, and ask the teacher for guidelines as to how often and how much other parents participate. The last thing your child wants is to be perceived as overly protected.

Teenagers, of course, are fanatic about independence issues. Overt gestures on your part to help find friends may be rejected out of hand. If they liked their old school and their friends there were an important part of their emerging sell they are likely to be resentful and resistant to the new school.

Let them and the school know you're willing to volunteer. Make an area of the house a good place for teenagers to hang out. Don't lose your cool if you *still* get told you're doing everything all wrong. Teenagers need both your support and your flexibility in trying new ways to live together.

Tip: Often times people move because of significant life changes. Jennifer VanDeWater, our assistant in putting this book together, told us how she moved to a new town at the age of twelve, when her father remarried. She had mixed feelings about the move. She missed her old friends, but she liked the chance to start over and make new ones. She was moving out of the town where her mother lived and into a home with new brothers and sisters.

Jennifer's father helped the family cope by organizing weekly meetings, where they became aware of how others were feeling and vented frustrations. Everyone talked openly about problems, and she appreciated her father's involvement.

In school, she preferred to make friends without the help of family members. She joined extracurricular activities, such as plays and dance committees, and felt free to grow into a different kind of person from what she had been in the old school.

When to Worry

Although a few children settle in quickly, for most—particularly teenagers—it takes time. Dr. Stevanne Auerbach, director at the Institute for Childhood Resources and author of *The Whole Child* and other books for parents, reassures us that most children will make the adjustment and find new friends, but we need to follow their progress. "Good communication and understanding what the child is feeling are especially important before and after the move," she emphasizes. "Make it a point to have private talks about how things are going. Be sure to listen to the child carefully."

If a young, toilet-trained child has occasional relapses, not to worry. Let her know that this is natural and to be expected in times of big changes, says Dr. Auerbach. If it persists, your child's pediatrician can offer help on what you may be able to do to assist the child.

The major symptoms of overwhelming stress are consistent unhappiness and/or a significant physical or personality change. You should be particularly concerned if unusual sleeplessness and/or inability to eat goes on for more than a week. Watch especially for the following emotional symptoms that continue for more than a month:

√ *The child is sullen, easily upset, persistently angry, or unnaturally quiet or shy.*
√ *She is unwilling or unable to focus on doing things she previously enjoyed.*
√ *She unrelentingly "hates school," is unable to do homework, and teachers report problems in the schoolroom.*

If there is no easing of these symptoms, consult with a child specialist, either at the school or privately, for additional help. "The child may need someone to talk to about her feelings at leaving," says Dr. Auerbach. "It may be easier to express the turmoil to a neutral person who is not invested in the move."

YOUR NEW JOB

Your new office also will present crucial challenges. You're walking into an unmarked battlefield, where smiles may mask resentment or fear and helpful hints can blow up into political infighting.

The first six months is a time when expectations are created, relationships formed, changes planned. You're in a period of glaring expectations with precious few guidelines.

Here are suggestions and observations collected from some of the IIP Frequent Mover Survey respondents and from *The Executive Female*, the publication for the National Association of Female Executives.

Build Knowledge

This is a two-lane highway. You need to 'get to know the organization and the people you're working with, and they need to get to know you. Most companies expect a round robin of one-on-one interviews with your superiors and colleagues. Don't make this a time for checking out office gossip or a meaningless flurry of "whistlestop" handshakes. It's your opportunity to set your course. Ask about:

√ The overall picture—both the good things that are happening and changes that are planned.

√ Your predecessor—her successes and problems, and how you can shoulder her load and help tackle things that need to be done.

√ Current priorities and projects you're assigned to, and how they interact with others' assignments.

√ Corporate culture.

Your new company may not set up these orientation interviews for you, have a "Let's go to lunch" ritual, or even give you a welcome at your first staff meeting. If it doesn't, mount your own "Lunch today?" and "Have you got time to give me a fifteen-minute 'how-to?'" initiatives. Try to contact as many people as possible, including those outside your department, and even customers and suppliers.

Build Commitment

Ceri Evans and John Por, management consultants interviewed by *Executive Female.*, recommend that once the knowledge-building phase is in hand, new supervisors should move into the commitment-building phase. Work with your team to come up with an action plan. "Creating an agenda that is as specific as possible—a virtual blueprint of what people will be expected to do—will help solidify commitment."

Take Action

Evans and Por advise carrying out your changes quickly and decisively. Donna Hansen, speaking from her experience as the Fort Myers, Florida, police chief, says that you need to get the lay of the land from both those who've been there and those who've recently joined. The best advice she got? "Go with your own style."

YOUR NEW LOCAL TELEPHONE BOOK

If you haven't gotten a new personal telephone book yet, get one now. Look for one that you can distinguish easily from your old one, and start entering your new friends and contacts.

> *Tip: This is a great time to try one of the pocket electronic organizers or put your personal telephone book on disk with software. In addition to the sleek Palm Pilot, Clyde recommends the Sharp or Casio electronic organizers, because you can send the contact and appointment information to your computer to print it out.*

The first few weeks after you've moved, you'll have to devote a major part of your time to unpacking, setting up the household, and getting out to know your new community. Still, it's important to be sure your new personal life "support staff" is in place, so that, if you suddenly have an emergency, you can immediately call a plumber or a doctor or your car insurance agent or whatever.

Go over your "Change-of-Address Checklist" to get names, addresses, and numbers that you've already researched. If you're missing any of the vital ones under personal consultants, utilities, money matters, or insurance, contact your new friends and colleagues for suggestions. Make it a goal to have these blanks filled in within your first thirty days in your new home.

THE HOUSEWARMING PARTY

If you're moving into a new development or a very friendly community that has a tradition of throwing housewarming parties for newcomers, sit back and enjoy the fuss.

If not, Miss Manners won't come and whack you for hosting your own housewarming. The hard part is filling oat the list of whom to invite, since you may not know many people by last name, much less by address.

Bobble Sakkema, enthusiastic and energetic founder of Events, Etc., a party planning group, advises a keep-it-simple strategy.

"I've known lots of people who wanted to have a housewarming, but they kept putting it off, thinking they should finish the interior decorating or the garden or something else to make their new place perfect. It's better to just jump in with something easy—maybe even before the furniture arrives. Doing an informal champagne 'Getting to Know Everybody' couple of hours can be lots of fun and budget effective. Make up some invitations and drop them off to neighbors and work colleagues."

Kathryn Rudman, a genius at theme parties with an eclectic guest list, who recently moved from an inner-city location to a small, upscale suburb, recommends taking an entirely different tack.

"We thought about having a housewarming, then didn't, and I'm glad. We've got small children, and we want to make friends with parents of other kids the same age. We've gotten to know other parents though children's activities and play groups we found through notices at the library and in the local weekly newspaper. Then we've done potlucks and projects with the kids."

However you decide to plan it, have fun, and be open to friendship opportunities. It's the best part of settling in.

THIRTEEN

Your Countdown
Moving Timetable:
What to Do When

TWENTY-FOUR TO TWELVE MONTHS
IN ADVANCE

If you're considering relocating or establishing a business in a new location, start researching the economic opportunities in possible locations as well as investigating whether you'll like living there. Read through Chapter 1.

If you're moving abroad, apply for passports for the entire family. Contact the destination country consulate and apply for any visas or other documentation needed. Find but what inoculations will be necessary. See "Contacts and Resources" (Appendix C) for alternative move lead sources and "Overseas Options" in Chapter 7.

If you're moving to the United States for the first time, contact the nearest U.S. consulate for a visa long before your planned trip. If you're going to be working in the United States, your company also will have to file permit documentation.

Set up a Decision Day deadline for making a commitment to the move and selecting a destination.

SIX TO TWELVE MONTHS IN ADVANCE

Research possible destinations, and rank them in the "City Evaluator" from Appendix A. See Chapter 1, which deals with site selection and city evaluation. Review the "Job Change/Transfer Deductions" and "Homeowner's Moving Deductions" summaries in Appendix D to see if there are any deadlines that will make a difference in your move scheduling. Read Chapter 4 and have a strategy meeting with your tax advisor.

FIVE TO SIX MONTHS IN ADVANCE

Investigate trial moves and other alternatives described in Chapter 3. Attend conferences or take a vacation in your target location(s).

Subscribe to destination location newspapers, real estate photo advertisers, and professional newsletters. Review the "Contacts and Resources" directory in Appendix C.

Work up the numbers on the "Monthly Budget Estimator" in Appendix D for your target location(s). See "Budgeting Your New Location" in Chapter 1.

Bring the whole family together to talk about the move. See "Psyching Up the Whole Family for Change" in Chapter 2.

Make the final decision on whether to move and select your target location.

Start the other family member job search in the new location. Read through "Long Distance Job-Hunt Strategies" in Chapter 5.

Obtain maps of destination location(s) and start asking contacts about neighborhood selections. See Chapter 7 for "The Three Maps You Absolutely Must Have."

Contact destination authorities for any restrictions on your bringing pets or plants there.

Decide if you will take your pet with you. If not, start finding a new home for her. Taking a pet means familiarizing her with riding in a car, walking on a leash, and thinking of a travel carrier as her "portable home." Make only short trips at first. Give your animal(s) lots of love and affection at the end of each ride. Your pet(s) will travel better with practice, even if they'll be flying. See "Of Pets and Pitfalls" in Chapter 2 and "Pack Kids and Pets First" in Chapter 11.

THREE TO FOUR MONTHS IN ADVANCE

Decide on a range of Moving Day dates. Start interviewing moving and alternative shipping companies and fill in the "Moving Company/Options Evaluator" in Appendix A. Set appointments with their estimators. See "Moving Company Profiles" and "Selection Interviewing Tips" in Chapter 10.

Talk with children's school advisors and activity leaders about the move and get suggestions about destination schools, classes, and activities.

Check destination school schedules and enrollment requirements.

If you are being transferred or hired by a company, negotiate with human resources for company relocation benefits. See "Negotiating Your Best Deal with Your Employer" in Chapter 5.

Follow up on alternative move responses, and decide which, if any, you're going to take. See Chapter 3 and "Alternative Move Lead Sources" in Appendix C.

Interview real estate agents using the "Seller's Real Estate Agent Evaluator" in Appendix A. Select one to list your home. Ask the agent about average number of days on the market and estimated amount of time for escrow to close, so that you can determine if you need to arrange for interim housing. See "Points to Cover When Interviewing Prospective Agents" in Chapter 6.

Contact a credit bureau to get a copy of your credit report. Review and notify the bureau if there's any inaccurate information. See "Credit Record Redux" in Chapter 9.

Call lenders and mortgage brokers advertising in destination newspapers. Interview them using the "Loan Evaluator" from Appendix A. Decide on a program that works for you, apply, and have your loan advisor send you a pre-qualification commitment letter. Read "Mounting a No-Fear Attack on Financing" in Chapter 8.

Decide on your new home price and area. Go over the family's "Home" and "Neighborhood" evaluators to be sure everyone agrees on priorities. See "Dollar Basics—Deciding What to Spend" and "Determining Market Value" in Chapter 7, and read through Chapter 9.

Telephone realty or rental agents in your destination. Interview them using the "Buyer's Real Estate Agent Evaluator" in Appendix A. Decide if you want to work with several real estate agents or exclusively with a buyer's agent. See Chapter 8.

Review your current home's marketing progress with your listing agent. When you accept a purchase offer, fill in the sale "Escrow Timetable and Checklist" from Appendix B. See "The Escrow Timetable—Avoiding Last Minute Surprises" in Chapter 6.

Start calling packing material sources for prices. Start collecting boxes. See Chapter 11 and Appendix C.

TWO TO THREE MONTHS IN ADVANCE

Do your homehunting trip(s). Select your new home. Read through Chapters 7 and 9.

If you're buying, negotiate price and terms and set the closing date. Arrange for inspections. Review documents. Make sure your sale contract on your existing home is solid prior to committing to buy another. See Chapter 9 for "Buyer's Follow-Up Strategies."

As soon as you're in contract to buy a new home, fill in a second "Escrow Timetable and Checklist" (Appendix B) on your purchase transaction to be sure you don't miss any deadlines on either transaction.

If you're renting, make an application and reserve a move-in date. See "Renter's Follow-up Strategies" in Chapter 9.

Be sure to reserve elevator service if your new home is in a highrise building.

As soon as you have a new destination address, order address labels and fill in the "Change-of-Address Checklist" from Appendix B. When the labels arrive, use them on the Change-of-Address postcards you get from the post office. See "Letting People Know" in Chapter 7.

Fill in the "Steiners Furniture Checklist" from Appendix B. Decide which pieces will go with you, which will be sold or given away, and which are "maybe's." Check to be sure that large pieces will fit in the new location, color schemes will work, and appliances will operate. Read through Chapter 10.

Sell expensive items you've decided against taking with you in newspaper classifieds.

Contact your tax advisor to obtain copies of all tax documents you'll need to take with you and obtain possible accountant referrals for your destination. See Chapter 4 and Appendix D.

If you're doing a trial move, decide whether you want to forward all mail or maintain a mail drop in your existing hometown.

Use Appendix C and publications from the destination area to research children's activities there. Get suggestions from teachers and others and see if any pen pal correspondence can be initiated.

ONE TO TWO MONTHS IN ADVANCE

Notify your landlord that you're moving. Set a date to go over the "Renter's Move-in/Move-out Property Condition Checklist" (Appendix B) and receive your deposit refund. See "Dealing with the Leviathan Landlord" in Chapter 6.

Have carpets and drapes cleaned. Keep them in the dry cleaner's bags for shipping.

Go over the floor plan of your new home. Determine how your present furniture will fit, and make up your final list of the things you'll be moving. Read "Deciding What to Leave Behind" in Chapter 10.

Set family doctor's appointments and obtain medical records. Get referrals to destination health facilities. See also "Health Hurdles" in Chapter 2.

Take pet(s) to the veterinarian for inoculations, health records, health certificates, tattooing, and registration. Discuss destination area and needs for new inoculations and/or medicine. Get referrals. Read "Of Pets and Pitfalls" in Chapter 2.

Contact the Motor Vehicle Bureau in your new location, and obtain forms for new driver's license and vehicle registration. Find out if there are any special restrictions, and if your vehicle might need retrofitting in the new location. See "Cutting Vehicle Red Tape" in Chapter 8.

Have children mark up their own photocopies of maps of the moving trip route you're going to take and research locations that will make for good rest stops or mini-vacations along the way.

Make reservations for travel and any overnight stays en route. If you need pet accommodations, make sure these are possible.

Make reservations for people, pets, or items flying separately from the rest of the family to the new location.

Contact insurance agents to arrange for coverage of your new home and contents and automobile as per your "Change-of-Address Checklist" in Appendix B.

Select a bank in your new location, establish accounts, and obtain a safety deposit box. Set up charge accounts with new local merchants. Do not close old accounts until your new credit is established. Leave enough in the old checking account to cover moving and at least two weeks' living expenses.

ONE MONTH IN ADVANCE

If you still have not found a new home, rent a mail box for mail forwarding. See "The One-Week Home-Hunting Blitz Trip" in Chapter 9.

Contact utility companies and delivery services such as newspapers and diaper laundry on your "Change-of-Address Checklist" in Appendix B with information regarding turn-off/turn-on dates. Obtain any "perfect payment" utility records, and make arrangements for any refunds or deposits. You don't want to be stuck in your new home with no lights or telephone.

If you've been leasing your telephone, take it back to the company, get your deposit back, and buy a phone for your new residence.

Set your moving date with the moving company or van rental agency. Ship items going via a separate service. Make arrangements for your car to be transported if you're taking it but not driving it yourself. See "Alternate Shipping Possibilities" in Chapter 10.

Reverify your "Escrow Timetable and Checklist" (Appendix B) and your move-out/move-in schedules with real estate agents or landlords. If problems exist, arrange for interim housing.

Set up appointments with real estate agents and/or landlords to hand over the keys to your current residence and to obtain keys to your new home. Try to get new home keys prior to arrival, so that—whether you run into moving trip delays or you arrive early—you still can get into your new home without a problem.

Hold your garage sale and/or give away everything you no longer need.

TWO WEEKS IN ADVANCE

Have moving-away parties or get-togethers with a few friends at a time.

Take your children around to say goodbye to friends. Have them make arrangements to stay in touch and get together again during the next summer vacation. Read through "Anticipating Children's Concerns" in Chapter 2.

Finish the packing except final items you'll need for day-to-day living until Moving Day. See "Packing Strategies" in Chapter 11.

If you're doing your own packing, go over your "Steiners Furniture Checklist" (Appendix B). Coordinate with the number and types of boxes you've assembled to be sure there's enough. Doublecheck that you have the bracing needed for the movable parts in pendulum clocks, computers, and appliances. See "Organization" in Chapter 11.

Reconfirm dates for packing, pickup, and delivery with your mover or vehicle rental agency. Make sure packing party friends and/or professional helpers will be on hand for Moving Day.

Settle any outstanding bills. Take all books back to the library.

Arrange for hazardous waste pickup of old paint cans, cleaners, oil and gas drained from your power equipment. Burn off any excess fuel in barbecue equipment. See the "Household Hazardous Waste Checklist" in Appendix B.

Take any plants and/or pets you can't take with you to their new homes.

Arrange for a Moving Day sitter for your kids and any pets going with you.

Have car serviced. If you are having car shipped via a "drive-away" service, be sure the operations manual is in the glove compartment and stick a label with your new address and telephone number under the dashboard.

MOVING WEEK

Arrange for traveler's checks for trip expenses and—if necessary—a certified bank check that you cosign when you pay the movers.

Finish packing your "Take-It-with-Me Tote" for each member of the family. See that section in Chapter 11.

Empty your freezer, clean it, and dry it out. Give or throw away any perishable food you won't eat in the next few days.

Disconnect all appliances and brace moving parts. Box anything you're packing yourself. If you're using any appliances as containers, pack them with lightweight items. Read "Packing Strategies" and "Organization" in Chapter 11.

Use only necessary household items, such as towels, sheets, pans, a coffee pot, and a few tools. Everything else should be packed. Take advantage of paper plates and disposable utensils.

If you're doing a home trade, fill in the "Home Trade Move-in/Move-Out Checklist" from Appendix B. Read through Chapter 3.

MOVING DAY

Take the kids and pets to a sitter. Reassure children that you *will* be back to pick them up.

Hold a packing and loading party, if you're not using movers. Meet the movers, review forms, and oversee the inventory list, packing, and loading.

Before the movers leave, check through the house with the driver to make sure nothing was missed. Remember to check the attic, basement, closets, cupboards, and drawers. See "Van Loading" in Chapter 11.

After movers leave, meet landlord, review the checkout form, and either receive a refund or a "Landlord/Tenant Move-Out Deposit Refund Agreement." (See sample in Appendix E.) Turn over your keys.

Read through "Pack Kids and Pets First," "My Take-It-with-Me-Tote—a Checklist," and "Trip Tips" in Chapter 11.

If you've sold your home, meet the real estate agent or buyers and turn over the keys and any other necessary items, such as the garage door opener.

Stay overnight in a hotel or with friends or family so you can start your moving trip fresh.

ARRIVAL DAY

Try to schedule one day to prepare your new home prior to bringing in furniture, even if you've driven your furniture yourself in a rental van.

Clean the new house and use disinfectant in the kitchen and bath. Vacuum the rooms before movers arrive. If you're allergic to animals and there was a pet there previously, have a professional cleaning company come in and give the place an antiallergy treatment. Read through Chapter 12.

Change locks, make repairs, do child- and pet-proofing. See "Child Customizing From Day 1" and "Pet Customizing Too" in Chapter 12.

Arrange for any help you need in unloading van.

Arrange for sitter for children and pets for Move-in Day.

MOVE-IN DAY

Take children and pets to stay with a sitter while furniture is being moved around.

If movers are unloading, still schedule two people to help— one to oversee the condition of boxes and furniture and check off the inventory list, the other to direct the movers to furniture locations. See "Unloading and Checking for Damage" and "When to Tip" in Chapter 11.

If you're unloading a rented or borrowed vehicle, be sure everything is off the truck and that you've replaced any rented equipment (dollies, strapping, etc.) before returning to the truck to the friend or rental agency.

FIRST MONTH

Call at least five "new buddy" contacts. See "Five Calls You Absolutely Must Make Within Twenty-Four Hours of Moving In" Chapter 12. Plan a mini-vacation excursion.

Unpack. If you have boxes of things that won't be used for a while, open them and review the contents for breakage. Get claims forms and file a claim, if needed. See "Unpacking and Claims that Get Results" in Chapter 11.

Fill in the practical and personal consultant sections of your new telephone book. See "Your New Local Telephone Book" in Chapter 12.

Start getting acquainted with your new shopping areas, leisure/tourist spots, and clubs and activities.

Mount a campaign to initiate activities with children, new neighbors, and work colleagues.

Hold a housewarming party. See "The Housewarming Party" in Chapter 12.

Appendix A
FILL-IN EVALUATOR CHARTS

CITY EVALUATOR

SELLER'S REAL ESTATE AGENT EVALUATOR

BUYER'S REAL ESTATE AGENT EVALUATOR

NEIGHBORHOOD EVALUATOR

HOME EVALUATOR

LOAN EVALUATOR

MOVING COMPANY / OPTIONS EVALUATOR

DO-IT-YOURSELF MOVING EVALUATOR

CITY EVALUATOR

Mark only those items important to you. Use a scale of low=1 to high=5. Use separate charts for your current & each possible new location.

Location_____

Info Contact _____

Phone _____

JOB AVAILABILITY

___ Jobs in Your Career Path

___ Many Jobs in Many Fields

___ Strong Business/Entrepreneurial Prospects

___ Good Prospects for Spouse Job

___ Strong University/Adult Ed/Training Programs

___ Strong Part-Time Job Market

___ Good Airport for Frequent Business Travel

___ _____

COST OF LIVING

___ Affordability of Homes I Like

___ Good Average Wages to Cost of Living Ratio

___ Low Costs for Fixed Income Living

___ Low Health Care Costs

___ Inexpensive Living

___ Shopping Variety

___ Luxury Living

___ _____

CLIMATE / ENVIRONMENT

___ Mild Winters

___ Mild Summers

___ Mild All Year

___ Clearly Defined Seasons

___ Sunny more than 75% of the year

___ Hilly with Trees, Good Views

___ Flat, Easy to Get Around

___ Low Smog Count

___ Low Pollen Count

___ Ocean/Fresh Water within 1 Hour Drive

___ Mountains within 1 Hour Drive

___ _____

CHILDREN'S WORLD

___ Good Schools/Child Care

___ Friendly Neighborhoods

___ Many Supervised Activities
___ Much Open Space or Parks
___ Active Parent Groups
___ Strict Upbringing Prevalent
___ Liberal Upbringing Prevalent
___ Many Newcomer Children in Area
___ Good Colleges and Universities

___ _____
___ _____

SOCIAL LIFE / PERSONAL SAFETY
___ Relatives/Friends/Business Contacts in Place
___ Openness to Newcomers
___ Active Singles Community
___ Active Family Community
___ Cultural/Ethnic Homogeneity
___ Cultural/Ethnic Variety
___ Political Orientation
___ Active Church
___ Active Club(s)
___ Many Health Club Options
___ Many Hospitals/Health Service Options
___ Low Crime Rate
___ Good Freeway System
___ Good Public Transport
___ Good Newspapers/Libraries

___ _____

ENTERTAINMENT / LEISURE
___ Variety of Cultural Activities
    Special Cultural Activity (fill in interest):

___ _____
___ Variety of Sports Activities
    Special Sports (fill in interest):

___ _____
___ _____

___ Good Restaurants
___ Elegant Clubs
___ Fun Clubs
___ Many Weekend Getaway Places

___ _____
___ _____

___ **TOTAL POINTS**

SELLER'S REAL ESTATE AGENT EVALUATOR

Each set of questions has a set maximum number of points to be awarded. We like to delay scoring until after the interview, taking time to think about what's been said, and grading agents against each other. Select the top three scores and ask those agents for personal listing presentations. Score again to select your agent.

Agent Name: _____

Agency: _____

Tel#:_____

Address:_____

Number of Agents in Company: _____

Referred by: _____

Area Knowledge (Maximum Points = 30)   Score_____
Look for: A quick, informed market overview of your neighborhood and two or three other similar areas. Knowledge of neighborhood schools, etc., will help sell your home.
　　What neighborhoods do you specialize in and why?

　　How many homes have you sold in my area in the past two years?

　　How many Days on the Market (DOM) were these homes and at what prices did they sell?

　　Which are direct price comparables for my home?

Marketing and Advertising Services (Maximum Points = 20)
　　　　　　　　　　　　　　　　　　　　　　　　　Score_____
Look for: Feasible strategy to make your home more saleable including suggestions for painting and fixing. Check number, size and style of agency's ads in both newspaper and real estate photo magazines. Be sure you are guaranteed all marketing listing services and Open House frequency in writing.
　　What marketing strategy do you recommend?

　　What do you recommend for my asking price?

　　Where does your company advertise and how often will you advertise my home?

SELLER'S REAL ESTATE AGENT EVALUATOR

Are advertising frequency, Open House schedules, and MLS exposure in your written listing contract?

What similar homes are you now selling?

What kind of Comparable Market Analysis (CMA) do you provide?

Who holds Open Houses and how often?

Do you use any other marketing tools?

Personality/Working Style (Maximum Points = 20)   Score_____
Look for: Willingness to make frequent progress reports and to modify sales strategy.
Describe how you interface with seller during the listing period.

Professionalism (Maximum Points = 10)   Score_____
Look for: Full-time interest in selling as well as official credentials. Ask the references about agent's effectiveness and whether they would use same agent again.
Are you a full-time or a part-time salesperson?

Do you belong to the local real estate board?

What continuing education classes have you taken in the last year?

Give me the names and phone number references of three clients whose homes you have sold.

Contracts (Maximum Points = 10)   Score_____
Look for: A 3- or 4-month exclusive listing and willingness to negotiate commission.
What is your listing contract duration?

What is your fee structure?

Company (Maximum Points = 10)   Score_____
© 1999 C & S Steiner

SELLER'S REAL ESTATE AGENT EVALUATOR

Look for: Full cooperation with other agencies who can bring in buyers as well as specialization in similar type neighborhoods. Company should have a working relationship with mortgage brokers and bank loan officers. Be sure the competitors are on your interview list.

What other neighborhoods does your company specialize in?

Does it have branch offices in each area?

What percentage of sales of total agency sales are in my neighborhood?

What is your commission policy with other agencies?

What is your policy toward Buyer's Agents?

How do you help with buyer's financing?

What are your agency's biggest advantages?

Who are your competitors?

TOTAL SCORE _____

BUYER'S REAL ESTATE AGENT EVALUATOR

We like to delay scoring until after the interview, taking time to think about what's been said, and grading agents against each other. Assign points within the limits set for each section.

Area Knowledge (Maximum Points = 30)   Score_____

Look for: A quick, informed market overview of many neighborhoods with specific rather than generalized information on schools etc. Knowledge of developers should include their reputations and market overview. Any forms and charts should be easy to understand.

What neighborhoods should I look at and why?

Please send me a copy of your MLS comparable and Days on the Market (DOM) printouts and graphs showing monthly and year-on-year price trends.

Tell me about schools, commute times, public transport, and amenities in the neighborhoods you recommend.

Who is building new houses in the area in my price range and what financial inducements are available?

Services to Buyers (Maximum Points = 20)   Score_____

Look for: Recommendations for support services from contractors and lenders after the sale, as well as hand holding before the sale.

Do you have an Orientation Packet or Video on the area?

Will you arrange an Area Orientation Tour?

Do you offer a Computerized Loan Origination service with a list of lenders' fees?

Which inspection services (Home, Pest, etc.) and other experts do you have in your Referral Data Bank?

Personality/Working Style (Maximum Points = 20)   Score_____

Look for: Detailed questioning to solicit the features you want in a home, as well as the offer to pre-select homes for you to see. The agent should take you to houses at times convenient to you. Agent should offer a negotiating strategy on offer prices and terms that suit the current market conditions.

SELLER'S REAL ESTATE AGENT EVALUATOR

How often do you check in with a client?

Describe how you work with a client.

What are the main things you need to know about my housing needs?

How will you help me in negotiating an offer?

Contracts (Maximum Points = 10)   Score_____
Look for: Buyer's Agent fee setup. Buyer's Agents should not have dual loyalties. If the agent also represents sellers, you should not pay a fee.
Do you represent sellers or are you exclusively a Buyer's Agent?

Do you insist on a contract with buyers?

What is your fee structure?

Professionalism (Maximum Points = 10)   Score_____
Look for: Commitment to the profession both through credentials and actual performance.
Are you a full-time or a part-time salesperson?

Do you belong to the local real estate board?

What continuing education class(es) have you taken in the last year?

How many homes did your clients buy through you in the past two years?

What were their addresses, property descriptions, days on the market(DOM) and actual sales prices?

SELLER'S REAL ESTATE AGENT EVALUATOR

Names and phone numbers of people who have bought
homes through you.

Company (Maximum Points = 10)   Score_____

Look for: Working relationship with more than one lender. Company should share
commissions with other companies to give you the widest selection of homes. Add
competitors to your contact list.

What assistance can your company provide in obtaining a mortgage?

How do you work with other listing companies in the
Multiple Listing Service (MLS)?

What are your agency's biggest advantages?

Who are your competitors?

TOTAL SCORE _____

NEIGHBORHOOD EVALUATOR

Neighborhood _____

Mark only items important to
your own quality of life, using a scale of poor=1 to
ideal=5.

Boundaries _____

Real Estate Agent Phone _____

AMENITIES

___ City Proximity
___ Neighborhood Appeal
___ School District
___ Children's Activities
___ Medical Care
___ Hospital
___ Church
___ Sports Fields
___ Health Clubs
___ Adult Education
___ Cultural Facilities
___ Low Traffic Flow
___ Low Crime Rate
___ Zoning
___ Views
___ Commute Time
___ Shopping
___ Entertainment
___ Parks
___ _____
___ _____

___ **TOTAL POINTS**

LIVING COSTS (yearly)

Housing	$ _____
Real Estate Taxes	$ _____
Home Insurance	$ _____
Health Insurance	$ _____
Groceries	$ _____
Appliances	$ _____
Furniture	$ _____
Schools	$ _____
Car -Taxes	$ _____
Car -Parking Fees	$ _____
Car -Gas	$ _____
Car -Insurance	$ _____
Other Transportation	$ _____
_____	$ _____
_____	$ _____

TOTAL YEAR COSTS

$ _____

COMMENTS

_____
_____
_____
_____

HOME EVALUATOR

Rate suitability from low=1 to high=5 based on actual inspection of property.

Address _____

Contact _____

Phone _____

Asking $_____   Offer $_____   Seller Finance (Y/N)

FEATURES
___ Home Layout
___ Amount of Light
___ Levels / # Floors
___ Living Room
___ Family Room
___ Formal Dining
___ Fireplace
___ Beams
___ Woodwork
___ Hardwood Floors
___ Carpets
___ Stairs

BEDROOMS
___ Master Bedroom
___ Bedroom 2
___ Bedroom 3
___ Bedroom 4
___ Closet Space

KITCHEN
___ Appliances
___ Cabinets
___ Counters Tops
___ Flooring
___ Other

DEN/OFFICE
___ Built-Ins
___ Other

BATHROOM
___ Tiles
___ Fixtures
___ Jacuzzi

YARD/GARDEN
___ Pool
___ Type of View

___ Wind exposure
___ Size
___ Landscaping
___ Other

UTILITY AREAS
___ Garage
___ Laundry Room
___ Storage Room
___ Workshop
___ Attic
___ Basement
___ Out Buildings
___ Expansion Space
___ Other

CONDITION
___ Foundation
___ Brickwork
___ Insulation
___ Exterior Siding
___ Exterior Paint
___ Entrance Doors
___ Windows
___ Double Glazing
___ Screens
___ Roof Age
___ Gutters
___ Downspouts
___ Chimney
___ Fences
___ Decking
___ Garage
___ Driveway
___ Sidewalks
___ Landscaping

___ Interior Walls
___ Ceilings
___ Interior Doors
___ Basement
___ Attic
___ Other

SYSTEMS
___ Plumbing copper
___ Plumbing other
___ Heating
___ Hot Water Heater
___ Water Pressure
___ Electrical Amps
___ 220 Volt Line
___ Electrical Sockets
___ Air Conditioning
___ Pool Equipment
___ Sprinkler System
___ Other

Subtract for Hazards:
___ Environmental
___ Asbestos

____ **TOTAL POINTS**

COMMENTS

_____

_____

_____

LOAN EVALUATOR

Enter loan programs and terms from each lender on a separate photocopy of this form. See "Six Steps to Savvy Loan Shopping" in Chapter 8, "Finding the New Homestead."

INSTITUTION			
Contact			
Phone #			
Credentials			
Referral			
BASIC INTERVIEW		**ADJUSTABLE MORTGAGE**	
Loan Program		Periodic Cap	
Adjustable or Fixed		Life Cap	
Negative or No Negative		Rate Adjustment Schedule	
Initial Payment Rate		Max Payment Scenario*	
Origination Fee in $		1st Yr Monthly Payment in $	
Pre-qualification Letter		Max 2nd Yr Payment in $	
Turnaround Time –Lock In		Max 3rd Yr Payment in 3	
Turnaround Time –Funding		Max 4th Yr Payment in $	
Rate Sheet Sent		Max 5th Yr Payment in $	
NOTES:			
FOLLOW-UP INTERVIEW		Borrower Qualifying Ratios	
Downpayment % Required		Prepay Penalty	
Documentation Required		Assumable	
Amortized/Years		Application Fee in $	
Due/Years		Total Lender Charges	

*Calculations to be based on rates going to their maximum as quickly as possible and remaining there. Negative Amortization loan payments to INCLUDE all amounts that could be negatively amortized.

MOVING COMPANY OPTIONS EVALUATOR

Company Name			Estimate Total Cost $	
Contact				Helpful Y/N
Phone #				
Referred By				
Estimator				Helpful Y/N
National/Local Affiliation				Rapid Follow-up Info Y/N
ICC Perfomance Rating	Frequent Destination Shiping Y/N	Direct Transport to Destination Y/N	Relay to Another Truck Y/N	
Takes Antiques, etc. Y/N	Local Service Persons Y/N	Reassembles Antiques, etc. Y/N	Personal Auto Transport $	
Charge per 100 Pounds $	Charge per Cubic Ft $	Stair Surcharge $	Specific Date Charge $	
Charge per Hr $	Time Starts at Door	Overtime Charge $	Extra Helper Charge $	
Weekend Charge $	Extra Pickup Charge $	Truck Fridge Hookup	Tariff Increase Expected Y/N	
Packing Hr Rate $	Packing Rate Overtime $	Box Purchase $	Box Rental $	
Free Written Estimate Y/N	Non-Binding Estimate Only Y/N	Binding Estimate Y/N	Not-To-Exceed Estimate Y/N	
Price Cut-off Date	Poundage Breakpoints	Trade Excess Wt for Storage Y/N	Senior/Army/etc. Discount %	
Season Discount $	Mid-Week Discount $	Mid-Month Discount $	Other Discount $	
Performance Guarantee Y/N	Days Advance to Reserve	Time Payment Interest %	Credit Cards OK Y/N	
Free Storage Time Y/N	Daily Rate $	Monthly Rate $	Unload Charge $	
Perm Storage Rate $	Mini Storage Rate $	Other		

DO-IT-YOURSELF MOVING

Make copies for each alternative company you consider using.

Company Name		Est. Total Cost $	
Telephone #			
Referred By			
Contact			
Helpers & Phones			
Helpers & Phones			
Van Size & Rate $	Extra Day Charge $	Weekday Discounts $	Free Days
Free Milage	Extra Mile Charge $	Return Vehicle Charge $	Car Tow Bar $
Dolly $	Auto Trailer $	Road Service Charge $	Road Service 800 #
Helper Hr Rate $	# of Boxes	Box Cost $	Padding Cost $
Added Insurance $	Gas $	Motels $	Own Labor $
Food $	Tolls $	Other $	Other $
Freebies			

ALTERNATIVE SHIPPING:

Air Cargo	$	Rail Companies	$
Freight Forwarding	$	Steamship & Cruise Lines	$
Frieght Consolidating	$	United Parcel Service Ground	$
Mailing Services	$	Trucking	$
Packaging Services	$	Packing & Crating Services	$
US Parcel Post		Other	$

NOTES:

Appendix B
CHECKLISTS

ALTERNATIVE MOVE:

    Home Trade Move-in/Move-out Checklist

    Info/Emergency/People/Phone List

    Fun Things to Do List

    Bill Tracking List

CHANGE OF ADDRESS CHECKLIST

RENTER'S MOVE-IN/MOVE-OUT PROPERTY

    Condition Checklist

ESCROW TIMETABLE AND CHECKLIST

STEINERS FURNITURE CHECKLIST

HOUSEHOLD HAZARDOUS WASTE CHECKLIST

HOME TRADE MOVE-IN/MOVE-OUT CHECK LIST*

DATE DONE	PREPARING YOUR HOME
	Prepare your home for your exchange partners as you would for any other special guests--make sure that it is clean and ready for their arrival.
	Provide the necessary linens and a minimum amount of food staples so that your guests can get off to a comfortable start. It's nice to leave a special welcome--a homemade cake, flowers, or a local handicraft.
	Leave notes in appropriate places on how to operate appliances and where to find essentials, e.g., the fuse box, main shut off for gas, water, and electricity.
	Leave list of where to shop for food, recommended auto repair shops, good restaurants, parks, recreational facilities and entertainment spots for adults and children.
	Leave instructions for care of plants and pets. Include veterinarian's name and number in case of an emergency.
	Leave note pad next to telephone for recording important telephone calls or mail that you want your trade partners to forward.
	Leave list specifying any parts of the home to be off-limits or equipment not to be used.
	Leave keys in the agreed upon place or with designated friends. Leave two sets of keys--the extra set should stay with friends to be used in the event the first set is lost.
	Ask friends and neighbors to welcome your guests.
	Arrange storage for irreplaceable antiques and personal items if there is concern about breakage.
	If auto is to be exchanged, determine that insurance coverage is adequate. Make sure that there is gas in the car and leave maps of the local area.
	Make sure that homeowner's insurance coverage is adequate.
	Provide adequate closet and drawer space for guests.
	Make sure that everything that is to be turned off is turned off and everything that is to be turned on is turned on.
	Empty refrigerator, except for staples.

*(*Based, with permission, on the list used by Intervac, one of the largest and oldest home exchange clubs in the world. For further information, contact Intervac, (800) 756-HOME.)*

HOME TRADE MOVE-IN/MOVE-OUT CHECK LIST*

DATE DONE	THEIR HOME WHEN YOU LEAVE
	Replace food staples and leave linens, as arranged.
	Clean home and leave everything in the same order in which you found it. Remember some people have standards different from yours--when you use their home you should meet their standards or better. Leave a check for long distance telephone calls and any other agreed upon items.
	Leave note on any problems, incidents or telephone calls that the owners would be interested in knowing about.
	Leave a thank you note and perhaps a small gift as a token of appreciation for a wonderful time and all the money you saved by exchanging homes.
	If you depart early for any reason make sure that your exchange partners and their neighbors are notified.
	Make sure that everything that is to be turned off is turned off and everything that is to be turned on is turned on.
	Return keys to designated location.

(*Based, with permission, on the list used by Intervac, one of the largest and oldest home exchange clubs in the world. For further information, contact Intervac, (800) 756-HOME.)

INFO/ EMERGENCY/ PEOPLE/ PHONE LIST

These check lists will make settling in much easier for your home trade partners. They can also be terrific goodwill builders if you are renting (or selling) your home. You may want to ask the people in the home you'll be staying in to fill in a blank photocopy of these forms for you, as well.

Leave this list next to telephone for easy reference.

Home Trade Partner:	
Contact with Keys:	
Emergency Info Contact:	
Neighborhood Lore contact:	
Others to meet:	
Fire:	Police:
Ambulance:	
Doctor:	
Dentist:	
Pediatrician:	
Babysitter:	
Auto Repair:	
Auto Insurance:	
Household Contents Insurance:	
Property Insurance:	
Gas Company:	Electrical Company:
Water Company:	Garbage Company:
Telephone Company:	Cable TV Company:
Plumber:	
Electrician:	
Roofer:	
General Contractor:	
Handyperson:	
Gardener:	

INFO/ EMERGENCY/ PEOPLE/ PHONE LIST

OTHER CONTACTS	TELEPHONE

FUN THINGS TO DO LIST

Best local park:
Best entertainment:
Best restaurants:
Best local paper for entertainment and events:
Things locals like to do that tourists don't know about:
Best shopping:
Supermarkets:
Beauty Salons:
Drycleaners:
Bookstores:
Discount stores:
Other shops:
Things to do with kids:
Interesting classes:
Excursions:
Our club memberships:

BILL TRACKING LIST - ARRIVAL

In the attached envelope, we've left checks for our balance due on the following bills. The bills should be arriving over the next few weeks. Please use these checks to pay them, and add whatever additional you need to cover extra charges since we left.

VENDOR	BILL AMOUNT	OUR CK AMOUNT	OUR CK NUMBER	YOUR CK AMOUNT	YOUR CK NUMBER
Gas					
Electricity					
Telephone					
Water					
Garbage					
Newspaper					
Other					

BILL TRACKING LIST - DEPARTURE

Please call the utilities, get your Balance Due and leave us checks to cover them for your last month's stay in the envelope. We'll add any long distance phone calls and send you a copy of that bill in determining reimbursements on either side. Thanks for keeping track of these things. We hope you have a wonderful stay!

VENDOR	BILL AMOUNT	OUR CK AMOUNT	OUR CK NUMBER	YOUR CK AMOUNT	YOUR CK NUMBER
Gas					
Electricity					
Telephone					
Water					
Garbage					
Newspaper					
Other					

CHANGE OF ADDRESS CHECK LIST

Here is a list of those who need your new address. Date each change of address notice when sent. Retain a copy of tax notification for your records.

DATE	OLD ADDRESS / PHONE	DATE	
	NEW ADDRESS / PHONE		
	GOVERNMENT		**INSURANCE**
	IRS (Form 8822)		Automobile
	Government Benefits		Business
	State and Local Tax Offices		Disability
	Motor Vehicles Department		Fire
	Post Office		Health
	Voter Registration		Household (Renter's/Homeowner's)
	Other		Life
			Other Vehicle
	GROUPS		Valuables
	Church		Other
	Colleagues		
	Family		**MONEY MATTERS**
	Friends		Accountant
	Libraries		Automobile Loan
	Neighbors		Bank
	Schools		Consumer Loans
	Social Associations		Credit Cards
	Sport Clubs		Credit Union
	Trade Associations		Department Stores
	Unions		Employees (Babysitters)
	Other		Landlord
			Mortgages

[www.usps.com/moversguide]
[to change address - even for magazines]

CHANGE OF ADDRESS CHECK LIST

Here is a list of those who need your new address. Date each change of address notice when sent. Retain a copy of tax notification for your records.

DATE		DATE	
	MONEY MATTERS (Cont)		**SUBSCRIPTIONS**
	Savings & Loan		Book Clubs
	Home Loan		Catalogs
	Student Loans		Journals
	Employer		Magazines
	Mutual Fund/CD		Newspapers
	Pension		Newsletters
	Social Security		Record Clubs
	Stock Broker		Other
	Other		
			UTILITIES
	CONSULTANTS		Cable TV
	Doctors		Electric Company
	Hospital		Garbage Disposal
	Dentist		Gas Company
	Lawyer		Telephone Company
	Veterinarian		Water Company
	Other		Other

RENTER'S Move-In / Move-Out CONDITION LIST

Mark condition B-ad, F-air, or G-ood in this list with building owner both when you move in and when you move out. Owner should initial and date each sheet here to indicate agreement:

	In	Out	Repair $		In	Out	Repair $
EXTERIOR				**INTERIOR**			
DECK/PATIO				BATHROOMS			
Doors				Cabinets/Shelves			
Floor				Ceiling			
Handrails				Closets			
Other				CurtainRack/Door			
				Doors/Locks			
GARAGE/CAR PORT				Outlets/Switches			
Closets/Shelves				Exhaust Fan			
Doors Opener				Floor/Coverings			
Driveway/Parking				Lighting/Fixtures			
Other				Mirror			
LANDSCAPING				Screens/Shades			
Children's Area				Shower/Tub			
Lawns				Sink/Faucets			
Trees/Shrubs				Toilet			
Garden Tools				Towel Racks			
Other				Walls/Coverings			
				Windows/Coverings			
POOL				Other			
Deck							
Furniture				MASTER BEDROOM			
Pump				Ceiling			
Cleaning Equipment				Closets			
Water Quality				Doors/Locks			
Other				Outlets/Switches			
				Smoke Alarm			

© 1999 C & S Steiner

RENTER'S Move-In / Move-Out CONDITION LIST

Mark condition B-ad, F-air, or G-ood in this list with building owner both when you move in and when you move out. Owner should initial and date each sheet here to indicate agreement:

	In	Out	Repair $		In	Out	Repair $
Floor/Covering				Lighting/Fixtures			
Lighting/Fixtures				Screens/Shades			
Screens/Shades				Walls/Coverings			
Walls/Coverings				Windows/Coverings			
Windows/Coverings				Other			
Other							
				DINING AREA			
BEDROOM 2				Ceiling			
Ceiling				Outlets/Switches			
Closets				Floor/Covering			
Doors/Locks				Lighting/Fixtures			
Outlets/Switches				Screens			
Smoke Alarm				Walls/Coverings			
Floor/Covering				Windows/Coverings			
Lighting/Fixtures				Other			
Screens/Shades							
Walls/Coverings				ENTRANCE/HALLS			
Windows/Coverings				Ceilings			
Other				Closets			
				Doors			
BEDROOM 3				Outlets/Switches			
Ceiling				Fire Alarms			
Closets				Floors/Coverings			
Doors/Locks				Handrails			
Outlets/Switches				Hardware/Locks			
Smoke Alarm				Lighting/Fixtures			
Floor/Covering				Steps/Landings			

RENTER'S Move-In / Move-Out CONDITION LIST

Mark condition B-ad, F-air, or G-ood in this list with building owner both when you move in and when you move out. Owner should initial and date each sheet here to indicate agreement:

	In	Out	Repair $		In	Out	Repair $
Walls/Coverings				LIVING ROOM			
Windows/Coverings				Ceiling			
Other				Closets			
				Outlets/Switches			
KITCHEN				Fireplace			
Cabinets				Floor/Covering			
Ceiling				Lighting/Fixtures			
Closets/Pantry				Walls/Coverings			
Counter Tops				Windows/Coverings/			
Dishwasher				Other			
Garbage Disposal							
Doors				OTHER ROOM 1			
Outlets/Switches				Ceilings			
Exhaust Fan/Lights				Closets			
Fire Alarms				Doors/Locks			
Floor/Covering				Outlets/Switches			
Lighting/Fixtures				Floors/Coverings			
Range/Oven				Lighting/Fixtures			
Refrigerator				Screens			
Screens/Shades				Stairs			
Sinks/Faucets				Walls/Coverings			
Walls/Coverings				Windows/Coverings			
Sinks/Faucets				Other			
Walls/Coverings							
Washer/Dryer				OTHER ROOM 2			
Windows/Coverings				Ceilings			
Other				Closets			

RENTER'S Move-In / Move-Out CONDITION LIST

Mark condition **B**-ad, **F**-air, or **G**-ood in this list with building owner both when you move in and when you move out. Owner should initial and date each sheet here to indicate agreement:

	In	Out	Repair $		In	Out	Repair $
Doors/Locks				SAFETY			
Outlets/Switches				Burglar Alarms			
Floors/Coverings				Door Locks			
Lighting/Fixtures				Fire Extinguisher			
Screens				Security Gate			
Stairs				Smoke/Fire Alarms			
Walls/Coverings				Stairs/Handrails			
Windows/Coverings/				Window Locks			
Other				Other			
HEAT/PLUMBING							
Air Conditioning							
Heating							
Hot Water Heater							
Plumbing							
Washer/Dryer							
Other							
EQUIPMENT							
Doorbell/Intercom							
Gutters							
Roof							
Thermostat							
Other							

ESCROW TIMETABLE & CHECK LIST

Attorney / Escrow Co. _____

Contact _____ Phone_____

Real Estate Agency _____

Agent _____ Phone _____

Lender _____ Phone _____

Insurance _____ Phone _____

Inspectors _____

_____

Fill in the deadlines from your contract. Cross out any that do not apply. Highlight the events which are most important to you on charts on next pages.

Important: Deadlines assume:

1. Each contingency is reviewed and accepted by both Buyer and Seller. Contract should state that if a contingency is not accepted by the deadline, the contract may be terminated.

2. Buyer and Seller give written acceptance or refusal of each respective contingency. Failure or refusal by the relevant party to give written acceptance or refusal by a deadline can *automatically* either terminate or lock-in many contracts.

ESCROW TIMETABLE & CHECK LIST

DEADLINE	COMPLETED	DOCUMENT REVIEW
		Escrow opened
		Buyer $_____ Earnest Money Escrow Deposit
		Preliminary Title Search delivered to Buyer/Seller
		Title accepted or problems discovered
		Problems eliminated/Buyer acceptance
		Order City/County Inspection Report/Zoning Forms
		City/County Report(s) received/accepted
		Property Disclosure Statement given to Buyer
		Property Disclosure Statement accepted by Buyer
		INSPECTIONS
		Pest Control Inspection
		Pest Control Report delivered to Seller/Buyer
		Pest Control accepted by Seller/Buyer
		Pest Control correction work ordered
		Pest Control work completed/accepted/paid
		Pay Pest Control correction at Close of Escrow
		Home Building Inspection/General Contractor
		Roof
		Environmental Hazards
		Appliances
		Pool
		Other

DEADLINE	COMPLETE	LENDING & INSURANCE
		Buyer's Deposit increased to $
		Home Protection Warranty issued
		Loan Application submitted
		Loan Application approved
		Lender's Disclosure Documents to Buyer
		Buyer removes Financing Contingency
		Note in favor of Seller drawn
		Note in favor of Seller accepted by Buyer/Seller
		Buyer's Hazard Insurance placed
		Hazard Insurance to include Seller as Loss Payee
		Bill of Sale for Personal Property drawn
		Pre-Close Walk-Through completed
		Escrow/Closing Instructions drawn
		Buyer/Seller Closing Papers signed & notarized
		Closing Papers to Escrow Holder and funds ordered
		Record Deed of Trust (Mortgage) in favor of Lender
		Record Deed of Trust (Mortgage) in favor of Seller
		Policies of Title Insurance for Buyer/Lender issued
		FUNDS DISPERSED
		Previous Loan paid
		Post-Close Occupancy Funds to Buyer or Seller
		Cancel Hazard Insurance Policy /refund to Seller
		Taxes & Pro Rata monies allocated to Buyer/Seller
		Inspection Fees paid
		Commission Check(s) to Agent(s) drawn
		Deferred Maintenance Holdback escrow funded
		Seller's Proceeds Check drawn
		Keys turned over to Buyer's Real Estate Agent

ESCROW TIMETABLE & CHECK LIST

STEINER'S FURNITURE CHECK LIST

This checklist provides you with a way to organize moving your household goods. It lists the information you need to make intelligent decisions about what to take and what to sell. These standardized estimates of the weight and volume of common household items make it possible for you estimate shipment size for renting a self move truck. Item weight is used by moving companies in calculating charges. The checklists have been compiled from information from the U.S. Government, commercial catalogs and personal experience. If you have more rooms than listed, make extra copies of the appropriate pages before you begin your inventory.

Column headings are:
Len=Length
Dpth=Depth or width
Ht=Height
LoWt=Lowest weight (lbs)
AvWt=Average Weight (lbs)
HiWt=High weight (lbs)
CuFt=Cubic feet
Sell=Mark for garage sale
Take=Take with you as you travel
Need=Need to pack for your new home
$$$$=Replacement price or Selling price
Qty=Number of pieces
ToCu=Total Cubic from Qty times CuFt
ToWt=Total weight from Qty times Lo/Hi Wt

BEDROOM CHECK LIST

FURNISHINGS	Len	Dpth	Ht	LoWt	AvWt	HiWt	CuFt	Sell	Take	Need	$$$$	Qty	ToCu	ToWt
Armoire, wardrobe/cupboard	5.00	1.00	6.00	130.0	195.0	260.0	30.0							
Bed, Captain	7.80	3.10	3.50	92.0	115.0	138.0	84.6							
Bed, Folding Cot	2.50	6.00	1.00	20.0	26.0	30.0	15.0							
Bed, Futon Frame	5.00	3.00	3.60	50.0	75.0	100.0	54.0							
Bed, Headboard w Shelves	5.30	0.75	3.58	260.0	325.0	390.0	14.2							
Bed, Headboard, Queen	5.10	0.17	3.60	20.8	26.0	31.2	3.1		✓			2	6.2	62
Bed, Mattress Set Full/Double	6.30	1.30	4.50	108.0	114.0	120.0	36.9		✓				36.9	114
Bed, Mattress Set King	6.70	1.30	6.30	100.0	145.0	190.0	54.9							
Bed, Mattress Set Queen	6.70	1.30	5.00	134.0	138.5	143.0	43.6		✓				43.6	139
Bed, Mattress Set Twin	6.30	1.30	3.30	79.0	86.0	93.0	27.0							
Bed, Rollaway	3.50	3.50	1.50	40.0	54.0	69.0	18.4							
Bed, Single Hollywood	6.20	1.70	3.30	52.0	62.5	73.0	34.8							
Bed, Sofabed, Twin Foam	2.00	2.50	2.10	50.0	65.0	80.0	10.5							
Bed, Water Platform	7.80	6.20	3.50	56.0	70.0	84.0	169.3							
Bed, Youth/Twin	6.50	3.60	5.50	88.0	99.0	110.0	128.7							

BEDROOM CHECK LIST

FURNISHINGS	Len	Dpth	Ht	LoWt	AvWt	HiWt	CuFt	Sell	Take	Need	$$$	Qty	ToCu	ToWt
Bed, Trundle Bunk	6.60	3.40	5.00	75.0	82.5	90.0	112.2							
Blanket	1.00	1.00	0.50	2.0	4.0	6.0	0.5							
Boots	1.00	1.00	0.50	3.0	3.8	4.5	0.5							
Canopy	6.58	3.50	5.60	40.0	50.0	60.0	129.0							
Chair, Boudoir	2.50	1.50	3.00	15	17	20	11.3		✓			1		17
Chest of Drawers/Bureau/Dresser	4.30	4.60	2.30	128.0	207.0	285.0	45.5		✓					128
Chest of Drawers/Bureau/Dresser	2.60	1.50	3.90	70.0	113.0	155.0	15.2							
Comforter	2.00	1.50	1.00	6.5	8.8	11.0	3.0							
Drape Set	5.25	0.20	7.10	2.8	6.4	10.0	7.5							
Dresser/Vanity Bench	2.00	1.00	1.50	12.0	15.0	18.0	3.0							
Fan	1.00	0.50	1.00	7.0	13.0	20.0	0.5							
Fern/Plant Stands	3.00	1.00	1.00	8.0	10.0	12.0	3.0							
Heater, Gas/Electric	2.00	1.00	4.50	24.0	30.0	36.0	9.0							

BEDROOM CHECK LIST

FURNISHINGS	Len	Dpth	Ht	LoWt	AvWt	HiWt	CuFt	Sell	Take	Need	$$$$	Qty	ToCu	ToWt
Lamp	1.00	1.00	1.60	3.2	4.0	4.8	1.6							
Mirror, Rectangle	3.00	0.30	4.50	35.0	42.5	50.0	4.1							
Pillow	2.50	1.50	0.50	2.0	3.5	5.0	1.9							
Pillow Case/Sheet Set	1.00	1.00	0.25	2.0	3.5	5.0	0.3							
Rocking Chair	2.00	3.00	4.50	25.0	37.5	50.0	27.0							
Table, Night	1.50	2.50	3.00	30.0	40.0	50.0	11.3							
Wastepaper Basket	1.00	1.00	1.50	2.4	3.0	3.6	1.5							
CLOTHING														
Pants	1.00	1.00	0.50	1.8	1.8	2.2	0.5							
Shirts/Blouses	1.00	1.00	0.25	0.5	0.8	1.0	0.3							
Shoes	1.00	0.50	0.50	1.5	2.0	2.5	0.3							
Suit	2.50	2.00	0.50	1.8	3.2	4.5	2.5							
Jacket	2.00	1.50	1.00	2.3	2.3	2.8	0.2							
GRAND TOTAL														

DEN CHECK LIST

FURNISHINGS	Len	Dpth	Ht	LoWt	AvWt	HiWt	CuFt	Sell	Take	Need	$$$$	Qty	ToCu	ToWt
Cabinet, Filing 2 Door	1.30	2.10	2.30	50.0	55.0	65.0	6.3							
Cabinet, Filing 4 Door	1.30	2.10	4.30	105.0	116.0	127.0	11.7							
Cabinets, Filing (per drawer)	2.00	1.50	3.00	16.0	20.0	24.0	9.0							
Chair, Desk Swivel	3.00	2.50	4.00	20.0	30.0	40.0	30.0							
Chair, Typing	1.50	1.50	3.00	10.0	20.0	30.0	6.8							
Chairs, Card Table (each)	2.50	3.00	0.50	4.0	5.0	6.0	3.8							
Computer	2.50	2.50	0.50	5.0	27.5	50.0	3.1							
Computer Moniter	1.50	1.50	1.50	10.0	12.0	15.0	3.4							
Computer Printer	2.50	2.50	1.50	30.0	37.5	45.0	9.4							
Copier	2.50	2.50	2.00	25.0	37.5	50.0	12.5							
Desk	3.50	2.50	2.50	50.0	200.0	350.0	21.9							
Fax	2.00	1.50	1.50	15.0	20.0	25.0	4.5							
Safe	1.50	1.70	1.90	0.0	0.0	0.0	4.8							
Table, Card	3.00	3.00	0.50	8.0	10.0	12.0	4.5							
Typewriter	2.00	1.50	1.00	10.0	20.0	30.0	3.0							
GRAND TOTAL														

DINING ROOM CHECK LIST

FURNISHINGS	Len	Dpth	Ht	LoWt	AvWt	HiWt	CuFt	Sell	Take	Need	$$$$	Qty	ToCu	ToWt
Buffet	3.50	2.00	3.00	100.0	110.0	120.0	21.0							
Cabinets, China/Curio	3.00	1.50	7.00	50.0	75.0	125.0	31.5							
Chair, Dining	2.50	2.50	3.00	15.0	20.0	25.0	18.8							
Hutch	3.50	2.00	4.00	90.0	110.0	120.0	28.0							
Table, Dining	3.00	5.00	2.50	50.0	100.0	150.0	37.5							
Tea Cart	1.50	2.50	3.00	15.0	20.0	25.0	11.3							
GRAND TOTAL														

BATH CHECK LIST

FURNISHINGS	Len	Dpth	Ht	LoWt	AvWt	HiWt	CuFt	Sell	Take	Need	$$$$	Qty	ToCu	ToWt
Bathroom, Cabinet	1.70	1.25	2.18	16.0	20.0	24.0	4.6							
Clothes Hamper	1.60	1.00	1.90	6.0	7.5	9.0	3.0							
GRAND TOTAL														

FAMILY ROOM CHECK LIST

FURNISHINGS	Len	Dpth	Ht	LoWt	AvWt	HiWt	CuFt	Sell	Take	Need	$$$$	Qty	ToCu	ToWt
Bowling Ball	1.20	1.00	0.75	12.0	15.0	18.0	0.9							
Cedar Chest	3.00	1.50	1.50	20.0	40.0	50.0	6.8							
Ceiling Fan	4.50	4.50	1.50	16.0	20.0	24.0	30.4							
Cue & Ball Set	1.00	1.00	4.00	24.0	30.0	36.0	4.0							
Dehumidifier	1.30	1.70	2.00	0.0	0.0	0.0	4.4							
Exercise, Bicycle	3.10	1.50	4.10	32.0	40.0	48.0	19.1							
Exercise, Total System	6.10	4.50	6.50	240.0	300.0	360.0	178.4							
Fitness, Ski Machine	4.10	1.60	4.10	40.0	50.0	60.0	26.9							
Golf Bag	0.70	0.70	3.50	7.0	10.0	12.0	1.7							
Guitar	1.25	0.40	3.50	4.0	8.0	12.0	1.8							
Ping Pong Table	5.00	1.80	6.00	0.0	0.0	0.0	54.0							
Pool Table	8.30	4.60	2.60	120.0	435.0	750.0	99.3							
Sewing Machine, Portable	1.40	0.80	1.30	20.0	35.0	50.0	1.5							
Tanning Bed	6.50	2.30	2.30	81.6	102.0	122.4	34.4							
Toy Box	1.00	1.00	1.50	8.0	10.0	12.0	1.5							
GRAND TOTAL														

KITCHEN CHECK LIST

FURNISHINGS	Len	Dpth	Ht	LoWt	AvWt	HiWt	CuFt	Sell	Take	Need	$$$$	Qty	ToCu	ToWt
Bulletin Board	1.50	2.00	0.50	4.0	5.0	6.0	1.5							
Cart, microwave oven	2.50	1.50	3.00	15.0	20.0	30.0	11.3							
Chair, Wood	2.00	2.00	3.50	15.0	17.5	20.0	14.0							
Freezer	3.90	2.50	3.00	150.0	225.0	300.0	29.3							
Gas/Electric Stove	2.50	2.30	3.80	150.0	175.0	200.0	21.9							
Wolf/Viking Stove	4.00	3.00	3.00	580.0	620.0	980.0	36.0							
Ironing Board	4.50	1.20	3.00	10.0	13.0	17.0	16.2							
Microwave	1.70	1.20	1.30	35.0	45.0	55.0	2.7							
Portable Dishwasher	2.00	2.20	3.00	150.0	160.0	170.0	13.2							
Refrigerator	2.45	2.45	5.50	170.0	258.0	345.0	33.0							
Refrigerator, Under Counter	1.60	1.60	2.80	56.0	70.0	84.0	7.2							
Stool	1.50	1.50	2.50	15.0	25.0	35.0	5.6							
Table, Kitchen	3.50	3.50	2.40	50.0	62.5	75.0	29.4							
Table, Radio	1.00	0.40	0.40	3.0	4.0	5.0	0.2							
Trash Compactor	1.25	2.00	2.80	150.0	160.0	170.0	7.0							
GRAND TOTAL														

LIVING ROOM CHECK LIST

FURNISHINGS	Len	Dpth	Ht	LoWt	AvWt	HiWt	CuFt	Sell	Take	Need	$$$$	Qty	ToCu	ToWt
Air Conditioner	2.20	1.60	2.40	90.0	160.0	260.0	8.4							
Answering Machine	0.71	0.54	0.16	2.5	6.3	6.0	0.1							
Antennae, TV, roof	1.00	1.00	6.00	16.0	20.0	24.0	6.0							
Aquarium	2.00	1.00	2.00	20.0	25.0	30.0	4.0							
Aquarium, Stand	2.50	1.50	2.50	28.0	35.0	42.0	9.4							
Bar, portable	3.00	1.50	2.50	96.0	120.0	144.0	11.3							
Bar, stool	1.00	1.00	3.00	16.0	20.0	24.0	3.0							
Bench, Fireside/Piano	2.50	1.00	2.00	15.0	20.0	25.0	5.0							
Bookcase 2 Shelf	2.50	3.00	1.00	44.0	51.5	59.0	7.5							
Bookcase 6 Shelf	6.00	3.00	1.00	69.0	89.5	110.0	18.0							
Cabinets, Korean	3.00	1.50	3.00	140.0	175.0	210.0	13.5							
Cabinets, Record/Stereo	5.00	1.50	4.00	132.0	165.0	198.0	30.0							
Carpet Padding per square yard	0.00	0.00	0.00	2.0	3.0	4.0	0.0							
Carpet per square yard	0.00	0.00	0.00	2.0	4.0	6.0	0.0							
Chair, Arm	2.50	2.75	3.30	48.0	60.0	72.0	22.7							

LIVING ROOM CHECK LIST

FURNISHINGS	Len	Dpth	Ht	LoWt	AvWt	HiWt	CuFt	Sell	Take	Need	$$$$	Qty	ToCu	ToWt
Chair, Recliner	2.50	2.75	3.30	60.0	70.0	80.0	22.7							
Clock, Grandfather	1.80	0.60	4.40	50.0	60.0	80.0	4.8							
Drape Set	7.10	5.25	0.10	2.8	6.4	10.0	3.7							
Entertainment Center	3.60	1.60	6.50	165.0	200.0	235.0	37.4							
Fireplace Tong Set/Screen	2.00	0.50	2.50	5.0	7.0	10.0	2.5							
Footstool/Ottoman	3.00	1.80	1.40	25.0	30.0	35.0	7.6							
Hall Tree Rack	3.00	1.50	1.50	3.0	5.0	7.0	6.8							
Lamp, Floor	1.30	1.30	4.60	12.0	13.0	14.0	7.8							
Lamp, Table	1.60	1.60	2.00	9.0	12.0	15.0	5.1							
Magazine Rack	1.60	1.00	1.50	5.0	7.0	10.0	2.4							
Piano, Baby Grand	6.00	6.00	3.00	800.0	900.0	1000	108.0							
Piano, Upright	3.00	2.00	4.00	300.0	400.0	500.0	24.0							
Rocking Chair	2.00	3.00	4.50	25.0	37.5	50.0	27.0							
Sofa Sectional	6.80	8.00	2.50	250.0	275.0	300.0	136.0							

LIVING ROOM CHECK LIST

FURNISHINGS	Len	Dpth	Ht	LoWt	AvWt	HiWt	CuFt	Sell	Take	Need	$$$	Qty	ToCu	ToWt
Sofa, 2 cushions	5.00	3.00	2.90	92.0	126.0	160.0	43.5							
Sofa, 3 cushions	6.90	3.00	2.90	120.0	169.0	217.0	60.0							
Stereo Speakers	1.20	0.80	3.10	40.0	50.0	60.0	3.0							
Stereo System	1.20	1.40	3.10	100.0	115.0	125.0	5.2							
TV, Camcorder	1.50	0.50	0.80	6.0	13.0	20.0	0.6							
TV Set 19	1.60	1.58	1.56	40.0	50.0	60.0	3.9							
TV Set 24	2.00	1.50	1.80	56.0	70.0	84.0	5.4							
TV Set 27	2.20	1.60	2.00	80.0	100.0	120.0	7.0							
TV Set 45	3.40	2.00	3.80	200.0	250.0	300.0	25.8							
TV Stand	2.00	1.50	2.50	30.0	50.0	60.0	7.5							
Table, Coffee	3.00	3.00	1.40	60.0	70.0	80.0	12.6							
Table, End	2.25	1.75	1.66	25.0	30.0	35.0	6.5							
Telephone	0.70	0.70	0.70	2.5	3.0	3.5	0.3							
Trunk	3.00	1.50	3.00	30.0	40.0	50.0	13.5							
VCR	1.50	2.00	0.50	15.0	17.5	20.0	1.5							
GRAND TOTAL														

NURSERY CHECK LIST

FURNISHINGS	Len	Dpth	Ht	LoWt	AvWt	HiWt	CuFt	Sell	Take	Need	$$$$	Qty	ToCu	ToWt
Bassinette/Cradle	3.00	2.50	1.50	10.2	12.8	15.4	11.3							
Bathinette	3.00	2.50	2.50	8.0	10.0	12.0	18.8							
Bed, Headboard, Twin	3.40	2.50	0.80	40.0	45.0	50.0	6.8							
Chair, Child	1.00	1.00	2.00	3.0	5.0	7.0	2.0							
Chair, High	1.50	1.50	3.50	10.0	12.0	15.0	7.9							
Chest	3.00	1.50	1.50	10.0	20.0	30.0	6.8							
Crib, Baby Bed	4.50	2.50	3.70	50.0	60.0	70.0	41.6							
Playpen	3.30	3.30	2.30	20.0	25.0	30.0	25.0							
Table, Childs	2.00	2.00	2.00	5.0	10.0	15.0	8.0							
GRAND TOTAL														

UTILITY CHECK LIST

FURNISHINGS	Len	Dpth	Ht	LoWt	AvWt	HiWt	CuFt	Sell	Take	Need	$$$$	Qty	ToCu	ToWt
Archery Set, complete	4.30	1.40	0.50	7.0	10.0	12.0	3.0							
BBQ Grill	2.00	2.00	3.00	0.0	0.0	0.0	12.0							
Barbecue/Garden Cart	2.50	1.50	3.00	20.0	50.0	60.0	11.3							
Bench, Wood	4.00	1.50	2.50	15.0	20.0	30.0	15.0							
Bicycle	5.00	2.00	3.50	20.0	40.0	50.0	35.0							
Bird Bath	2.00	2.00	2.00	18.0	20.0	25.0	8.0							
Chairs, Metal	1.50	1.50	3.50	7.0	10.0	12.0	7.9							
Chairs, Wood	2.00	2.00	3.50	20.0	25.0	30.0	14.0							
Chaise Lounge	5.00	3.00	4.00	8.0	10.0	12.0	60.0							
Child Gym	15.00	6.00	8.00	120.0	200.0	220.0	720.0							
Child Slide	10.00	2.00	8.00	60.0	70.0	80.0	160.0							
Garden Hose	1.50	1.50	0.50	5.0	12.0	15.0	1.1							
Garden Hose Cart	1.00	1.00	2.00	10.0	15.0	17.0	2.0							
Garden Tractor	5.50	4.00	3.25	550.0	650.0	750.0	71.5							
Ladder, 6' Step	6.00	1.50	0.60	24.0	30.0	36.0	5.4							

UTILITY CHECK LIST

FURNISHINGS	Len	Dpth	Ht	LoWt	AvWt	HiWt	CuFt	Sell	Take	Need	$$$$	Qty	ToCu	ToWt
Ladder, 8' Metal	8.00	1.50	0.60	32.0	40.0	48.0	7.2							
Ladder, Extension	12.00	1.50	0.60	40.0	50.0	60.0	10.8							
Lawn Mower, Hand	2.00	0.50	4.00	10.0	15.0	20.0	4.0							
Lawn Mower, Riding	4.60	3.00	3.00	270.0	300.0	400.0	41.4							
Leaf Blower	2.00	2.00	2.00	20.0	25.0	30.0	8.0							
Power Mower	2.00	2.00	4.00	65.0	85.0	105.0	16.0							
Roller, Lawn	3.00	1.50	1.50	64.0	80.0	96.0	6.8							
Swing Sets	4.00	11.00	7.00	100.0	150.0	200.0	308.0							
Table	3.50	3.50	2.50	60.0	70.0	80.0	30.6							
Umbrella, Patio	1.00	1.00	5.00	5.0	10.0	20.0	5.0							
Wheelbarrow	3.00	2.30	0.75	20.0	40.0	60.0	5.2							
GRAND TOTAL														

HAZARDOUS HOUSEHOLD WASTE LIST

The following is a list of some common household items which cause damage to the environment if thrown away with your regular garbage. If you need to dispose of these items or others like them, contact your local community hazardous waste removal service.

4	PRODUCT	4	PRODUCT
	Aerosols		Kerosene
	Ammonia and ammonia cleaners		Mercury thermometers
	Antifreeze		Metal cleaners and polishes
	Asbestos		Oils (e.g., linseed, mineral, motor)
	Asphalt driveway topping		Oven cleaners
	Auto batteries		Paint (oil-base, latex, acrylic, etc.)
	Bleach		Paint stripper/remover
	Brake fluid		Pesticides
	Chemistry sets		Photographic chemicals
	Denatured alcohol		Pool chemicals
	Drain cleaners		Rodenticide (rat poison)
	Fertilizers		Roofing cement
	Fingernail polish and remover		Rug and upholstery cleaner
	Flea powder and shampoo		Solvents
	Floor/furniture polish		Thinners
	Gasoline		Transmission fluid
	Glues and adhesives		Turpentine
	Hair bleach and dye		Used motor oil
	Herbicides		Waxes
	Hydrogen peroxide		Wood filler/putty
	Insect killers		Wood preservatives
	Insecticides		

Appendix C

A LISTING OF NATIONAL, INTERNATIONAL TELEPHONE & INTERNET CONTACT SOURCES

TAKING CONTROL GENERAL INFORMATION SOURCES
Books, Maps, and Community Information Sources
ALTERNATIVE MOVE LEAD SOURCES
Directories, Exchange Clubs, Student/Work
Exchange Clubs, Short Term Rental Networks
CONSUMER ECONOMIC ASSISTANCE
Non-Profit Consumer Credit Counseling,
Overseas Banking, Credit Check Issuers, Tax
Information
FAMILY AND HEALTH SERVICES
National Adult Education Course Networks,
Health Support Groups and Resources, Parenting
Publication Networks, Senior Services and
Publications
HOME BUYING, RENTING AND AUXILIARY SERVICES
Real Estate/Rental Photo Advertising Magazine
Chains, Map Sources
JOB HUNT, BUSINESS AND ENTREPRENEUR SERVICES
Trade/Professional/Job Hunting/Networking
Organizations, Contacts and Publications
NEWSPAPERS AND PUBLICATIONS
OUTDOOR AND GETAWAY INFORMATION
RELOCATION AND MOVING SERVICES

CONTACTS & RESOURCES

The following are national and international addresses, telephone numbers, and websites to help you research your relocation.

Taking Control General Information Sources

www.amazon.com The first online bookstore. Easy to use and fast. Currently has more book reviews than its competitors.

www.barnesandnoble.com Currently touts the biggest list of books, but has fewer reviews than Amazon.

Before You Move, Inc., will send your change of address to all your magazines, credit cards and other places you regularly correspond with (including mom!). The service, Totalmove, is paid for by large companies wanting to send you information about their services in your new location. (800) MOVE-595, www.movecentral.com

Book Passage, (800) 321-9785. Call for their knowledgeable advice about the best new (or classic) books. Particularly strong list of international cultural, travel and language books.

Federal Information Sources. Searchable data bases of community and business information. Census information- www.census.gov Federal Bureau of Labor Statistics- www.bls.gov

www.geocities.com Alphabetized and mapped lists of businesses and services in various cities. Like the telephone yellow pages, there is the basic information of address, phone numbers and email info. Featured listings have ads with web addresses/links and further information. Some cities seem very well covered, others are skimpy or non existent. The cities with good listings have more coverage than their corresponding Yellow Pages because of the mapping and ease of website linkup.

www.homefair.com Large relocation site with numerous helpful calculators, including a salary calculator, a lifestyle optimizer worksheet, that interrelates with data from hundreds of cities across the nation, a household moving calculator and a timeline "wizard" that customizes the general things you need to do into a schedule that works for your situation. Also has hundreds of links to mortgage and real estate sites.

The Learning Annex 291 Geary Street, #510 San Francisco, CA 94102; (415) 788-5500; www.thelearningannex.com Nationwide adult education organization offering a wide range of short term educational courses. Emphasis on business and personal growth subjects. Main offices are in New York, Washington, DC, San Francisco, San Diego, and Toronto. Call or check website for local organization information and current course catalog.

National Directory of Address and Telephone Numbers, The Pac Bell SMART Resource Center. Also Sells national and international telephone directories. (800) 848-8000.

www.msn.sidewalk.com Listings and mapping of grocery stores, parks and schools in the vicinity are very helpful for investigating a new neighborhood, as are other links to entertainment, car registration, and utilities.

Newcomers News, 775A Commercial Street San Francisco, CA 94108; (415) 989-0278. National newspaper for Asians moving to New York, Boston, Los Angeles and San Francisco.

Rand McNally, www.randmcnally.com or your bookstore. A wide variety of maps including Flash Maps, for ease of use (800) 322-4070.

Runzheimer International. Special reports on national and international cost of living comparison data, Runzheimer Park, Rochester, WI 53167-0009. (800) 558-1702, www.runzheimer.com

Thomas Brothers Guides. Area maps for California, Seattle, Portland and Phoenix which lie flat and have big print; (800) 899-MAPS; www.thomas.com

Travel Discount Coupon Books. Coupon books offering highway maps, travel info and discount coupons to motels and hotels in areas throughout the country. They're free on stands at some gas stations and restaurants in the area covered, or you can order them ahead of your trip from:

Traveler Discount Guides. $4.00 (extra express mail), (352) 371-3948; www.exitguide.com

Traveler Coupon Guide. $3.95, 7051 Alvarado Rd., Ste B, La Mesa, CA 91941-9915; www.exitinfo.com

U.S. Geological Survey. Source of information on areas prone to earthquakes, flooding or other geological problems. Federal Center, Box 25286, Denver, CO 80225. (800) USA-MAPS, www.map.usgs.gov

www.virtualrelocation.com cost-of-living database for over 500 American cities.

Wishcraft, How to Get What You Really Want, a Unique, Step-by-Step Plan to Pinpoint Your Goals and Make Your Dreams Come True, by Barbara Sher. Great psychotherapist's insights and worksheets to help you find new directions in your life.

Alternate Move Lead Sources

Note: The overseas service organizations also have extensive listings of homes available inside the U.S.

American-International Homestays, Inc. PO Box 1754 Nederland, CO 80466-1754; (800) 876-2048; www.spectravel.com/homes

An Invented City Home Exchange 41 Sutter Street -- Suite 1090 San Francisco, California 94104; (415) 252-1141; www.invented-city.com

At Home Abroad, 405 East 56th Street, Suite 6-H, New York, NY 10022-2466; (212) 421-9165; www.members.aol.com/athomabrod

Au Pair/Homestay Abroad, World Learning, Inc., 1015 15th Street NW, Suite 750, Washington, DC 20005; (800) 287-2477. Arranges for 18-26 year olds to work as legal au pairs in Argentina, France, Germany, Great Britain, the Netherlands, Norway and Spain. Language proficiency is required for Argentina, France, Germany and Spain. Positions range from 3-18 months (6-12 months is standard), and extended stays are an option except in the UK, where stays are set at six months. Room and board are provided. A monthly stipend is included, as is time to attend classes in the host country. Application deadlines vary, but should be made at least three months before desired departure month.

Bridgestreet Accommodations (800) 778-2250; www.bridgestreet.com

Council on International Education Exchange, *Work, Study, Travel Abroad: The Whole World Handbook,* Council on International Education Exchange (CIEE) International Administration Center 205 East 42nd Street, New York, NY 10017-5706; (212) 822-2600; www.ciee.org

Educational Travel Programs, American Institute for Foreign Study, Dept. P-1, 102 Greenwich Avenue, Greenwich, CT 06830, (800) 727-2437; www.aifs.com

El Monte RV Center. Nationwide RV rentals for temporary stays. 12818 Firestone Blvd, Santa Fe Springs, CA 90670; (800) 367-3687; www.elmonte.com

Four Star Living PO Box 1273, Millbrook, NY 12545; (914) 378 3288.

Hideaways International, 767 Islington St., Portsmith NH 03801; (800) 843-4433; www.hideaways.com

HomeExchange Post Office Box 30085 Santa Barbara, CA, 93130; (805) 898-9660 or (805) 898-9199; www.HomeExchange.com

Home Exchange Vacationing–Your Guide to Free Accommodations, Bill Barbour, 1996.

Holiday Homes, 1989 British Tourist Authority (800) 462-2748 (within New York call (212) 986-2200); www.visitbritain.com

Home Rental Guide 95 Calle Vadito NW Albuquerque, NM 87120; (505) 836-8626; www.homerentalguide.com

Intercultural Press, (207) 846-5168. PO box 700 Yarmouth, ME 04096 International cultural information publications, with a large selection for those moving abroad. www.interculturalpress.com

Inter Exchange Au Pair USA; (212) 924-0446; www.interexchange.org

InterService Home Exchange Box 87 Glen Echo, MD 20812; (301) 229-7567.

INTERVAC International, PO Box 590504, San Francisco, CA 94159, (415) 435-3497; www.intervac.com Well established international network, with a large teacher interchange base. Has over 10,000 homes in 30 countries.

Travel To Go 6790 Top Gun St. #7, San Diego, CA 92121; (800) 477-6331.

Transitions Abroad Publishing Inc. PO Box 1300, Amherst, MA 01004-1300 (413) 256-3414, www.transitionsabroad.com

World Learning Inc. (formerly Experiment in International Living), (212) 924-0446.

Consumer Economic Assistance and Information

www.banxquote.com, www.bestrate.com, www.quicken.com and www.loanweb.com all have financial information websites, with information on mortgages, etc., and the ability to fill in a form and get your credit report quickly e-mailed to you for about $10. We like banxquote best, because it has a very consumer oriented list of best rate credit card services, mortgages and other banking services, while the others are mostly limited to advertisers.

Bauer Financial Reports, PO Drawer 145510, Coral Gables, FL 33114-5510, (800) 388-6686; www.bauerfinancial.com Private rating company which assesses the financial health of banks, and will issue individual reports to consumers.

Council of Better Business Bureaus, 4200 Wilson Blvd #800 Arlington, VA 22203; (703) 276-0100; www.bbb.org Contact for general business information, how to contact local Bureaus and direct links to local sites with a searchable database of business and charity organization reports.

CitiBank's Personal Banking for Overseas Employees, (212) 307-8511; www.citibank.com/pboe Expedites American checking accounts abroad.

Consumer Credit Counseling Service, (800) 388-CCCS; www.cccsebay.org National, nonprofit organization which offers a full program of credit repair classes, individual counseling and credit negotiating assistance for little or no fee. Check your phone book for a local branch.

Consumer Information Center which publishes over 200 free or low-cost government publications on topics like health, nutrition, careers, money management, and federal benefits. Of particular interest is the *Consumer Resource Handbook*, with lists of thousands of government and trade contacts throughout the country. Voice (719 948-4000; fax (719) 948-9724; www.pueblo.gsa.gov

Equifax (was CBI) PO Box 105873 Atlanta, GA 30348. Contact to pull your own credit report. (800) 685-1111 or www.equifax.com

Experian (was TRW) Contact to pull your own credit report. (800) 682-7654 or (888) 397-3742 or www.experian.com

FDIC (800) 934-3342. Handles questions or complaints about banks.

Tax information, IRS General Information, (800) TAX-1040. Tax forms and publications, (800) TAX-3676.

Veribanc, PO Box 461, Wakefield, MA 01880, (800) 442-2657. Private rating company which assesses the financial health of banks and issues reports to individuals.

Family Health Information and Services

American Association of Homes and Services for the Aging. News and information on housing and services. www.aahsa.com

AARP American Association of Retired Persons has various information and service sources. Several of their financial and homeowner services are listed separately, but to find out about their information on *How to Help Older Adults in Your Community Live Independently* (publication D16431) and other brochures and/or services, call AARP at (202) 434-3980 or look up their calendar of activities at www.aarp.org

Alzheimer's Disease and Related Disorders Programs, (800) 621-0379. 919 N Michigan Ave, #1000, Chicago, IL 60611-1676 www.alz.org Nationwide 24-hour information and referral line for assistance or information with nearby chapters and affiliates.

American Board of Medical Specialties, 47 Perimeter Center E. #500 Atlanta, GA 30346; (800) 776-CERT x 2378; www.certifieddoctor.org Operators answer questions about whether a particular physician is board-certified, the year certified, and the boards under which she received certification.

American Lung Association, 1-800-LUNG-USA (1-800-586-4872) www.lungusa.org

Arthritis Foundation HelpLine, (800) 283-7800. Newsletters describing local free therapy classes, support groups, etc.

www.barrier-free.com Catalog site explaining how to set up your home for independent living and listing some products for sale directly from the site.

Child Care Aware. Child care listing service. (800) 424-2246.

Child Care listings also available at www.rentnet.com

County Mental Health Association. Most counties operate a geriatric mental health program that offers a variety of services to the elderly and/or the children caring for them. Ask for free pamphlets addressed to grown children of aging parents, and about sliding-scale fees. Call the county Mental Health Association for help in assessing and dealing with the problems of your aging parents.

Diabetic Traveler, The, PO Box 8223, Stamford, CT 06905. Quarterly newsletter.

Diabetes Publishing. Catalog of mail-order diabetic supplies, including the Diapack, a travelling case which keeps insulin cold for hours without refrigeration. (800) 473-4636.

The Eldercare Locator. A public service of the Administration on Aging, U.S. Department of Health and Human Services and is administered by the National Association of Area Agencies on Aging and the National Association of State Units on Aging. Lists community assistance programs for seniors throughout the country. (800) 677-1116

National Association of Home Builders' Research Center Directory, 400 Prince George's Boulevard, Upper Marlboro, MD 20774. Look for their *Directory of Accessible Building Products.* (301) 249-4000; www.nahbrc.org

National Association of Child Care Resource and Referral Agencies. Child care information. To obtain a copy of *The Complete Guide to Choosing Child Care* published by the same organization, call (800) 462 1660.

National Association for the Education of Young Children, 1509 16th NW Washington DC 20036-1426; (800) 424 2460, www.naeyc.org Child care information and referrals. Send a stamped, self-addressed envelop requesting a list of accredited child care facilities in the region you want. You can call or reach them via email, but they prefer written requests.

National Child Care Information Center 243 Church Street, NW, 2nd Floor Vienna, VA 22180 Telephone: 800-616-2242 Fax: 800-716-2242 TTY: 800-516-2242. www.nccic.org

Easy Access Home Remodeling Information
- *Easy Access Housing for Easier Living*
- *Lifetime Homes,* Floorplans for fully accessible homes.
- *Resource List,* Organizations that can assist in building or adapting a home for accessibility.
Free Brochures from participating Century 21 offices, send an SASE or review the website of National Easter Seal Society, 230 West Monroe Street Suite 1800 Chicago, IL 60606; 800-221-6827; www.seals.com/html/easy_access/ eahousing.html

Parenting Publications of America. Nationwide list of local publications that cover events and information on local services for parents with children up to college level. (210) 492-9057; www.parentingpublications.org

Pets. www.pets.com lists products online, but no moving services. Ditto www.cyberpets.com (smaller site). www.AirAnimal.com only moves pets internationally for company employees who are relocating. www.spca.org has many suggestions and local SPCA addresses.

Senior Housing Development and Services. Offers tours of model apartments outfitted for the differently abled and elderly who are living independently. Stein Gerontological Institute, 5200 NE Second Ave. Miami, FL 33137 (305) 762-1465

www.seniornet.com List of senior citizen apartment complexes and retirement homes throughout the country.

www.utility.com helps you find alternative sources of electricity, gas and other utilities.

Home Buying, Renting and Auxiliary Services

AARP Home Equity Information Center. Ask for their brochure, "Home-Made Money: A Consumer's Guide to Home Equity Conversion" and a list of reverse mortgage lenders across the country. PO Box 2400, Long Beach, CA 90901-2400.

AARP Mobile Home Insurance Program, Foremost Insurance Group, Dept. 2701, PO Box 164, Grand Rapids, MI 49501, (800) 752-2441 www.foremost.com/aarp
Air Animal, (800) 635-3448. Moves pets all over the world.

American Society of Home Inspectors, 2625 Oakton Glen Drive, Vienna, VA 22181, (703) 938-1044.

Appraisal Institute, (312) 335-4100. 875 N Michigan Ave #2400 Chicago, IL 60611 Call for a list of local members.

ASPCA, Education Department, 441 East 92nd Street, New York, NY 10128. Write for $4 booklet, *Traveling With Your Pet*, with vaccination and quarantine requirements worldwide. www.aspca.org

Buyer's Agent, National franchise and network of buyer's real estate agents. 1255 A Lynnfield #273 Memphis TN 38119; (800) 766-8728, www.forbuyers.com.

Buyer's Resource. A national listing of Buyer's Agents. (800) 359-4092; www.buyersresource.com

Buyers Best Home Warranty. Warranty program for appliances and the mechanical systems of a home after it's been purchased. (818) 841-2320.

Buying a Home When You're Single, Donna G. Albrecht, 1993.

Deloitte & Touche (was PHH Fantus) www.us.deloitte.com/ Realest/Specialties/FANTUS.htm. Performs worldwide relocation research services for corporations. See USAA Relocation Service below for information on their real estate services to independent homebuyers (203) 834-8500.

Economic Research Institute. Issues compiled demographic and budget reports on various locations. (800) 627-3697.

Equity Sharing Book: How to Buy a Home Even if You Can't Afford the Down Payment, Bull, Diana, Elaine St. James.

For Sale by Owner: All the Contracts and Instructions Necessary to Sell Your Own California House, George Devine, 1999. Look for other books on selling without an agent in your home state.

For Rent Magazine. Chain of nearly two dozen national real estate photo advertisers covering major metropolitan areas. Each issue includes extensive picture ads of upscale apartment complexes, a real estate area map, grids comparing advertisers rentals by neighborhood and other helpful information. Free on local distribution stands. $4 a copy to be sent outside the area. (900) 420-0040.

Harmon Homes Magazine. Large, nationwide chain of real estate photo advertisers listing homes on sale with photographs and real estate agent contacts. Call to order copies for your targeted city (or cities) and surrounding area. (800) 955-5516.

Home Equity Sharing Manual, The, David Andrew Sirkin, 1994. Deal lawyers' extensive and knowledgeable explanation of using investor money to get started with a home in an expensive area.

HomePool Cooperative Resource Services. Offers counseling on both selling and buying your home, gives references on real estate agents nationwide, and works with a mortgage company that can do a "Home Pre-qualification," i.e., they'll

appraise your home and send you a letter stating that it qualifies for an 80 percent loan of a certain amount. (800) 321-
8000.

www.homes.com Extensive home listing site.

Homes and Land Magazine. One of the largest national
chains of homes for sale magazines. Call for subscription in
your destination location. (800) 277-7800.

Housing Guide Magazine. Published in more than 20 metropolitan areas in 15 states, with photos, features, prices and
easy-to-read maps. Lists new homes only. (800) HGA-3579,

*How Home Sellers, Buyers and Realty Agents Can Profit
from Lease Options,* Robert Bruss, $4.00, Tribune Publishing
Company, 75 East Amelia Street, Orlando, FL, 32801.

www.improvenet.com for finding contractors, but must fill
in a complicated and detailed form with information a homeowner unlikely to know, and then they'll search data base to
send you up to four contractors who fit your profile.

National Association of Home Builders offers area information, how to select a builder information and a nationwide
database of new home projects searchable by location.
www.nahb.org

National Association of Realtors multiple listing service
and area information. NAR hosts the largest online database of
homes for sale in the world. Unfortunately, this abbreviated
version of the MLS real estate agents use at their desks to pinpoint just the right home for their clients usually omits crucial
information like price and address. It is, however, the best way
to browse the market. Search for homes in your price range to
determine likely neighborhoods and agents. Or browse a global
search engine listings of local agencies and/or the local newspaper listings. www.realtor.com

National Center for Home Equity Conversion. Provides a
list of reverse mortgage lenders and information on sale leaseback; 348 West Main Street, Marshal, MN 56358.

Real Estate Book, The. Chain of nearly two dozen national real estate photo advertisers covering major metropolitan areas. Issues include extensive color photo ads from real estate companies, real estate area maps and other information. Free copies. (800) 841-3401. www.treb.com

Relocation Resources, (800) 422-2461. Buyer's Agents listings.

www.rent.net Has a similar list of apartment complexes as Springstreet (see below), but doesn't seem to have as many cities. Makes up for this by having numerous supplemental lists like complexes catering specifically to seniors, childcare services in various cities, etc.

www.springstreet.com (was www.allapartments.com) Lists large apartment complexes in almost every city of 500,000+. Many of the listings have ads, giving pictures and listing amenities, although currently the majority are simple listings of address (with map), phone number, email, and starting rent for various size units. Does NOT currently have individual homes or small complexes. Also, two other problems--they don't organize the list by price, so the best way to browse is to print out the list--and they only give fifty listings, then make you go back and revise your query to get more (which can overlap). Links to www.msn.sidewalk.com for listings and mapping of grocery stores, parks and schools in the vicinity very helpful, as are other links to entertainment, car registration, and utilities.

www.utility.com helps you find alternative sources of electricity, gas and other utilities.

USAA Banking Service Real Estate Assistance Program, (800) 582-8722. Families of active or retired military officers can receive free services of a Deloitte & Touche affiliated relocation consultant and discount real estate agency services by joining USAA.

Job Hunt, Business and Entrepreneur Services

ACCESS: Networking in the Public Interest. National non-profit employment listings. Large newsstands, libraries or 1001 Connecticut Ave., NW Suite 838 Washington, DC 20036 Phone: (202) 785-4233; www.communityjobs.org

American Business Women's Association, 9100 Ward Parkway, Kansas City, MO 64114, (816) 361-6621.

American City Business Journals, 120 W Morehead St. #400 Charlotte 28202 www.amcity.com (704) 375-7404. Call to find their publication nearest your new location.

American Society of Women Accountants, District of Columbia Chapter, 11350 Random Hills Road, Suite 800, Fairfax, VA 22030, (703) 938-7114.

American Women's Society of CPA's, 401 North Michigan Avenue, Chicago, IL 60611, (312) 644-6610.

Association of Outplacement Consultation Firms, 364 Parsippany Road, Parsippany, NJ 07054.

Business Assistance Service, Office of Business Liaison, 14th & Constitution, Room U.S. Department of Commerce, www.doc.gov/agencies/oca/index.html (202) 482-5001.

Business & Professional Women's Foundation, 2012 Massachusetts Avenue NW, Washington, DC 20036, (202) 293-1100.

Cooperative Education Consumer Education Catalog, Consumer Information Center-2C, PO Box 100, Pueblo, CO 81002. Catalog of consumer information brochures including "Job Outlook for College Grads 2000," "The Job Outlook in Brief," and "Matching Yourself with the World of Work Requirements." They also have brochures on other topics (see Consumer Assistance)

Crain Communications Inc. Publishes a national chain of local business newspapers headquartered in Chicago. Contact to find out if there's one in your new location, and/or subscribe. (312) 649 5200.

The Directory of Executive Recruiters, Kennedy Publications, (603) 585-6544. www.kennedyinfo.com

Directory of Women Business Owners, U.S. Chamber of Commerce, Superintendent of Documents, U.S. Government Printing Office, Washington, DC 20404-9325.

Dow Jones National Business Employment Weekly, (800) JOB-HUNT (800 562-4868). Mainly managerial and sales positions, plus articles on workplace trends. Newsstands, libraries or 3-month subscription.

Encyclopedia of Associations. The ultimate resource list of associations related to your business or industry. Call local chapters in likely organizations to see if you can attend a meeting on an investigatory trip to ask questions about job opportunities.

Encyclopedia of Business Information Sources, by James Woy.

Executive Female Magazine, National Association for Female Executives, (800) 634-NAFE (6233).

www.entrepreneurmag.com helpful, well executed online version of magazine, with links to other startup, home office, entrepreneur publications, etc.

Financial Women International, 200 North Glebe Rd., Suite 820 Arlington, VA 22203 (703) 807-2007 www.fwi.org

Government Resource Guides, 2392 Morse Avenue, PO Box 19787, Irvine, CA 92713-9438, (800) 421-2300. Information on how to start a business for entrepreneurs. See also Score, below.

How to Get a Job In... (various locations nationwide) Surrey Books, Inc., 230 E. Ohio St, #120, Chicago, IL 60611 Series of directories of job sources for various cities across the country. In most bookstores and libraries, or contact the publisher.

How to Get a Job Overseas, Casewit, Curtis W., Arco Publishing, 215 Park Ave S., New York, N.Y. 10003. Lists job opportunities worldwide, with insider's tips on what different countries and positions are like. Bookstores, libraries or write publisher.

International Council for Small Business/USASBE, 975 University Avenue, Room 3260, Madison, WI 53706, (608) 262-9982. Professional association to promote small business entrepreneurs.

International Employment Gazette. Large newsstands, libraries or (800) 882-9188 or www.intemployment.com for subscription. Competes with the *WSJ National Employment Weekly*, emphasis on ads for international positions.

...*JobBank*, Series, various editors. Adams Media Corp., (800) USA-JOBS (800 872-5627) or MA (781) 767-8100. Job source directories for more than 20 metropolitan areas nationwide. Adams also does a number of career guides. Available in bookstores, libraries, and from publisher.

National Association for Female Executives, 800-634-6233 www.nafe.com Chapters throughout the country for networking. Caters to both corporate and entrepreneur women. Services include health coverage, credit cards, car insurance, etc.

National Directory of Address and Telephone Numbers, The SMART Resource Center, (800) 848-8000. Sells national and international telephone directories.

National Association for the Cottage Industries, PO Box 14850, Chicago, IL 60614, (773) 472-8116.

National Association of Black Women Entrepreneurs Inc. PO Box 1375 Detroit, MI 48231 (313) 341-7400

National Association of Corporate & Professional Recruiters, 4000 Woodstone Way, Louisville, KY 40241.

National Association of Executive Recruiters, 222 South Westmonte Drive, Suite 101, Altamonte Springs, FL 32714. Membership Directory & Annual Directory of professional and trade associations nationwide.

National Association of Negro Business & Professional Women, 1806 New Hampshire Avenue NW, Washington, DC 20009, (202) 483-4206.

National Association of Small Business Investment Companies; 11th Street, NW; Suite 750 Washington DC 20001; (202) 628-5055; www.nasbic.org

National Association of Women Business Owners (NAWBO), 1100 Wayne Avenue, Suite 830 Silver Spring, MD 20910 800 55-NAWBO; www.nawbo.org

National Association of Women in Construction, 327 South Adam Street, Fort Worth, TX 76104, (817) 877-5551. www.nawic.org

National Federation of Independent Business (NFIB). The country's largest small business association, with more than 500,000 member business owners. In addition to representing small business interests to state and federal governments, it distributes educational information and publications. 600 Maryland Avenue SW, Suite 700, Washington, DC 20024, (202) 554-9000. www.nfibonline.com

National Network of Commercial Real Estate Women, 1201 Wakarusa Drive #1A; Lawrence, KA 66049; (888) 8NN-CREW. www.nncrew.org

National Women's Economic Alliance Foundation, 808 17th Street NW, #600, Washington, DC 20006, (202) 393-5257.

Network of City Business Journals, (800) 433-4565. Publishes 69 local business newspapers nationwide. Great sources for local business trend information, event calendars and contacts for job hunters.

"Occupational Outlook Quarterly," *Consumer Information Catalog,* Consumer Information Center-2C, PO Box 100, Pueblo, CO 81002. For job seekers and employment counselors. Overviews of new occupations, salary and job trends, and more. Annual subscription. Four issues. $6.50.

Omnigraphics, (800) 234-1340. Publishes area *Sourcebooks* of site selection information.

Organization of Chinese American Women 4641 Montgomery Avenue., #208 Bethesda, MD 20814 Phone (301) 907-3898 Fax (301) 907-3899.

Quill Corporation P.O. Box 94080 Palatine, IL 60094-4080 (800) 789-1331 www.quill-office-supplies.com Discount office products with free delivery.

Score. Small Business Administration assisted local classes, libraries and contact organization. Look them up in the government section of your local phone book, or check out their website at www.score.org

Management Consultant Network Intl. 858 Longview Road Burlingame, CA 94010 Phone: (415) 342-5259 Fax: (415) 344-5005 www.mcni.com

U.S. Hispanic Chamber of Commerce. Promotes Hispanic participation in business and business leadership. Conducts conferences, workshops and management training sessions, and compiles statistics and reports on Hispanics in business. 1019 19th St. NW, Suite 200, Washington, DC 20036 Phone: (202) 842-1212 Fax (202) 842-3221 www.ushcc.com

What Color is Your Parachute?, Richard Bowles, classic how-to-find a new job handbook. Re-edited and issued annually.

WSJ National Employment Weekly. Published by the *Wall Street Journal*, this is the largest and best known national job available newspaper. Almost 100% managerial positions. Newsstands or libraries (800) JOB-HUNT.

Walter Drake, (800) 525-9291 Economically priced return address stamps, printed letterheads and envelopes, business cards, starter stationery sets for setting up in your new location.

Women Construction Owners & Executives, (800) 788-3548. National trade organization with branches throughout the country.

Women in Government Relations, Inc., 1029 Vermont Avenue NW, Suite 510, Washington, DC 20005, (202) 347-5432.

Women's Guide To Starting a Business, Holt, Rhinehart, Winston, Genie Chips, Claudia Jessup, New York, NY. Explains how to organize a business and keep it running, as well as how to calculate cost, pick a location, raise money, and other issues.

Catalogs for Odds and Ends as You Settle In

Catalogs, 951 Broken Sound Pkwy NW, Building 190, PO Box 5057, Boca Raton, FL 33431-0857. This is a catalog of catalogs, including stained glass windows, antique clocks, carpentry tools, etc.

Damark, (800) 827-6767. Don't go for their membership club, their basic catalog is just as good for closeouts on computers, home and office accessories, furnishings, etc.

J.C. Whitney & Co., (312) 431-6102. Automotive parts and accessories.

Outdoor and Getaway Information

American Wilderness Experience, PO Box 1486, Boulder, CO 80306-1486, (800) 444-0099.

Backroads Bicycle Touring, 801 Cedar Street, Berkeley, CA 94710, (800) 245-3874.

Canoe Magazine, (425) 827-6363.

Echo: The Wilderness Company, 6529 Telegraph Avenue, Oakland, CA 94609, (510) 652-1600.

Sierra Club, 85 Second Street, Second Floor, San Francisco CA, 94105-3441, Telephone 415-977-5500; Fax 415-977-5799. www.sierraclub.org, Nonprofit association promoting nationwide environmental education. Conducts wilderness lectures and tours worldwide.

Relocation and Moving Publications and Services

American Moving and Storage Association. Trade association of the large household transportation companies, which runs an arbitration system for individuals in disputes with moving companies. Website also has other helpful information plus links to members' local websites and a worksheet to estimate your moving costs. Call, write or fill in their online form. 1611 Duke Street, Alexandria, VA 22314. Contact (703) 683-7410 general number or (703) 706-4978 for the arbitration department or review the website at www.moving.org

Bradley's. Discount packing materials. Call for extensive catalog. (800) 621-7864.

Employee Relocation Council Directory, Employee Relocation Council. Relocation service industry trade group. Annual Directory of relocation service companies that work mainly with companies. 1720 "N" Street NW, Washington, DC 20036, (202) 857-0857

Interstate Commerce Commission's Office of Compliance and Consumer Assistance (the ICC) was a governmental office where consumers could take complainants about interstate moving companies. It was not outstandingly effective, and was abolished in 1996. Currently consumers can only take their intra state complaints to state utility company and interstate complaints to the trade oversight group, the American Moving and Storage Association (see this section of the Contact Directory, above).

www.moverquotes.com Wonderful site listing all kinds of moving companies, including less than load (LTL) shippers and services that do just your loading or driving. Includes calculators giving average costs of various transportation options fitted toyour specs.

RELO International. The largest international network of independent real estate agencies. Can supply a list of companies in both current and destination locations. (312) 616-0400. www.relo.com

Appendix D

BUDGETING BASICS

MONTHLY BUDGET ESTIMATOR

MOVING RELATED
IRS TAX INFORMATION PUBLICATIONS

THE WHY'S AND WHEREFORE'S OF
TAX FORM 3903

SAMPLE TAX FORM 3903

FIXER-UPPER BUDGET ESTIMATOR

LOAN PAYMENT CALCULATOR

LOAN QUALIFICATION WORKSHEET

LOAN QUALIFICATION LOOK-UP TABLES

If we make $50,000 in Omaha, we need to make $63,000 in Portland

MONTHLY BUDGET ESTIMATOR

Runzheimer International, (800) 558-1702 and BTA Economic Research Institute, (800) 627-3697, both corporate relocation assistance companies, can supply living costs for a number of cities in the U.S. and abroad. Below is an estimator you can create on your own using salaries you expect and research sources such as local newspaper ads, shopper ads, and real estate photo advertisers.

ITEM	CURRENT	NEW	DIFFERENCE
INCOME			
Salary			
Investments			
Other			
TOTAL INCOME			
HOME COSTS —RENTED			
Rent			
Deposit			
Renter's Insurance			
HOME OWNERSHIP			
Mortgage Principle & Interest (Use our Loan Payment Calculator that follows for new amounts.)			
Homeowner's Insurance			
Real Estate Taxes			
Remodeling			
Pool, Gardening etc.			
Maintenance			
Other			
UTILITIES			
Water (high water usage charges in some areas may change your water use habits)			
Garbage			

Electric			
Gas			
Telephone			
Other			
INSURANCE			
Health			
Life			
Car			
Other			
HOUSEHOLD EXPENSES			
Food			
Clothing			
Sales/Other Local Taxes			
State Income Tax			
Schooling			
Entertainment			
Other			
TRANSPORTATION			
Public Transport			
Commute			
Gas			
Auto Insurance			
Auto Loan			
Auto Maintenance			
Taxes			
Other			
TOTAL EXPENSES			
DISCRETIONARY FUNDS REMAINING			

MOVING RELATED IRS TAX INFORMATION PUBLICATIONS

You can get further information and the following publications from a local IRS office or the Internet at www.irs.gov or call the national help lines at (800) 829-1040 and (800) 829-4477. For free filing forms and publications call (800) 829-3676. *Note:* Besides the booklets listed below, the IRS has instruction sheets for each form required. Also, many of the publications and form instructions are available in Spanish.

GENERAL GUIDES
#3	"Tax Information for Military Personnel (Including Reservists Called to Active Duty)"
#4	"Student's Guide to Federal Income Taxes"
#17	"Your Federal Income Tax for Individuals"
#463	"Travel, Entertainment and Gift Expenses" (for temporary moves and jobhunting expenses)
#509	"Tax Calendars for (the current year)"
#521	"Moving Expenses"
#529	"Miscellaneous Deductions"
#552	"Recordkeeping for Individuals"
#554	"Tax Information for Older Americans"
#907	"Tax Information for Persons with Handicaps or Disabilities"
#910	"Guide to Free Tax Services"

BUSINESSES
#15	"Employer's Tax Guide"
#334	"General Tax Guide for Small Business"
#583	"Taxpayers Starting a Business"
#937	"Employment Taxes"
#953	"International Tax Information for Business"

CIVILIANS GOING ABROAD
#54	"Tax Guide for U.S. Citizens and Resident Aliens Abroad"
#514	"Foreign Tax Credit for Individuals"
#516	"Tax Information for U.S. Government Civilian Employees Stationed Abroad"
#593	"Tax Highlights for U.S. Citizens and Residents Going Abroad"
#597	"Information on the United States-Canada Income Tax Treaty"
#686	"Certification for Reduced Tax Rates in Tax Treaty Countries"
#901	"U.S. Tax Treaties"

CIVILIANS COMING TO THE UNITED STATES
#513	"Tax Information for Visitors to the United States"
#514	"Foreign Tax Credit for Individuals"
#515	"Withholding of Tax on Nonresident Aliens and Foreign Corporations"
#519	"U.S. Tax Guide for Aliens"

HOMEOWNERS/PROPERTY OWNERS
#523   "Tax Information on Selling Your Home"
#527   "Residential Rental Property"
#530   "Tax Information for First-Time Homeowners"
#534   "Depreciation"
#537   "Installment Sales"
#544   "Sales and Other Dispositions of Assets"
#551   "Basis of Assets"
#555   "Federal Tax Information on Community Property"
#587   "Business Use of Your Home"
#924   "Reporting of Real Estate Transactions to IRS"
#925   "Passive Activity and at Risk Rules"
#936   "Home Mortgage and Interest Deduction"
#946   "How to Begin Depreciating Your Property"

CRISIS MOVES
#504   "Tax Information for Divorced or Separated Individuals"
#547   "Nonbusiness Disasters, Casualties, and Thefts"
#559   "Tax Information for Survivors, Executors, and Administrators"
#584   "Nonbusiness Disaster, Casualty, and Theft Loss Workbook"

MOVING SPECIFIC FORMS
(should include instruction sheet)
Schedule D (incl Capital Gain Income on Sale of Personal Residence)
#2119 Sale of Home
#3903 Moving Expenses
#6252 Installation Sale Income
#8822 Change of Address
#8396 MCC Mortgage Interest Credit
#8829 Expenses for Business Use of Your Home

THE WHY'S AND WHEREFORE'S OF
TAX FORM 3903

Important Note: Before you take the time to fill out this form, review any reimbursements from your employer. If your reimbursements matched your deductible expenses and were distributed via an accountable plan, you don't need to fill out this form because the reimbursement income was not subject to withholding (see Chapter 4 for more explanation).

Lines 1-3 The Mileage Test.

Here's where you determine whether or not your new job is far enough away to qualify you for moving expense deductions.

Lines 4-6 Deductible Expenses.

It's important to keep all receipts, not just the major ones from the moving and storage companies. Check with your tax preparer about including other possible expenses like piano tuning fees, shipping a pet, etc.

Your deductible moving trip expenses currently include 100 percent deductions for travel (airline tickets, car/trailer expenses, etc.) and lodging both along the way and on the first night after the movers take your furniture before departure and the first night of arrival.

Note that you can NOT deduct meal expenses, and if you don't itemize car expenses with receipts, etc., mileage can only be written off at a proscribed rate per a mile (which is currently less than the amount allowed for business car expenses). Be careful to keep expenses "reasonable." Don't throw in a side trip to Orlando in a move from Boston to Atlanta.

Mark which receipts your employer is reimbursing, and check your records against the reimbursement record your employer gives you. Store all of this information with your tax returns (the IRS doesn't want it unless they audit you).

Line 7 - Employer's Reimbursements NOT Included as Wages.

Here's where you match up your deductible expenses against reimbursements that did not have withholding taken out. Your employer should have reported them on your W-2 in a specified box, not with wages.

Line 8 - Final Calculation.

Deduct your reimbursements from your expenses. If you happen to have more reimbursements than expenses, you must transfer the extra into your taxable income. You can only deduct expenses in excess of your reimbursements. Enter this number as a deduction in the Adjustments to Income section on the front page of your IRS.

Note: Unlike Job Search Expenses, which are listed with Other Miscellaneous Deductions on Schedule A, Moving Expenses are **not** subject to any floor or other Schedule A restrictions (see text in Chapter 4).

If you enjoy creative physical challenges and you have patience to

SAMPLE IRS FORM 3903

Form **3903**
(Rev. October 1998)
Department of the Treasury
Internal Revenue Service

Moving Expenses

▶ Attach to Form 1040.

OMB No. 1545-0062

Attachment
Sequence No. **62**

Name(s) shown on Form 1040

Your social security number

Before you begin, see the Distance Test and Time Test in the instructions to make sure you can take this deduction. If you are a member of the armed forces, see the instructions to find out how to complete this form.

1	Enter the amount you paid for transportation and storage of household goods and personal effects (see instructions)	1
2	Enter the amount you paid for travel and lodging expenses in moving from your old home to your new home. Do not include meals (see instructions)	2
3	Add lines 1 and 2	3
4	Enter the total amount your employer paid you for the expenses listed on lines 1 and 2 that is not included in the wages box (box 1) of your W-2 form. This amount should be identified with code P in box 13 of your W-2 form	4
	Is line 3 more than line 4?	
	Yes. Go to line 5.	
	No. You cannot deduct your moving expenses. If line 3 is less than line 4, subtract line 3 from line 4 and include the result on the "Wages, salaries, tips, etc." line of Form 1040.	
5	Subtract line 4 from line 3. Enter the result here and on the "Moving expenses" line of Form 1040. This is your **moving expense deduction**	5

FIXER-UPPER BUDGET ESTIMATOR

overcome repetitive setbacks, you may want to consider transforming a fixer upper into your own version of a castle. The crucial questions are how much is it *really* going to cost and will it be *worth* the cost.

Here is a sample budget/required resale value estimator for a renovation that needed extensive work before we could move in. Along with the "hard costs" of supplies, repairs and workmen, we calculated our own "Project Manager Fee" to make up for the wages lost on other projects while we worked on this rehab. We also included mortgage carrying costs while the place was unlivable to the overall project cost. The mortgage costs will not be added in if you opt to live in the property while you're rehabbing, to avoid paying lenders on both your new purchase and your existing home.

ITEM	OURS	YOURS
Purchase Price	$100,000	_____
Rehab Work (get several bids for every item)		
Roof	not needed	_____
Electrical	$ 5,400	_____
Plumbing	$ 4,300	_____
Carpentry	$ 4,800	_____
New Kitchen Cabinets		
and Appliances	$ 2,300	_____
New Bath Fixtures	$ 1,200	_____
Foundation	$ 7,000	_____
Total Rehab Work	$ 25,000	_____
Time Needed to Do Work	6 months	_____
Mortgage Payments During Work	$ 4,250	_____
Plus Unexpected Disaster Fund	$ 5,000	_____
(Estimate @ 20% of Tot Rehab $25,000)		
Total Cash Needed to Do Work	$34,250	_____
Plus Our Fee as Project Managers	$18,000	_____
(Estimate @ $3,000 / Mo)		
Plus Our Fee as Venture Capitalists	$17,125	_____
(We Want 50% Profit on the		
Total $34,250 Cash Needed—also known		
as our "Raging and Weeping" fee)		
REQUIRED Total Value of Home		
Upon Completion	$169,375	_____

Check the comparable remodeled properties in the same neighborhood as the fixer you've found. If they're selling for a price above the REQUIRED Total Value of your completed home, you've got a good deal, value wise.

LOAN PAYMENT CALCULATOR FOR EACH $1,000 OF LOAN

Monthly and Annual Total Principle & Interest Payment Factor for Each $1 Borrowed.
Steps:
1. Find your interest rate in the left-hand column.
2. Go across the row to the applicable length of loan term column.
3. Multiply the factor found times the amount of your loan (see next page example).

Interest Rate	30 Yr Monthly Payment	30 Yr Annual Payment	15 Yr Monthly Payment	15 Yr Annual Payment
3.00%	0.00422	0.05059	0.00691	0.08287
3.25%	0.00435	0.05222	0.00703	0.08432
3.50%	0.00449	0.05389	0.00715	0.08579
3.75%	0.00463	0.05557	0.00727	0.08727
4.00%	0.00477	0.05729	0.00740	0.08876
4.25%	0.00492	0.05903	0.00752	0.09027
4.50%	0.00507	0.06080	0.00765	0.09180
4.75%	0.00522	0.06260	0.00778	0.09334
5.00%	0.00537	0.06442	0.00791	0.09490
5.25%	0.00552	0.06626	0.00804	0.09647
5.50%	0.00568	0.06813	0.00817	0.09805
5.75%	0.00584	0.07003	0.00830	0.09965
6.00%	0.00600	0.07195	0.00844	0.10126
6.25%	0.00616	0.07389	0.00857	0.10289
6.50%	0.00632	0.07585	0.00871	0.10453
6.75%	0.00649	0.07783	0.00885	0.10619
7.00%	0.00665	0.07984	0.00899	0.10786
7.25%	0.00682	0.08186	0.00913	0.10954
7.50%	0.00699	0.08391	0.00927	0.11124
7.75%	0.00716	0.08597	0.00941	0.11295
8.00%	0.00734	0.08805	0.00956	0.11468
8.25%	0.00751	0.09015	0.00970	0.11642

LOAN PAYMENT CALCULATOR FOR EACH $1,000 OF LOAN

Example: You need to find out how much your annual loan payment would be for a
5175,000 loan, amortized for 30 years, at a 90/6 interest rate:

$175,000 x .09655 = $16,896 annually

Note: These factor figures have been rounded off at five decimal places. Your bank's
calculation of your total annual loan payment may vary slightly. Also, sometimes ads
and lender's rate sheets give you a factor to be used per $1,000 borrowed. The calcu-
lation is the same, except you have to divide your loan amount by $1,000, then multiply
the result by the factor given.

Interest Rate	30 Yr Monthly Payment	30 Yr Annual Payment	15 Yr Monthly Payment	15 Yr Annual Payment
8.50%	0.00769	0.09227	0.00985	0.11817
8.75%	0.00787	0.09440	0.00999	0.11993
9.00%	0.00805	0.09655	0.01014	0.12171
9.25%	0.00823	0.09872	0.01029	0.12350
9.50%	0.00841	0.10090	0.01044	0.12531
9.75%	0.00859	0.10310	0.01059	0.12712
10.00%	0.00878	0.10531	0.01075	0.12895
10.25%	0.00896	0.10753	0.01090	0.13079
10.50%	0.00915	0.10977	0.01105	0.13265
10.75%	0.00933	0.11202	0.01121	0.13451
11.00%	0.00952	0.11428	0.01137	0.13639
11.25%	0.00971	0.11655	0.01152	0.13828
11.50%	0.00990	0.11883	0.01168	0.14018
11.75%	0.01009	0.12113	0.01184	0.14210
12.00%	0.01029	0.12343	0.01200	0.14402
12.25%	0.01048	0.12575	0.01216	0.14596
12.50%	0.01067	0.12807	0.01233	0.14790
12.75%	0.01087	0.13040	0.01249	0.14986
13.00%	0.01106	0.13274	0.01265	0.15183
13.25%	0.01126	0.13509	0.01282	0.15381
13.50%	0.01145	0.13745	0.01298	0.15580
13.75%	0.01165	0.13981	0.01315	0.15780

LOAN QUALIFICATION WORKSHEET

Lenders use this formula to determine the size of the annual loan payment you can make, and therefore, how much you qualify to borrow. They're concerned with both the ratio of your mortgage payments to your total annual income and the ratio of all your reoccurring payments on other debts to your total annual income. Below, the sample lender sets the "PITI" (Principle, Interest, Taxes and Insurance) ratio at 28% and the borrower's total Debt Ratio at 36 %. Your lender's ratios may be different. Ask your lender what expenses they include in your total family debt.

1. Fill in the blanks on rows "b, c, & q" in your Lender Ratio column with the percentages (Borrower Qualification Ratios) that your lender gives you.
2. Fill in the last column with your personal budget dollars.
3. Calculate Preliminary "PI" (Principle and Interest) yearly payment on row "g," subtracting "b" from "f."
4. Calculate the annual amount your Lender considers to be your maximum "PI" (Principle and Interest) yearly loan payment on row "p."
5. Coordinate your "PI" from row "p" with the loan rate column on the following Loan Qualification Look-Up Table to determine

	Catagories	Sample Lender Ratio %	Sample Budget	Your Lender Ratio %	Your Budget
	Salary, Borrower #1		$36,800		$
	Salary, Borrower #2		$33,500		$
	Self-Employment Income		$5,800		$
	Investment & Interest Income		$1,000		$
	Other Income				$
a	TOTAL ANNUAL INCOME	100%	$77,100	100%	$

LOAN QUALIFICATION WORKSHEET

	Categories	Sample	Sample	Your Lender	Your Budget
b	Max. "PITI" (Principle, Interest, Taxes, Insurance) Allowed (Lender % x Your Total Annual Income from row (a))	28%	$21,588	%	$
c	Max. Family Debt Allowed (Lender % x Total Annual Income)	36%	$27,756	%	$
d	Real Estate Taxes (New Home) "T"		$2,633		$
e	Insurance (New Home) "I"		$1,322		$
f	Total House Obligations "T" (d + e)		$3,955		$
g	PRELIMINARY Qualified "PI" (LOAN) Payment (b-f)		$17,634		$
h	Student Loan Yearly Payment		$2,436		$
i	Auto Loan Yearly Payment		$3,072		$
j	Credit Card Yearly Payment		$243		$
k	Alimony Yearly Payment		$0		$
l	Vacation Home Yearly Mortgage Payment		$0		$
m	Other Yearly Payment		$551		$
n	Total Fixed Household Payments (add d thru m)		$27,890		$
o	Excess Debt if n is larger than c, subtract c-n, or enter Zero)		($134)		$ ( )
p	MAX. Qualified "PI" Payment (subtract g-o)		$17,500		$
q	MAX. Loan Amt. Allowed at Current Lender Loan Rate	9%	$181,244	%	$

LOAN QUALIFICATION LOOK-UP TABLES

Loan Rate	Max PI $10,000	Max PI $12,500	Max PI $15,000	Max PI $17,500	Max PI $20,000	Max PI $22,500	Max PI $25,000
4.00	$174,551	$218,189	$261,827	$305,464	$349,102	$392,740	$436,378
4.25	$169,397	$211,747	$254,096	$296,445	$338,795	$381,144	$423,493
4.50	$164,468	$205,585	$246,701	$287,818	$328,935	$370,052	$411,169
4.75	$159,750	$199,688	$239,625	$279,563	$319,501	$359,438	$399,376
5.00	$155,235	$194,043	$232,852	$271,661	$310,469	$349,278	$388,087
5.25	$150,910	$188,638	$226,366	$264,093	$301,821	$339,549	$377,276
5.50	$146,768	$183,460	$220,152	$256,844	$293,536	$330,228	$366,920
5.75	$142,799	$178,498	$214,198	$249,897	$285,597	$321,297	$356,996
6.00	$138,993	$173,741	$208,490	$243,238	$277,986	$312,734	$347,483
6.25	$135,344	$169,179	$203,015	$236,851	$270,687	$304,523	$338,359
6.50	$131,842	$164,803	$197,764	$230,724	$263,685	$296,645	$329,606
6.75	$128,482	$160,603	$192,723	$224,844	$256,964	$289,085	$321,206
7.00	$125,256	$156,570	$187,884	$219,199	$250,513	$281,827	$313,141
7.25	$122,158	$152,698	$183,237	$213,777	$244,316	$274,856	$305,395
7.50	$119,181	$148,977	$178,772	$208,567	$238,363	$268,158	$297,953
7.75	$116,320	$145,400	$174,481	$203,561	$232,641	$261,721	$290,801
8.00	$113,570	$141,962	$170,354	$198,747	$227,139	$255,532	$283,924
8.25	$110,924	$138,655	$166,386	$194,117	$221,848	$249,579	$277,309
8.50	$108,378	$135,473	$162,567	$189,662	$216,756	$243,851	$270,945
8.75	$105,928	$132,410	$158,891	$185,373	$211,855	$238,337	$264,819
9.00	$103,568	$129,460	$155,352	$181,244	$207,136	$233,028	$258,921

LOAN QUALIFICATION LOOK-UP TABLES

Loan Rate	Max PI $10,000	Max PI $12,500	Max PI $15,000	Max PI $17,500	Max PI $20,000	Max PI $22,500	Max PI $25,000
9.25	$101,296	$126,619	$151,943	$177,267	$202,591	$227,915	$253,239
9.50	$99,106	$123,882	$148,658	$173,435	$198,211	$222,988	$247,764
9.75	$96,995	$121,243	$145,492	$169,741	$193,989	$218,238	$242,486
10.00	$94,959	$118,699	$142,439	$166,178	$189,918	$213,658	$237,398
10.25	$92,995	$116,244	$139,493	$162,742	$185,991	$209,240	$232,489
10.50	$91,101	$113,876	$136,651	$159,426	$182,201	$204,976	$227,752
10.75	$89,272	$111,589	$133,907	$156,225	$178,543	$200,861	$223,179
11.00	$87,505	$109,382	$131,258	$153,134	$175,011	$196,887	$218,763
11.25	$85,799	$107,249	$128,699	$150,148	$171,598	$193,048	$214,498
11.50	$84,150	$105,188	$126,225	$147,263	$168,301	$189,338	$210,376
11.75	$82,556	$103,196	$123,835	$144,474	$165,113	$185,752	$206,391
12.00	$81,015	$101,269	$121,523	$141,777	$162,031	$182,284	$202,538
12.25	$79,524	$99,405	$119,287	$139,168	$159,049	$178,930	$198,811
12.50	$78,082	$97,602	$117,123	$136,643	$156,163	$175,684	$195,204
12.75	$76,685	$95,857	$115,028	$134,199	$153,370	$172,542	$191,713
13.00	$75,333	$94,166	$113,000	$131,833	$150,666	$169,499	$188,333
13.25	$74,023	$92,529	$111,035	$129,541	$148,046	$166,552	$185,058
13.50	$72,754	$90,943	$109,131	$127,320	$145,508	$163,697	$181,885
13.75	$71,524	$89,405	$107,286	$125,167	$143,048	$160,929	$178,810
14.00	$70,331	$87,914	$105,497	$123,079	$140,662	$158,245	$175,828

Appendix E

SAMPLE CORRESPONDENCE, AGREEMENTS AND NEGOTIATING HIGHLIGHTS

SAMPLE ALTERNATIVE MOVE CORRESPONDENCE

Home Trade Query Letters

Potential Occupancy Agreement

Personal/Business Referral Letter

VERIFICATION OF CREDIT AND INCOME

LANDLORD/TENANT MOVE-OUT/DEPOSIT REFUND AGREEMENT

SELLER'S PROPERTY DISCLOSURE FORM

LEGAL DOCUMENT SOURCE LIST

SAMPLE ALTERNATIVE MOVE
CORRESPONDENCE

The following sample letters can be used as models for correspondence with out of towner's planning to stay in your home. These forms can also be used for Short Term Furnished Rentals or Homesharing. They are aimed at a house trade, because that is the most complex Alternative Move, but you can adapt them to fit any type of Alternative Move.

It's a big timesaver to fill these forms out once, and send photocopies to all potential occupants. You *must* keep a filled-in copy for yourself, because people are likely to call when they get it and ask questions.

The forms assume that residents will usually be two or more people, but if you are single, just change all the "we's" to "I's". It's important to customize the form for your specific use.

For example, you may not want people coming into your home to use your new stereo system. You can disconnect it and lock it away in a closet (the preferred plan with all fragile or irreplaceable items), or state clearly on the "off limits" line that this is an amenity you are *not* extending.

SAMPLE HOME TRADE QUERY LETTER

Dear _____ Date _____
We would like to trade homes with you.
Our house has ___ bedrooms and ___ baths. It is located
about ___ miles from the center of (city, state)
_____ in a (residential, suburban, young, etc.)
_____ community. The are both public
and private schools within (distance) _____. Shopping
is a short (distance) _____ drive and we have shopping malls
within ___ miles.
As you may know, (city/area) _____ is the center of (describe unique and enjoyable features of area)
_____ and there are theaters and
other cultural attractions in (location)_____.
My spouse (name) _____ and I wish to
trade for ___ months some time between (date) _____ and
(date) _____. We are coming to (destination)
_____ for (project, job, etc.)
_____. We are in our (ages) _____ and have
___ children, (ages) _____ and a (pets)_____.
We would like to exchange references and further information with you if our time period meshes with your plans. Looking forward to hearing from you.
Sincerely,
(name) _____
(address and phone) _____

PS: We got your name from (directory/ friends)
_____.

I'm enclosing photos of ourselves, our home and the general area to give you a better idea of what we are offering.

SAMPLE POTENTIAL OCCUPANCY AGREEMENT LETTER

Dear _____ Date_____

The following gives details on our home and the agreement we propose for your stay here. Please review. If you have any questions or things you need to do differently, please call us. Once everything is agreed, please photocopy, initial each page of both copies, sign the acknowledgment at the end of both copies and send us one copy with your "wet" signature.

Home Description:

Our home is _____ stories, _____ style. There are _____ bedrooms and ____ baths, and it is suitable for a MAXIMUM of ___ adults and ___ children. There is a (check all that apply) ___ living room, ___ den, ___ family room, ____ breakfast room, ___ dining room, ___ utility room, ___ sun porch, ___ garage, ___ carport, ___ street parking ____ other _____.

The things we like most about our home are

_____.

We also enjoy our views of (describe) _____ _____ _____, and relaxing around our ___ fireplace, ___ deck, ___ patio, ___ garden, ___ swimming pool.

The house is equipped with ___ television set(s), ___ VCR, ___ stereo set(s), ___ computer, ___ frost free refrigerator, ___ gas stove, ___ electric stove, ___ wall oven, ___ hot water heater, ___ micro wave, ___ dishwasher, ___ garbage disposal, ___ compactor, ___ bathtub, ___ jacuzzi, ___ shower, ___ bidet, ___ exercise equipment, — wall heaters, ___ radiators,___ air conditioner, ___ central heat and air, ___ furnace, ___ washer/dryer.

The furniture is mainly ___ modern, ___ traditional, ___ antique, ___ rustic. It ___ does//___ does not need careful handling. The only thing off limits is (explain equipment, belongings or rooms that are not to be used):

_____.

Our home is ___ owned //___ rented. If it is rented, the owner is ___ _____ at (telephone number)_____. A letter from him/her

___ will // ___ will not be furnished acknowledging our arrangement with you.

Our home is served by ___ city water, ___ public garbage collection, ___ gas company, ___ electrical company, ___ cable television, ___ daily mail, ___ telephone. These services are ___ very dependable, ___ dependable, ___ usually dependable. Explanation: _____
_____.

We ___ do // ___ do not have many pollen bearing plants in our area. The highest pollen count is usually (plants, count and active months) _____. Other environmental considerations are (list any high smog months, usual high/low temperatures at the time of year of the trade, extremes in heat or cold, etc.)
_____.

Our home is _____ miles from (list local scenic sites) _____ _____ and ___ miles from food and household item shopping in _____ (list closest shopping town). We'll be leaving behind information about how you can use our membership in (list any club memberships and privileges)
_____.

Chores:

We're ___ careful // ___ somewhat careful // ___ casual about housecleaning. WE AGREE TO LEAVE YOUR HOME JUST AS WE FOUND IT, AND TO REPAIR OR REPLACE ANYTHING THAT GETS BROKEN.

We're ___ making arrangements for someone else to take care of // ___ willing to trade the following chores: ___ taking care of our pet (describe) _____,
___ watering our house/garden plants, ___ gardening, ___ maintaining   pool,   ___   other
_____
_____.

We'll stock all supplies for the chores, so that you won't have any additional expenses.

We'll have the post office forward our mail. For the letters that get delivered by mistake, we'll leave behind several large pre-stamped envelops // ___ leave a box for you to store them

in. For magazines and advertisements please ___ store in box /
/___ throw away.

Food and Linens:

We'll leave out two clean sets of sheets and towels. We'd appreciate your having them washed when you leave. We'll leave stocks of sugar, coffee, tea, spices and some canned goods, plus a loaf of bread and some fruit in the refrigerator, so your first breakfast will be easy. We'd appreciate your leaving the same for us, at the end of your stay.

Vehicles:

A car ___ is //___ is not available for your use. It's a (give make, model, year, stick shift/automatic) _____ _____. It is ___ very dependable, ___ dependable, ___ usually dependable. Explain _____. We also have a (second car, recreational vehicle, boat, plane, other - describe) _____ for your use. We will leave you the name of our service shop.

Gasoline in our area runs $____ per gallon, and the car gets approximately ___ miles to the gallon.

If you want to use any of our vehicles, please send a photocopy of your current licenses with information on your insurance company for all vehicles you wish to use. List the information on your copy of this Agreement Letter, with the policy number, agent name and how to contact. That way, we can notify our insurance company and find out whether or not covering you will involve a surcharge. We'll prepay the basic insurance and will need you to send us your surcharge amount so you can prepay, as well. We'll send you a receipt from the insurance company.

We ___ do //___ do not wish to use your car. In order for us to be covered by your insurance policy, your insurance company may need the enclosed photocopy of our current drivers' licenses and our insurance information, which is (give company, policy number, agent name and telephone number) _____.
Please let us know if your company needs anything else and if there is any insurance surcharge to cover us so we can send you a check.

Household Insurance:
Our household insurance is (list agent name, company, policy number and whether or not contents are covered for fire, vandalism and theft) : _____.
Our insurance company tells us there ___ will // ___ will not be a surcharge to cover your possessions.   We ___ will // ___ will not need your insurance to cover our possessions, which we believe will have a value of $_____.
Please let us know if there will be any surcharge from your insurance, and we will send them a check to prepay that amount.

Other Bills:
We will pay our own ___ taxes, ___ mortgage, ___ rent via pre-written checks we've dated and left in an envelop for you to forward // ___ via an arrangement we've set up with separately. Other bills which we will be paying directly are
_____.
    Please OK with us any house repairs you wish us to reimburse that cost more than $_____ except for plumbing or other similar emergencies.   We'll leave a list of repair people contacts.
    We will expect you to pay the monthly utility and telephone bills you incur at our house, and we'll do the same at your house.   Our monthly utility bills for the time of year when you'll be here average $____ gas, $____ electricity, $____ water, $____ garbage, $____ cable tv, $____ telephone, $____ newspaper, $____   other   (describe)
_____.
    We will the utilities just before we leave to get the balance due on our share of bills, and we'll leave checks to pay that part. Please do the same.

People:
The people in our family who would be living in your house are _____
(adult(s), name(s), relationship) and _____
_____ (children, names, ages.) We ___ will // ___ will not have anyone else visiting us while we are at your house (describe)
_____. We
___ can // ___ cannot have children staying in our house. We
___ do // ___ do not have toys here for children to play with

(describe) _____.
We will leave the name of our babysitter.
　　Our profession is _____.
Our hobbies are _____. We're
particularly interested in finding out more about _____
_____ in your area, and would love
to meet people who _____.
Our children are active in _____,
and would like to meet other kids in those fields and/or find
out more about _____.
　　Exchange Dates:
　　At this time, we are ___ are not ___ certain that we will be
able to trade homes with you between (dates) _____ and
_____. We can make an absolute commitment by (date)
_____. Please confirm your commitment by (date)
_____.

　　We agree to the above:

_____

_____
Signature(s)   Date
Printed Name(s)

_____ _____

ACKNOWLEDGMENT

　　As potential Exchange Partners/Term Rental Tenants, we
have read this Agreement and the attached Check list, and agree
to exchange chores and pay bills as outlined.
　　Reviewed and Agreed:

_____

_____
Signature(s)   Date
Printed Name(s)

_____

SAMPLE PERSONAL/BUSINESS REFERRAL LETTER

It's a good idea to have several friends and/or business associates write you referral letters, and then have them be prepared to answer questions on the phone.

The following is a sample referral letter—don't have all your references copy it word for word, but it should give them some ideas about what to say.

Mr. Albert Brody, Branch Manager
1ST NATIONAL BANK OF CLEVELAND
1450 Allen Way
Cleveland, OH 87660
(510) 988 7566

January 30, 2000

Dear Sir/Madame:

This is a letter of referral for Mr. and Mrs. James Hobart of 13666 Sand Hill Drive in Cleveland.

I have worked with James Hobart, who has a small, but well run, contractor business here in Cleveland, for five years. During that time, his accounts are always kept paid, and the business has done well.

I have also been to the Hobart's home several times on social occasions, and enjoyed their outdoor barbecue parties.

If I were considering offering my home for a Trade or a Term Rental, I would certainly welcome the Hobarts.

Please call me at the above number if you have any questions.

Sincerely,

Albert Brody

VERIFICATION OF CREDIT AND INCOME

Please Complete a separate form for each adult who will be an occupant in the property. The information given will be treated as confidential and will not be revealed to outside parties. The acknowledgment at the bottom must be signed.

Name:
Hm Phone
Wk Phone
Soc Sec #
Date of Birth
Driver Lic #
Adult Co-Tenant(s) (Listed on Separate Application):
Accompanying Children Name(s)/Age(s):
Pets:
Present Address:
How Long at This Address:
Mo Rent$/Mo Mortgage:
Reason for Moving:
Landlord's Name:
Phone:
Prior Address:
How Long at This Address:
Prior Landlord's Name:
Phone:
Income
Present Occupation:
Employer:
Supervisor's Name:
Phone:

How long with this employer?
Gross Monthly Income:
Self-Employed D.B.A.
Type of Business:
How long with this business?
Fed EIN#
Gross Monthly Income:
Business Address:
Business Phone:
Previous Occupation:
Employer:
Supervisor's Name:
Phone:
How long with this employer?
Gross Monthly Income:
Other Income Sources (Stocks/Investments/Other):
Credit References
Bank/S&L:
Branch Tel:
Checking Account #:
Savings Account #:
Bank/S&L:
Branch Tel:
Checking Account #:
Savings Account #:
Major Credit Card #'s:
Car Make, Model, Year

Have you ever defaulted on a loan?
Filed bankruptcy?
Been evicted?
Personal References:
Name
Address
Tel #
Occupation
Relationship

I declare that the statements above are true and correct. I hereby authorize verification of all banking and other references given and herewith pay a non-refundable fee of $25 for obtaining of a full credit report. I agree that any misrepresentation herein is grounds for termination of any contract entered into on the basis of these statements:

Signed: _____ Tenant
Applicant Signature

Printed Name   Date

I hereby acknowledge receipt of $_____ non-refundable credit report fee

Signed: _____ Owner/
Agent Signature

Printed Name   Date

LANDLORD/TENANT MOVE OUT/DEPOSIT REFUND AGREEMENT

Tenant: _____ Apt#_____

Address:_____

Deposit: $_____

Move Out Date: _____

This is to certify that this tenant moved out of this apartment as of the date detailed above. At that time, the condition of the apartment was as detailed in the attached _____ Move In/Out Checklist _____ Initialed Photographs.

Charges were:

_____ Not assessed as apartment was vacated in good condition.

_____ To be determined by _____(date)

_____ Assessed as detailed below:

Explanation _____

_____

Amount Damage $	
Other $	
Cleaning $	
Rent/Other Fees $	

TOTAL $ _____

REFUND BALANCE DUE TENANT $_____

Landlord hereby agrees to:

___ pay the REFUND DUE TENANT immediately. BY SIGNING BELOW, THE TENANT ACKNOWLEDGES RECEIPT OF THE REFUND.

___ mail the REFUND DUE TENANT on or before _____ (date) to the address below:

Reviewed and Agreed:

Tenant _____ Date _____

Landlord/Manager _____ Date_____

New Address:

_____

_____

New Phone: _____

SELLER'S PROPERTY DISCLOSURE

NOTE: Sellers should answer the following questions to the best of their knowledge. Any YES answers should be explained in the "Notes" or on a separate sheet, citing applicable dates, names or reports, etc., and the current status of the condition described. Please also attach copies of any warranties or other relevant documents.

ITEM	YES	NO	NOTES
I. TITLE AND POSSESSION			
Is there anyone holding title interest in the property who has NOT signed the listing agreement			
Is there anyone holding a title interest in the property who is a licensed real estate agent			
Is there anyone holding a title interest in the property who is considered a "foreign person" under Section 1445 of the Internal Revenue Code			
Is there anyone who has an option to purchase, a first right of refusal to buy or a right to lease the property			
Is the property currently leased			
Are you (the Seller) aware of any notices of abatement or citations against the property			
Are you aware of deed restrictions or obligations			
Is there a Homeowners' or Condominium Association which has any authority over the subject property			
Do you know of any existing, pending or potential legal actions concerning the property or the Homeowners' Association			
Are you aware of any zoning violations, non-conforming uses, violations of "setback" requirements			
Do you have any notice(s) of violations relating to the property from any city, county or state agency			
Do you know of any violations of government regulations, ordinances or zoning laws regarding the property			
Are you aware of items shared in common with adjoining landowners-such as walls, fences, and driveways			
Do you know of any encroachments, easements, licenses, boundary disputes or third party claims affecting the property (i.e., rights of other people to interfere with the use of the property)			

Do you know of any pending real estate developments in your immediate area			
Are you aware of neighborhood noise problems or other nuisances			
Are you aware of any "common area" facilities-such as pools, tennis courts, walkways, or other areas-co-owned in undivided interest with others			
Have you ever had a survey of the property			
Are the property boundaries marked in any way			
2.LAND AND SOIL			
Do you know of any filled ground on the property			
Do you know of any past or present settling or soil movement problems on the property or on adjacent property			
Do you know of any past or present drainage, landslide, or flooding problems or damage on the property or on adjacent property			
Do you know of any active springs or streams on the property			
Do you know of any past or present problems with driveways, walkways, patios or retaining walls on the property or on adjacent properties due to drainage, flooding or soil movement (such as large cracks, potholes, raised sections, etc.)			
Is the property in a geological hazard zones or a flood control area			
Is the property in an area of occasional hurricane, tornado, earthquake, fire, or other natural disaster			
3. STRUCTURE			
Do you know of any defective or substandard conditions in the property			
Do you know of any settling, slanted floors, or cracks in walls, foundations, garage floors, driveways, chimneys or fireplaces			
Are you aware of any significant defect/malfunctions in any of the following:			
Chimneys/Fireplaces			
Solar heating			
Smoke detectors			

Water softener			
Electric garage door opener			
Burglar alarm			
Leased			
Owned			
Air conditioning			
Lawn sprinklers			
Sump pump			
Interior walls			
Lighting fixtures			
Ceilings			
Floor coverings			
Exterior walls			
Insulation			
Windows			
Doors			
Foundation or Basement			
Slab(s)			
Driveways			
Sidewalks			
Walls/Fences			
Do you know of any inspection reports, surveys, pest or insect infestation reports, studies, notices, etc., either private or by a public entity, concerning the condition of the property			
Do you know if the property is subject to radon emissions or if it contains underground tanks, asbestos, lead paint or other toxic substances			
Have you had pets on the property			
Have there been any problems with fleas or other parasites in the last year			
Do you know of any damage done to the property by insect pests			

During the course of your ownership have you made any structural additions or alterations to the property, or installed, altered, repaired or replaced significant components of the structures upon the property If so, please give all pertinent details including whether such additions, alterations, repairs or replacements were completed under an appropriate per-mit.			
Do you know of any structural additions or alterations which were made to the property, or installations, alterations, repairs or replacements of significant components of the structures upon the property by any previous owner If so, please give all pertinent details, including whether, to your knowledge, such additions, alterations, repairs or replacements were completed under an appropriate permit.			
Are you aware of any room additions, structural modifications, or other alterations or repairs made without necessary permits			
Are you aware of any room additions, structural modifications, or other alterations or repairs not in compliance with building codes			
When was the property constructed ___			
Are you aware of any major damage to the property or any of the structures from fire, earthquake, floods, or landslides			
4.ROOF			
Approximate age(years & Type)			
Do you know if there are any recurring leaks in the roof, gutters or chimney(s), around skylights and windows or from any other source			
Has the roof ever been repaired, patched or replaced while you have owned the property (Date)			
Is there a guarantee in effect on the roof(if so, please provide)			
5.PLUMBING SYSTEM			
Are water supply pipes other than copper (e.g.galvanized, plastic or a combination thereof)			
Do you know whether there is inadequate water pressure in your water supply from (City/Well/Private Utility)			
Do you know of any plumbing leaks on the property, including around and under sinks, toilets, showers or bathrooms			

Do you know whether any equipment for the pool, hot tub, spa, sauna (circle whichever applies) is defective or in need of replacement			
6.ELECTRICAL SYSTEMS			
220 volt			
Circuit breakers			
Fuses			
Do you know of any damaged or malfunctioning outlets			
Do you know of any damaged or malfunctioning switches			
Do you know of any defects, malfunctions or illegal installations of electrical equipment inside or outside of the building			
7.HEATING, AIR CONDITIONING			
Is the property NOT completely insulated If so, specify areas.			
Thickness and R-value of the insulation used			
Do you know of any problems with the heating system			
Type of heating system:			
Date of last inspection of heating equipment:			
Do you know of any problems associated with the operation of your water heater			
Type of air conditioner:			
Do you know if any heating or air conditioning equipment is in need of repair or replacement or has been installed improperly or without necessary permits			
8.BUILT-IN APPLIANCES			
The sale of the subject property will include the items circled below:			
Range, Oven, Microwave,Dishwasher, Trash Compactor, Garbage Disposal, Washer/Dryer & Hookups, Window Screens, TV Antenna, Satellite Dish, Intercom, Drapes, Chandeliers Heating, Central Air Conditioning, Evaporator Cooler(s), Wall/Window Air Conditioning, Septic Tank, Decking, Built-in Barbecue, Sauna, Pool, Hot Tub, Spa, Security Gate(s), Garage Door Openers & Number of Remote Controls			

Pool Heater (Gas/Solar/Electric)			
Water Heater (Gas/Solar/Electric)			
Gas Supply (Utility/Bottled)			

LEGAL FORMS AND INFORMATION SOURCE LIST

The best source of most real estate legal forms is your local Real Estate Board. But, as a trade organization, they often will not sell forms to the public. You may be able to obtain photocopies of sample contracts from a cooperative real estate agent or local law library. Otherwise, try:

Forms on Paper

Books of reproducible business forms are available at most book stores and often include the more common legal forms.

Professional Publishing Corporation, 122 Paul Drive, San Rafael, CA 94903; (415) 472-1964. Sells a range of more than 300 legal real estate forms and the industry standard, *The Realty Bluebook* giving insights on how to work with real estate transactions. Particularly geared towards California real estate agents, but expanding into other states, and the contract forms cover many issues that need to be addressed anywhere.

For California: Complete line of books covering the many issues facing Californians from landlording and tenanting to will revision to buying and/or selling a home. Authoritative books from a vanguard publisher for the do-it-yourself public. Nolo Press, 950 Parker, Berkeley, CA 94710 (510) 549 1976.

Forms on Disk to Use with Personal Computers

It's Legal—More than 35 forms including residential and commercial leases, promissory Note, Powers of Attorney, Request Credit Report, Challenge Credit Report, Bill of Sale, etc. Parson's Technology, One Parsons Drive, PO Box 100, Hiwatha, IA 52233-0100; (800) 223-6925.

Personal Law Firm - Most of the same standard forms, with more emphasis on small business forms for protecting trade secrets, notices on contract breach, etc. can be ordered through PC Produucts, TigerSoftware, PO Box 143376, Coral Gables, FL 33114-3376, (800) 888 4437.

Desktop Lawyer - Similar basic forms, includes more personal forms like pre and post nuptial agreements. Can be ordered from Power Up, 2929 Campus Drive, PO Box 7600, San Mateo, CA 94403-7600; (800) 851 2917.

Personal Lawyer - Similar basic forms, question and answer format. Bloc Publishing. Available in computer stores, Egghead or Comp USA (800) 451 7638.

Additional Sources of Legal Information
American Bar Association (ABA)
Lawyers Referral and Information Service
1155 East 60th Street
Chicago, IL 60637
(312) 332-1111
A staff member will refer individuals or groups making inquiries to a local legal referral service that can advise them of their options. The ABA answers calls from 9 a.m. to 5 p.m., CST.

NAACP Legal Defense and Educational Fund
99 Hudson Street
16th Floor
New York, NY 10013
(212) 219-1900
The staff at the NAACP Legal Defense Fund will put individuals or groups who feel that they have been discriminated against or "redlined" for housing in touch with an attorney who can help. The office is open weekdays from 9:30 a.m. to 5:30 p.m., EST.

National Center for Youth Law
1663 Mission Street
5th Floor
San Francisco, CA 94103
(415) 543-3307
Attorneys are available to help other attorneys who need advice on law applicable to youth including rejection of ac-

commodation for families with children. The office is open from 9 a.m. to 5 p.m., PST.

National Legal Aid and Defender Association
1625 K Street NW
8th Floor
Washington, DC 20006
(202) 452-0620
This association acts as a clearinghouse of organizations, providing legal services for those without the means to pay. The office is open from 9 a.m. to 5:30 p.m., EST.

National Resource Center for Consumers of Legal Services
3254 Jones Court NW
Washington, DC 20007
(202) 338-0714
This office is for people who need help in choosing a lawyer or who wish to complain about an incompetent one. A staff member offers help weekdays from 9 a.m. to 5 p.m., EST.

Women's Legal Defense Fund
2000 P Street NW
Washington, DC 20036
(202) 887-0364
This national organization is dedicated to securing women's rights through advocacy and litigation. Legal counseling is available on matters related to sexism, such as discrimination, economic inequality, and problems with legal documents in a woman's own name. Referrals are available. The office is open weekdays from 9 a.m. to 5 p.m., EST.

STEINERS COMPLETE
HOW TO TALK MORTGAGE TALK

Praise for the Steiner $12.95 Mortgage Guide.....

"This new book provides insight on some of the mortgage industry's dirty little secrets for the borrower's (not lender's) benefit, explaining key mortgage terms and procedures in everyday English."
— Robert Bruss, Chicago Tribune Syndicate dean of real estate columnists

♦ Easy-to-use steps and tips, plus details on the latest scams
♦ Financial jargon translated into plain English
♦ Fixed and adjustable side-by-side loan evaluations
♦ Balloons, principal paydowns and prepay penalties explained
♦ Dozens of contacts for FREE grants and counseling
♦ Negative amortization loans debunked
♦ Deals to avoid that can drop your home's value 20% in one day
♦ The silver bullet to save you from bait and switch traps
♦ All the information you need before you sign anything!

and many more loan agent SECRETS!

They've changed the rules—again—on getting a home mortgage. If you're buying a home, looking to refinance, get a home equity line or a reverse mortgage, you need to know what to look out for before you sign a piece of paper that will cost you more than your home, itself. This book is loaded with the latest practical strategies, checklists, and warnings about costly errors. Get the insider advice you need to deal with lenders for the best loans at the lowest rates.

Learn the 7 Steps to Save $1,000's
on Your Mortgage or Refinance

Steiners Complete How to Talk Mortgage Talk $12.95
ISBN 0-913733-12-1
Independent Information Publications Consumers Series

Phone 800-444-2524 ext 1
and order yours now.

ORDER FORM
Electronic Mortgage Hunter Kit

IIP Orders — Mortgagedisk
3357 - 21st Street
San Francisco, CA 94110

Please rush my timesaving mortgage disk

Mortgage Kit on disk $9.95 (plus $3.00 shipping and handling)

Name:_____(print)

Street:_____(print)

City/St/Zip:_____(print)

Credit Card #:_____

Expiration Date:____/____ Signature:_____

or Check Enclosed ( )

ORDER FORM
Steiners Complete How to Talk Mortgage Talk

IIP Orders — MortgageHandbook
3357 - 21st Street,
San Francisco, CA 94110

Please rush 152 page handbook

Complete How toTalk Mortgage Talk $12.95 (plus $3.95 shipping)

Name:_____(print)

Street:_____(print)

City/St/Zip:_____(print)

Credit Card #:_____

Expiration Date:____/____ Signature:_____

or Check Enclosed ( )